Dimensions of Mark in Higher Education

C000070637

Edited by Peter John and Joëlle Fanghanel

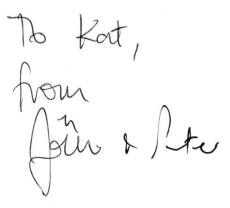

To Kat,
from
John & Peter

 Routledge
Taylor & Francis Group

LONDON AND NEW YORK

First published 2016
by Routledge
2 Park Square, Milton Park, Abingdon, Oxon OX14 4RN

and by Routledge
711 Third Avenue, New York, NY 10017

Routledge is an imprint of the Taylor & Francis Group, an informa business

British Library Cataloguing in Publication Data
A catalogue record for this book is available
from the British Library

Library of Congress Cataloging-in-Publication Data
A catalog record for this book has been requested

ISBN: 978-1-138-84512-1 (hbk)
ISBN: 978-1-138-84513-8 (pbk)
ISBN: 978-1-315-72833-9 (ebk)

Typeset in Galliard
by Apex CoVantage, LLC
Printed and bound in Great Britain by
Ashford Colour Press Ltd, Gosport, Hampshire

MIX
Paper from
responsible sources
FSC
www.fsc.org   FSC® C011748

This volume is dedicated to Roger Brown in recognition of his significant contribution to the higher education policy debate

Contents

Illustrations

Notes on contributors

Patrick Ainley is Professor at Greenwich University and has recently published *The Great Reversal: Young People, Education and Employment in a Declining Economy* and *Education Beyond the Coalition*, both with Martin Allen in 2013, and *The Great Apprenticeship Robbery* in 2014. Previous books include: *Lost Generation?* in 2010; *Learning Policy* in 1999; *Apprenticeship* (edited with Helen Rainbird) in 1999; *The Business of Learning, FE in the 1990s* (with Bill Bailey) in 1997; *Degrees of Difference, HE in the 1990s* in 1994; *Class and Skill* in 1993; *The Rise and Fall of the Manpower Services Commission* (with Mark Corney) in 1990; and *From School to YTS* in 1988.

Geoffrey Alderman is Professor of Politics and Contemporary History at the University of Buckingham. A graduate of the University of Oxford (from which he holds two doctorates), as well as a prize-winning journalist, Professor Alderman is the author and co-author of numerous monographs and learned articles on aspects of the British political system. He also enjoys an international reputation as an authority on the management of quality and standards in higher education.

Ronald Barnett is Emeritus Professor of Higher Education, Institute of Education, University of London. He is the author of twenty books (ten of which are sole-authored) on the concepts and theory of the university and higher education. His most recent book is *Imagining the University* (2013). A past Chair of the Society for Research into Higher Education (of which he is a Fellow), he has been an invited speaker in around thirty-five countries.

John Brennan is Emeritus Professor of Higher Education Research at the Open University and a Visiting Professor at the London School of Economics and at Bath and London Metropolitan universities. A sociologist by background, for nearly 20 years he directed the Centre for Higher Education Research and Information at the Open University. He has published several books and many reports and articles on higher education and its changing relationship with society.

Angela Brew is a Professorial Fellow in the Learning and Teaching Centre at Macquarie University, Australia. She is Honorary Associate Professor, University of Sydney and Visiting Professor, Gloucestershire University UK. She has published seven books and over 200 articles, book chapters, conference papers and reports. Her research is focused on the nature of research and its relation to teaching, learning and scholarship, models of research-led teaching and undergraduate research.

Tony Bruce is a higher education consultant who works principally on pension issues but also contributes to the work of the Higher Education Policy Institute. He was formerly Director of Policy Development and then Director of Research at Universities UK, 1992–2010, specialising in higher education funding issues. He is also a military historian who has published books on naval history and the First World War.

Helen Carasso's research concentrates on higher education policy, particularly in the context of undergraduate fees and funding in the UK. She is a member of the SKOPE research group in the Department of Education at the University of Oxford and sits on the Council of the Society for Research into Higher Education. Recently, Helen collaborated with Roger Brown as researcher and second author on *Everything for Sale? The marketisation of UK higher education* (2013).

Rob Cuthbert is Professor of Higher Education Management at the University of the West of England with 20 years' senior management experience as Dean, Deputy Vice-Chancellor and Acting Vice-Chancellor. His publications include six books and many reports, articles and papers on higher education policy, management, teaching and learning. A SRHE Fellow, he edits *Higher Education Review* and *SRHE News* and is co-director of the consultancy partnership *Practical Academics.*

Vaneeta D'Andrea is Professor Emerita at the University of the Arts London and has been a teaching scholar in the US and the UK for over 40 years. She has also been an international higher education consultant for over 2 decades in Africa, Central Asia, Europe, the Gulf States, North America and Southeast Asia. She has published on branding in higher education, educational development, educational research methods, higher education policy, quality enhancement in higher education, excellence in teaching in higher education and scholarship of teaching and learning (SoTL).

David D. Dill is Professor Emeritus of Public Policy at the University of North Carolina at Chapel Hill. He has been a Visiting Research Fellow at the University of Manchester Business School, a Visiting Fellow at Wolfson College, Cambridge, a Visiting Professor at the Center for Higher Education Policy Studies (CHEPS) at the University of Twente, and at the European University Institute. His research interests include public policy analysis, the regulation of academic quality (http://ppaq.web.unc.edu/) and research policy.

Joëlle Fanghanel is Associate Pro-Vice-Chancellor and Head of the Graduate School at the University of West London. She has published on academic identities and academic work, and higher education in a globalised context. A monograph on conceptions of teaching and learning based on her PhD was published in 2009. Her latest book *Being an Academic* examines the impact of higher education policies on academic practices in today's universities (Routledge, 2012).

Mick Healey is a higher education consultant and researcher based in the UK, who works across Australasia, Europe and North America. His main interest in the teaching-research nexus is in how research may best be integrated into higher education courses and programmes. Mick holds an Emeritus Professorship at the University of Gloucestershire, UK and is an Adjunct Professor at Macquarie University, Australia and a Visiting Professor at the University College London (www.mickhealey.co.uk).

Alan Jenkins has long taught and researched geography and contemporary China studies, in higher education in the UK and North America. He is now an educational developer and researcher on higher education and Emeritus Professor at Oxford Brookes University, UK. With Mick Healey he is editor for the International Section of the (US) *Council on Undergraduate Research Quarterly* and has published widely on the relationship between teaching and research (www.alanjenkins.info).

Peter John is the Vice-Chancellor and Chief Executive of the University of West London having formerly been Pro Vice-Chancellor (Education) and Deputy Vice-Chancellor (Academic) at the University of Plymouth. He has written widely on the policy and practice of education and is the author of six books and over eighty articles in academic journals. He sits on Universities UK student policy network, the board of London Higher and the executive board of the think-tank Million+.

Roger King is former Vice-Chancellor of the University of Lincoln and currently Visiting Professor at the University of Bath and at the University of Queensland in Australia. He is also a Research Associate at the Centre for the Analysis of Risk and Regulation at the London School of Economics and a Member of the Higher Education Commission (a Westminster think-tank). He has published numerous books and articles on governance, regulation and globalisation in higher education.

William Locke is Reader in Higher Education Studies and Co-Director of the Centre for Higher Education Studies at the Institute of Education, University of London. William was formerly Head of Learning and Teaching policy at HEFCE and has held positions at the Open University and Universities UK. He has a wide range of publications and has given keynote presentations at international conferences in North America, Japan, China, Australia and Europe.

Bernard Longden is Emeritus Professor of Higher Education Policy at Liverpool Hope University where he has been a teacher and a researcher. His research interests bear on the student experience and include student completion rates, performance indicator measures and the impact of funding mechanisms on higher education provision. More recently the focus of his work has been on higher education as a public good.

Robin Middlehurst is Professor of Higher Education at Kingston University, attached to the Vice-Chancellor's Office. She is also on secondment from Kingston, at the Leadership Foundation as Director of Strategy, Research and International (2004–2013) and since 2014 as Head of International Strategy at the Higher Education Academy. Robin's own research, teaching and consultancy is focused on higher education policy, management and practice at national and international levels.

Rajani Naidoo is Professor of Higher Education and Director of the International Centre for Higher Education Management, University of Bath. Her research focuses on transformations in global political economy, organisational change and the contribution of universities to the global public good. She has acted as expert advisor to international bodies including the Finnish Academy of Science. She is on the Editorial Board of the British Journal of Sociology of Education and the International Journal of Sociology of Education.

Lin Norton is a National Teaching Fellow (2007), Emeritus Professor of Pedagogical Research at Liverpool Hope University and Visiting Professor at the University of Ulster. Formerly Dean of Learning and Teaching at Liverpool Hope, she continues to actively champion pedagogical action research. She regularly publishes in this area including a book, book chapters, journal articles and conference papers. Lin is also an experienced journal editor.

Peter Scott is Professor of Higher Education Studies at the Institute of Education, University of London. He was formerly Vice-Chancellor of Kingston University. From 2000 to 2006, he was a member of the board of the Higher Education Funding Council for England. From 1976 to 1992, he was Editor of *The Times Higher Education Supplement*. His most recent book, with Claire Callender, is *Browne and Beyond: Modernizing English Higher Education* (2013).

Morgan White currently teaches part-time at Homerton College, University of Cambridge. He is a graduate of the Department of Government and Philosophy at the University of Manchester, where he received an Economic and Social Research Council doctoral studentship to research the structural transformation of higher education in Britain. His research interests are around normative political theory and education, especially the relations between economics, education and democracy. He is working on developing a 'political theory of the university'.

Gareth Williams is an Emeritus Professor at the Institute of Education. He has published extensively on higher education policy, especially in the area of higher education finance. While at the Institute, he founded the Centre for Higher Education Studies (CHES) and with Michael Shattock established the MBA in Higher Education Management at the Institute in 2004.

Joanna Williams is a Senior Lecturer in Higher Education and Academic Practice at the University of Kent. Her work explores the impact of government policy upon education. Most recently, this has taken a particular focus upon the marketisation of the higher education sector and the construction of students as consumers. Her book, *Consuming Higher Education: Why Learning Can't Be Bought*, was published by Bloomsbury in 2012. Joanna is education editor of Spiked Online and a regular contributor to *Times Higher Education*.

Foreword

Roger Brown is now recognized as the UK's leading chronicler of the rise of the market in higher education. Always challenging, he engages vice-chancellors and politicians alike with an easy familiarity but can always discriminate between the good, the bad and the downright ugly. In his writing and public persona, he always tries to separate suspicion and trust, lies and truth and the quick win from the long game. Always adept at explaining complexity, he does it in a way that increases accessibility while guiding us through the paraphernalia of policy with an independence that makes him so admired as 'the insider's outsider'. Above all, however, it is his cool skepticism using lessons from the past to illuminate contemporary assumptions that is policy writing at its very best.

His most recent piece highlights the many issues and ironies that have emerged during the move to the market, so much so that the UK is now behind only Chile and Korea in terms of the share of private expenditure spent on higher education (69.8 per cent compared with 23.2 per cent in 2006 and 11.3 per cent in 2000). Despite the many paradoxes, ambiguities and absurdities that led to this derogation of the public, the higher education system remains both robust and complicated. Universities differ not only in their histories, culture, missions, structures, resourcing, location and leadership but also in their position in what has become known as the higher education market. As a result, to varying degrees, the future of universities is now viewed through the lens of what Peter Scott describes as the awkward neologism 'marketisation'. This book sets out to explore and evaluate its many dimensions: the economics of higher education; students in a marketised environment; regulating a marketised sector; marketisation and higher education pedagogies; and the future of the sector.

Acknowledgements

As editors of this *Festschrift* for Roger Brown, we wish to acknowledge the authors in this collection, who are all Roger Brown's friends or colleagues and who have generously and enthusiastically contributed to this work. We are grateful too for the debates they have generated through their reflection on marketisation, particularly during the Brown Colloquium that was held at the University of West London on 25th September 2014 to prepare for this book and discuss, as an international group, the varied facets of marketisation in higher education.

Roger Brown is presently Visiting Professor at the Institute for Teaching, Innovation and Learning at the University of West London and a co-opted member of the Board of Governors. He is also Emeritus Professor of Higher Education Policy at Liverpool Hope University and was previously Vice-Chancellor of Southampton Solent University. He has held senior administrative positions as Chief Executive of the Higher Education Quality Council, Chief Executive of the Committee of Directors of Polytechnics and Secretary of the Polytechnics and Colleges Funding Council.

The colloquium and this collection celebrate Roger Brown's engagement with higher education policy, research and practice over the course of his career and his significant contribution to the field as a practitioner and thinker. His work and the many discussions with him over the past few years have provided the inspiration for this book, and we thank him for this.

We also thank our colleagues at the University of West London who have directly or indirectly contributed through discussions, writings, and attendance at policy seminars, to this global debate on the present state and future directions for higher education.

Peter John and Joëlle Fanghanel

Abbreviations

ACRU	Australasian Council of Undergraduate Research
ALTC	Australian Learning and Teaching Council
BIS	Department for Business, Innovation and Skills
CEO	Chief Executive Officer
CNAA	Council for National Academic Awards
DfE	Department for Education
EU	European Union
FE	Further Education
HE	Higher Education
HEFCE	Higher Education Funding Council
HEI	Higher Education Institution
HEQC	Higher Education Quality Council
IFS	Institute of Fiscal Studies
KIS	Key Information Set(s)
NCIHE	National Committee of Inquiry into Higher Education
NSS	National Student Survey
OECD	Organisation for Economic Co-operation and Development
OFFA	Office for Fair Access
QA	Quality Assurance
QAA	Quality Assurance Agency
QE	Quality Enhancement
SFC	Scottish Funding Committee
SRHE	Society for Research into Higher Education
UCU	Universities and Colleges Union
UGC	University Grant Committee
UK	United Kingdom
UKBA	United Kingdom Border Agency
UKVI	United Kingdom Visas and Immigration
US	United States
UUK	Universities United Kingdom

Editors' introduction

'Fearful symmetry?'
Higher education and the
logic of the market

Peter John and Joëlle Fanghanel

It should come as no surprise that the trajectory higher education has taken over the last 3 decades has been closely associated with the emergence of neo-liberalism, the introduction of market principles in the public realm and the rise of the New Public Management. All three grew out of the triumph of the Thatcherite settlement in the early 1990s, the fall of the Berlin Wall, the end of the Soviet Union and the rise of globalisation. The latter was viewed as the inevitable consequence of the changes and is often conceived of as a process that unleashes a series of strong (and sometimes overpowering) homogenising tendencies often without any counter-veiling currents (Hay, 2000). This view finds its clearest expression in Fukuyama's 'End of History' (1992) thesis and Zuckerman's (1998) confident assertion of the dawning of a 'Second American Century'. It is, however, possible to de-homogenise gloablisation by referring to the tensions that highlight differences, exclusion and inequities (Appadurai, 2005; Falk, 1994; Marginson, 2008). We focus on some of these tensions in this introduction.

In the context of a globalised economy, given the cost of keeping at the top of competition in a free market, governments in many developed countries, pro-pelled by declining faith in statist solutions to the rising cost of and demand for public services, sought a magic bullet that would solve their long-term funding problems. Seduced by the apparent success of free market mechanisms in secur-ing economic growth, politicians particularly in the US and the UK looked to the market to finance and provide most of their hitherto public services. This process of 'marketisation' denotes the transfer of goods and services from the public into the realm of the market (Crouch, 2009; Dicken, 2011). It also refers to the mar-ket exchange as a social production addressing capitalism's inherent potential to commodify (Cochoy *et al.*, 2010; Berndt and Broeckler, 2012). Higher educa-tion has not been immune to these movements and for more than 3 decades, the sector has been both accommodating with and adapting to what has been termed the 'quasi-market' (Le Grande and Bartlett, 1993).

In the UK, these trends have been depicted as the shift from the public to the private to relieve governments of the cost burden combined with defined improve-ments in efficiency and effectiveness (Williams, 1992, 1995; Brown, 2009, 2011).

The latter was viewed as part of the modernisation and minimisation drive of the state, which in the UK straddled the Conservative administrations of Thatcher and Major and the New Labour governments of Blair and Brown. At the heart of the modernisation agenda was targeted funding and flexible budgeting while minimisation was aimed at shrinking the state in part through outsourcing and the hollowing out of public functions (Shattock, 2008). For higher education institutions (HEIs), this meant that any future state funding would be issued on account, and with clearly defined output measures based on audited results (Williams, 2004). This form of contractual funding administered through the Higher Education Funding Council for England (HEFCE) saw universities take on the role of 'audited vendors' of a knowledge product (Williams, 2004: 246) through enhanced regulation and competitive tendering. Given that the core resources to be distributed in the quasi-market were mostly generated through taxation and borrowing, governments of all persuasions looked to improve the efficiency and effectiveness of their investment.

Despite these inherent contradictions within the quasi-market, HEIs were driven towards it to garner funding for teaching and research because it was the only conceivable way of reversing the decline in the unit of resource (by 1997 this had dropped to 76 per cent of its 1980 value, and sunk further to 63 per cent of its 1980 value in 2002) and to stem the stop-go recruitment practices and attendant financial lurches (Pritchard, 1994). As Unterhalter and Carpentier (2010) have shown, higher education systems and state funding ebb and flow in line with economic cycles although the ideological move to the market in the UK was lubricated by increasing austerity after 2008. In consequence, institutions became path dependent following government economic and social priorities (Middleton, 2000; Naidoo, 2008) while *pari passu* accepting the principle that students would have to make an ever-increasing contribution to the cost of their studies. The latter reached its apogee in the Browne Review of 2010, the subsequent white paper *Higher Education: Putting Students at the Heart of the System* (DBIS, 2011) and the raising of the fee to £9,000 in 2012.

These recent changes crystalised trends that had been emerging for over 3 decades. Roger Brown's (2015) excellent rendition of this process highlights the coercive convergence of many of the reforms that led to the residualisation of the public service model of universities. He explains that the removal of subsidies for international students in 1980, the separation of teaching and research funding in 1986, the introduction of top-up loans for student support in 1990 and the abolition of the binary line in 1992, presaged the more intensified marketisation of the first decade of the twenty-first century. This included the introduction of tuition fees in 1998 (£1,000), the variable fee in 2006 (£3,000) and the present fee arrangement in 2012 (£9,000). The result has been a near 70 per cent reduction in direct state funding for teaching and research with only a small number of subjects, predominantly science, technology, engineering and mathematics (STEM related), receiving direct subsidies (Brown, 2015). These changes to funding have been associated with a move towards greater diversification with new private providers entering the higher education arena. Brown with Carasso (2013) estimate that almost £1billion is being spent on students studying at such institutions compared to £104 million 3 years ago. Finally, the removal of the numbers cap in 2015 will allow providers to recruit as many of the students as they wish with selecting institutions having obvious advantages in the positional market.

This has exacerbated competition for resources and students, and triggered an increasing amount of external regulation. In reaction, universities have begun to resemble commercial organisations with income generating units, departmental cost centres, senior management structures, corporate plans and marketing strategies, all underpinned by governance structures that resemble the corporate world. The focus of successive governments on the economic contribution of universities has somewhat left aside any consideration of the University's educational and social functions. A reflection on the public non-commercial value of higher education provides a useful appendage to an analysis of the trends identified above.

In taking up this challenge, the authors in this collection will contest much of the discourse that surrounds the logic of the market; an approach that has made the 'marketising' drive appear inevitable in both economic and political terms. It will also problematise crucial areas of the debate, in particular the challenge the market represents to the notion of higher education as public good and the way it too often obscures the many intangible benefits that can be drawn from a university education. The book also explores the tensions and dilemmas marketisation brings into the educational environment for academics, students and academic leaders and managers – the price of engaging with students and supporting their development whilst in higher education; how to manage customer-oriented demands; keeping educational concerns at the centre of the academic endeavour. It argues that tensions can be managed through re-balancing the relation between the market dimension and the educational dimension. Debate and research about market-based policies are therefore essential to help shape answers and delineate the future of educational practices in universities.

In summary, the book focuses on what we term the 'logic of the market', which often seduces policy-makers, university leaders, regulators and even students to act without a critical understanding of the conditions required for efficient markets to operate and with very little recourse to empirical evidence (Regini, 2011). As a result, we might be heading into what King and Crewe (2014) call one of those 'Blunders of our Governments' as we balance precariously on what Malcolm Gladwell (2002) terms a 'tipping point' where even minor change could leave the sector permanently unrecognisable. This is exactly the kind of problem that Roger Brown revels in and one which will continue to feel the full force of his intellect.

In Part I the authors examine the economics of marketisation. Peter Scott focuses on the benefit bifurcation that has been at the heart of the debate on marketisation. In particular, whether universities' principal aim should be the conferring of private benefits on their students or should be primarily concerned with producing public goods, which have wider beneficiaries. Much of the debate concentrates on whether the sector operates within multiple markets linked to many different forms of public policy or whether it is possible to isolate the market from other instruments of state policy? He concludes by challenging the hyperbole surrounding the 'paradigm shift' that Lord Browne claimed after the publication of his report preferring instead to see the market-based reforms as more evolutionary than the 'ideological *furore* suggests'.

Using a diachronic approach, Helen Carasso and William Locke review the arguments that politicians and policy-makers adopted to justify the introduction of fees. They show that the three phases were characterised by the move from a shared investment approach in 1998 to a student contribution system in 2006, culminating in cost transfer in 2012. However, using an econometric methodology they challenge the approach used by Browne to justify the changes. The review calculated the market benefit of higher education being more than 50 per cent higher than the public benefits. Using McMahon's (2010) work on the private and social benefits of higher education, the authors show that such benefits make up close to 68 per cent of the total. They also remind us that a key phrase in the OECD Report used by Browne to justify the private benefit argument was conveniently ignored. It said: 'the net public return from an investment in tertiary education is . . . almost three times the amount of public investment' (OECD, 2010: 145). They end with a chilling reminder from Brown (2012) that too often major decisions are driven by 'policy-based evidence' rather than 'evidence-based policy'.

Rajani Naidoo continues in a similar vein. Her analysis highlights the ways in which the reforms of recent years have led to a particular type of learning market that sees students recast as consumers and one that automatically assumes positive outcomes. She claims that this tokenistic appeal to students may 'further entrench and reproduce widespread systemic inequality' across the sector. Her argument reflects Bourdieu's (1988) reference to this form of neo-liberalism as a 'doxa' that permeates all levels of society and where commodification is seen as destructive of the public good. She concludes with a plea for further theoretical and empirical research into the nature of this doxa so that the more corrosive effects of commodification in higher education can be challenged.

Rob Cuthbert likewise focuses on the student as consumer but uses the differentiating lens of both marketing and marketisation. He shows that there is no tension between marketing and educational values since the former was meant to restore academic principles as a corrective to what appeared to be 'producer capture'. He goes on to say that 'market forces' alone will never drive up standards as only academics themselves can achieve that, however, he notes that attempts to defend these values and standards largely failed for two reasons: they were 'reactive and oppositional'. He concludes by claiming that grand theories of opposition are impractical and prefers more subversive approaches which use marketing as a way of generating customer satisfaction and greater public interest.

The final piece in this opening section shifts the focus to Scotland. Here Tony Bruce reviews a number of recent developments north of the border where the transition to a more market-based system has been less intense and interrupted by the process of devolution after 1999. He analyses the main policy changes in the post-Browne era and shows that apart from some cross-border flows (Scotland continues to participate in the UK-wide quality assurance system, student admission arrangements, pay bargaining, pensions and data collection) the Scots have created a more distinctive system. This is characterised by a more limited market-oriented approach, a greater reliance on public funding, a rejection of the student contribution, a higher priority for widening access, less research selectivity and a greater focus on quality enhancement. He concludes by declaring that Scottish higher education 'now offers a distinct alternative to the market-based models being adopted in England'.

Part II of the book attends to the student experience in this marketised environment. Joanna Williams focuses on student charters and their use as marketing material and the effect they have in shifting students from learners to consumers. Drawing on an analysis of thirteen *in situ* student charters at a range of universities, the author concludes that despite some advantages (giving students the authority to negotiate the terms of their education and the ability to hold their teachers and institutions to account) they can infantilise students by removing the opportunities for them to develop individual responsibility for their learning. As a result, student identities become part of the commodification process where academics are positioned as service providers and students as instrumental learners.

In Chapter 7, Bernard Longden takes up the long debated question of league tables and their efficacy. He bases his argument on the fact that too often league tables are constructed using 'inappropriate manipulation and interpretation of data' which results in the reduction of complexity and the creation of skewed measures. Reflecting on the uses and abuses of league tables across the world he proposes an alternative approach based on the Carnegie Classification in the United States. The development of a prototype for use in the UK is an attempt to challenge the existing hierarchy of ranking where prestigious institutions remain at the top with others left 'land locked' competing for position based on less prestigious criteria. Using HESA data, a set of dimensions were constructed to generate a valid set of metrics. The resulting cluster analysis created a new classification system which (in the opinion of the author) better addressed the interests of the state, the students and the institutions. In a nutshell, Longden sums the advantages of the new system up by claiming that it reflects better what institutions did, who they taught and in what context.

Morgan White's chapter confronts the morality of envisaging a university education in economic terms. Using the notion of higher education as a 'post-experience good' where its value is determined less by its current or pre-experience consumption than by its more uncertain projected benefit, he challenges many current assumptions. Drawing on the work of Hannah Arendt (1993), White draws attention to the inter-generational need to pass on authority so that subsequent generations are able to renew themselves. He further examines this proposition by concentrating on the fiduciary relationship between the university teacher and the student within the context of an increasingly marketised system and uses the concept of a 'credence good' to further elaborate his ideas. White concludes by claiming that trust and authority (which lie at the heart of the tacit contract between teacher and learner) are being undermined by the instrumentalising effect of the higher education market.

Patrick Ainley quizzically asks why there has been so little resistance to the introduction of the market into English higher education. Using Rolfe's (2013) idea of the unravelling of the university embedded in the new market state, he explores the failed opposition of the two main campaigning groups and the lack of impact of the main academic trade union (University and College Union). His explanation highlights deeper structural changes that rendered any opposition nebulous and stymied any effective strategic defence of further and higher education. Focusing on the future, Ainley looks at the prospects for change (albeit within limited horizons) and sees the trend towards employability as problematic given rapidly changing employment patterns. He recognises that Labour's proposals for a more integrated higher and further education system might mitigate the competition between providers while allowing for more regional based solutions. However, he is less optimistic about higher education freeing itself from the economic framework within which it is embrocated and whether new governments will create an entitlement for young people to progress as citizens.

In Part III of the collection, the contributors explore regulation and risk management. Roger King presents a critique of risk-based regulation as an approach to quality assurance, preferring the latter to be underpinned by enhancement and collective staff buy-in at an institutional level. Beginning with the recognition that the state has slowly co-opted more non-state bodies into its regulatory systems, he explains that greater fragmentation, more agency-led and government-licensed self-regulation has emerged. With a clear emphasis on the 'risk business' King sees universities as acting in similar ways to corporate organisations with reputation management high on the risk agenda. As an antidote, King argues for a greater recognition of uncertainty within institutions which better represents the loose coupling and indeterminacy that characterises higher education as a whole. King concludes with a warning that the various agencies involved in quality assurance must avoid being drawn into areas that take them away from their core function and lead inexorably to more inspectorial approaches.

Geoffrey Alderman takes up this issue and traces how the Home Office got involved in the regulation of higher education as recent immigration controls began to effect institutions and their overseas recruitment patterns. The story has numerous twists and turns and takes us firmly into the private provider dimension of marketisation. Alderman shows that prior to 2012, Tier 4 students sponsored by a receiving institution (which operated outside the purview of the Quality Assurance Agency for Higher Education, QAA) were inspected by a number of designated bodies. This system was removed in 2012 as abuses became apparent, and the QAA were brought into the regulatory orbit of the Home Office and its satellites: the UK Border Agency (from 2008 to 2013) and its successor the UK Visa and Immigration. This invite to take 'educational oversight' of new providers resulted in the Home Office becoming a stakeholder in the regulation of quality and standards in the higher education sector. Alderman forensically chronicles these events and issues many warnings for institutions as further marketisation creates a more diverse and resource hungry sector.

John Brennan returns the reader to the ways in which the external regimes of quality assurance continue to undermine traditional academic autonomy. Using the past as guide he speculates on future directions particularly given the market propensity to construct students as consumers and higher education as providing products. With an emphasis on the student voice, the author draws on research which explores the student experience at thirteen UK universities. The key message emerging from the study is that students do not see an elision between their academic and personal development. In fact, the latter often had greater impact. As a result, Brennan argues for greater input from students in terms of quality measures combined with external academic peer-review of courses and processes. This, he argues, may help external quality assurance regimes take a wider perspective and ensure that the diverse values and demands of the market are taken into account.

In the opening chapter of Part IV of the collection, Angela Brew provides an Australian perspective on the changing relationship between research and teaching. Set within the shifting landscape of higher education and its relationship to the market, she reviews the evolving connection between teaching and research and the ways in which the scholarship of practice helped focus the debate. Brew concentrates on this nexus and the ways in which academic staff were encouraged to utilise their research in their teaching, which then gave way to the student being the key core mechanism within the relationship. This new wave of thinking, she argues, needs to be embedded within the 'very fabric of the university structure' if it is to be successful. Brew concludes by making a plea for the further professionalisation of teachers built on a new settlement where academic authority itself is problematised and students become co-creators of knowledge.

In Chapter 14, Lin Norton takes up the challenge posed by Angela Brew and advocates the use of pedagogical action research as a counterweight to the potential decline in the status of teaching. Building on an unintended consequence of the separation of funding for research and teaching, the author argues that focusing on the pedagogies in a critical way might not only improve practice but also the status of teaching in the academy. She concludes with the assertion that not only is such an approach a 'good' in itself but that it might give academics the confidence to resist some of the forces of marketisation that are becoming part of the status quo in institutions.

On the same theme, Alan Jenkins and Mick Healey describe the role played by the *Research and Teaching Forum* between 1998 and 2009 and how the changing terrain of higher education interacted with its many initiatives. Despite many successes in enhancing the profile of teaching and ensuring that national policies were shaped by the principles of the *Forum,* teaching strategies (not research) continued to be the vehicle for implementation. This meant that research continued to be seen as separate and supporting rather than integral and influential. In addition, according to the authors, the rise of 'massification' and the continuing subordination of universities and their activities to the demands of a productive economy further threaten the symbiotic connection between research and teaching. In particular, it might stymie the move towards student self-authorship and intellectual development where knowledge is viewed as contestable and uncertain – a conception of teaching and learning that was at the heart of the *Forum's* agenda.

Vaneeta D'Andrea continues on the topic of the research-teaching nexus with a personal perspective on the work of the same research and teaching group surveyed by Jenkins and Healey. She highlights Roger Brown's seminal contribution to the group which she claims had three main impacts: first, in creating a dialogue between the academic research community and policy-makers; second, by encouraging policy-makers to engage with international debates on issues of evidence-based policies; and third, by driving a changed narrative on the importance of the teaching-research nexus.

The final part of the book takes a more 'blue-skies' approach and seeks to tease out a number of the scenarios for universities as the quasi-market evolves. Robin Middlehurst begins with a reflection on the role of leadership during the period of marketisation. Starting from the position that debates surrounding the governance of higher education have become sterile, Middlehurst challenges current perceptions through a combination of experiential reflection interwoven with insights from the extant literature. She highlights the fact that overly controlling systems and poor relationships between management and academic staff can breed negative attitudes and poor behaviours on both sides of the divide. However, she firmly believes that this misalignment is not inevitable if the principles of 'challenge balanced with support' are applied systematically and fairly across institutions. She also posits that leadership theories from outside the sector can be beneficial and that often managerialism and its negative connotations are the result of poor practice rather than being inherently wrong. Quoting the work of Hamel (2007; 2012), she points to the need for higher education leadership to 'mend the soul' of management by embedding an 'ethos of community and citizenship to ensure that management serves a higher purpose'.

Gareth Williams in his chapter offers a career-long reflection on the higher education policy-practice nexus. Contrasting the paucity of information on universities existing during the period of the Robbins Review with the sheer volume of material now available, he questions the value of the corpus by evaluating its impact on policy and practice in the sector. Focusing on the two main categories in the field: one relating to teaching and learning and its relationship with research and scholarship; the other concerned mainly with student numbers, access, quality, finance and management. Quoting Dill (2014), he highlights some of the limitations of this literature in that it derives much of its substance from the personal positions and reflections of the authors rather than being based on rigorous empirical research. Proffering some questions on the economics of higher education in general and on the graduate earning question in particular, he argues for a more robust and wide ranging analysis of the needs of the graduate labour market to better inform policy especially around the means tested loans and their repayment. He also makes an appeal to researchers to explore the size and shape of the sector and to question whether growth has its limits. In conclusion, Williams says much remains to be done and ends with a conundrum: is higher education research a major driver of policy and practice or does it provide a *post-factum* justification for the whims and decisions of policy makers and managers?

In his chapter, David Dill explores the effect of the New Public Management and marketisation on academic quality and academic responsibility. He argues that the growing chasm between the collective good of the university and the rising tide of academic self-interest are creating numerous challenges for academic governance. To counteract these tendencies Dill offers Ostrom's (2005) commons model as an alternative to market forces and state regulation as the most effective institutional arrangement for re-establishing collegiate governance. At the heart of this approach is the confirmation of professional autonomy and responsibility as guiding concepts. Using a series of examples drawn from national policy areas, Dill develops a series of design principles that encourage collective academic action by members of the commons. In particular, Dill believes that refocusing on quality enhancement using Ostrom's principles will bring about a significant improvement in the quality of instruction and research. Such an approach will yield the best results if they operate at subject and course level where the engagement of academic staff can be most influential. Dill concludes with sentiments drawn from Craig Calhoun (2006) which emphasise the importance of the public sphere being re-established within institutions with the aim of serving the public good.

In the final chapter, Ronald Barnett presents a ten-fold policy framework that he claims can be found across the world and which provides a *lingua franca* of meetings and interactions within higher education policy circles. In this sense, the contemporary university is being shaped by converging global structures which are influencing teaching, research and enterprise – all driven by the digital revolution. In consequence, the idea of the corporate, entrepreneurial and digital university is being privileged over the engaged, civic university or the even the university of wisdom. However, Barnett warns us that holding on to the provisionality of these options can confuse the university as an idea with the university as an institution. This becomes relevant when discussing the policy formation that inevitably leads to a 'tinkering' with the relationships between the ten elements of the framework and the creation of a policy vacuum. Barnett then asks how might this vacuum be understood. And is the university constricted and preset by these global structures or does it have scope to create its own possibilities? His response is to see the university less as a space of reason and more as a space of imagining where its natural antagonism is not to be 'denied, repudiated or neglected'.

Bibliography

Appadurai, A. (2005) *Modernity at Large: Cultural Dimensions of Globalization.* Minneapolis: University of Minnesota Press

Arendt, H. (1993) *Between Past and Future.* London: Penguin

Berndt, C. and Broeckler, M. (2012) Geographies of Marketization. In T. Barnes, J. Peck and E. Sheppard (eds) *The Wiley-Blackwell Companion to Economic Geography.* Oxford: Wiley-Blackwell: 424–432

Bourdieu, P. (1988) *Homo Academicus.* Cambridge, UK: Polity Press

Brown, R. (2009) *The Role of the Market in Higher Education.* Oxford: Higher Education Policy Institute

Brown, R. (ed.) (2011) *Higher Education and the Market.* London: Routledge

Brown, R. (2012) The myth of student choice. *Vistas* 2 (2): 7–20

Brown, R. (2015) The marketisation of higher education: issues and ironies. *New Vistas* 1 (1): 3–9

Brown, R. with Carasso, H. (2013) *Everything for Sale: The Marketisation of Higher Education.* London: Routledge and the Society for Research into Higher Education

Calhoun, C. (2006) The university and the public good. *Thesis Eleven* 84 (1): 7–43

Cochoy, F., Giraudeau, M. and McFall, L. (2010) Performativities, economics and politics. *Journal of Cultural Economy* 3: 139–146

Crouch, C. (2009) Marketization. In M. Flinders, A. Gamble, C., Hay and M. Kenney (eds) *Oxford Handbook of British Politics.* Oxford: Oxford University Press: 879–895

Department of Business, Innovation and Skills (2011) *Students at the Heart of the System: White Paper on Higher Education.* London: DBIS

Dicken, P. (2011) *The Global Shift: Mapping the Changing Contours of the World Economy.* London: Sage

Dill, D.D. (2014) Assuring the Public Good in Higher Education: Essential Framework Conditions and Academic Values. In O. Filippakou and G. Williams (eds) *Higher Education as a Public Good: Critical Perspectives on Theory, Policy and Practice.* New York: Peter Lang: 141–162

Falk R. (1994) The Making of Global Citizenship. In B.V. Teenberge (ed.) *The Condition of Citizenship.* London: Sage: 127–140

Fukuyama, F. (1992) *The End of History and the Last Man.* London: Hamish Hamilton

Gladwell, M. (2002) *The Tipping Point: How Little Things Can Make a Big Difference.* San Francisco: Back Bay Books

Hamel, G. (2007) *The Future of Management.* Boston: Harvard Business School Press

Hamel, G. (2012) *What Matters Now: How to Win in a World of Relentless Change, Ferocious Competition and Unstoppable Innovation.* London: Jossey-Bass Wiley

Hay, C. (2000) Contemporary capitalism, globalization, regulation, and the persistence of national variation. *Review of International Studies* 20 (4): 509–531

King, A. and Crewe, I. (2014) *The Blunders of Our Governments.* London: Oneworld Publications

Le Grande, J. and Bartlett, W. (1993) *Quasi-Markets and Social Policy.* Basingstoke: Macmillan

Marginson, S. (2008) Global field and global imagining: Bourdieu and worldwide higher education. *British Journal of the Sociology of Education* 29 (3): 303–315

McMahon, W. (2010) The Private and Social Benefits of Higher Education: The Evidence, Their Value, and Policy Implications. *Advancing Higher Education*. New York: TIAA-CREF

Middleton, C. (2000) Models of state and market in the modernisation of higher education. *British Journal of the Sociology of Education* 21 (4): 537–554

Naidoo, R. (2008) Building or Eroding Intellectual Capital? Student Consumerism as Cultural Force in the Context of Knowledge Economy. In J. Valimaa and O-H. Ylijoki (eds) *Cultural Perspectives in Higher Education*. Netherlands: Springer: 43–55

OECD (2010) *Education at a Glance*. Paris: Organisation for Economic Co-operation and Development

Ostrom, E. (2005) *Understanding Institutional Diversity*. Princeton, NJ: Princeton University Press

Pritchard, R. O. (1994) Government power in British higher education. *Studies in Higher Education* 19 (3): 253–265

Regini, M. (ed.) (2011) *European Universities and the Challenge of the Market*. Cheltenham: Edward Elgar Publishing

Rolfe, G. (2013) *The University on Dissent: Scholarship in the Corporate University*. London: Routledge

Shattock, M. (2008) *Managing Good Governance in Higher Education*. London: Taylor & Francis

Unterhalter, E. and Carpentier, V. (2010) *Global Inequalities in Higher Education: Whose Interests Are We Serving?* Basingstoke: Palgrave

Williams, G. (1992) *Changing Patterns in Finance in Higher Education*. Buckingham: Open University Press

Williams, G. (1995) The 'Marketisation' of Higher Education Reforms and Potential Reforms in Higher Education Finance. In D. Dill and B. Sporn (eds) *Emerging Patterns of Social Demand and University Reform: Through a Glass Darkly*. Oxford: Pergamon Press: 170–193

Williams, G. (2004) The Higher Education Market in the United Kingdom. In P. Teixeira, B.B. Jongbloe., D.D. Dill and A. Amaral (eds) *Markets in Higher Education: Rhetoric or Reality*. Dordrecht: Kluwer Academic Publishers: 241–270

Zuckerman, M. (1998) A second American century. *Foreign Affairs* 77 (3): 18–31

Part I

The economics of
higher education

Chapter 1

Private commodities and public goods

Markets and values in higher education

Peter Scott

Introduction

Roger Brown has been one of the most terrier-like opponents of the introduction of an untrammelled market in English higher education since the publication of the Browne Report in the autumn of 2010, and the then Coalition Government's enthusiastic if uneven implementation of (the spirit if not the letter of) that report (Committee on Student Fees and Funding, 2010; BIS, 2011). But he has also been one of the most penetrating analysts of the effects, intended and unintended, of such a market through a stream of publications, from a full-length book through articles to more polemical pamphlets (Brown, 2009, 2011a,b; Brown with Carasso, 2013). To his political interventions he has brought an unremitting vigour, and to his intellectual analysis a commendable rigour.

'Marketisation' has now replaced 'massification' as a one-word characterisation of the general condition of higher education in England. One rather ugly neologism succeeding another, critics will say, and, like all one-word characterisations, it conceals as much as it reveals. But what it does reveal is important, and even scary – a shift from a largely publicly funded system to one now highly dependent on student fees (albeit one that is perhaps even more dependent on public funding in the short and medium term), that may lead to fundamental changes in the character of higher education – its institutional architecture, its organisational culture, its professional practices, even its normative foundations. For alerting us to the enormity of this change, the major credit must go to Roger Brown and a small number of fellow scholars (Marginson, 1997). Whether his interventions have succeeded in changing the political weather since 2010, or whether his analysis of markets in higher education has been convincing as well as compelling, are both secondary questions. Quite simply, he has put markets on the map of higher education.

This focus of this chapter is not initially on markets in an operational or even definitional sense, although in its final section it will consider whether it is right to characterise the post-Browne funding regime as a market.

Its primary focus is on the long, but still unresolved, debate about the extent to which modern higher education systems should be seen as predominantly conferring private benefits on their students, and graduates, in terms of improved earnings and life-chances more generally, or whether they should be regarded as producing public goods of which students are only one of a number of beneficiaries. To some degree, this is a technical debate based on economic calculations – but not entirely. This discussion makes up the first section of the chapter.

The second focuses on the characteristics of markets in general. No markets, of course, are pure; all are to some degree indirectly shaped political and social action and often directly regulated by the state. This raises the question of whether it is possible clearly to distinguish between markets and other instruments, notably state action as expressed through public policy, or whether it is more accurate instead to think in terms of a fuzzy spectrum made up of many different types of markets, more or less controlled, and many different forms of public policy, more or less market-like. The special characteristics of higher education, which may inhibit market development, are also considered.

The final section of this chapter considers whether the reforms of English higher education since 2010 can truly be characterised as a deliberate process of marketisation (perhaps so in terms of political ideology, but perhaps less certainly in terms of the implementation of these reforms). Are they best regarded as a 'paradigm shift', as Lord Browne himself claimed at the press conference introducing his report, or a further stage in a long-running process of more pragmatic evolution and adaptation?

Private benefits and public goods

The debate about the balance between the private benefits conferred and public goods produced by modern higher education is as old, and perhaps as unresolvable, as the rather similar debate about whether investment in higher education makes countries rich or whether only rich countries can afford elaborate higher education systems. The answer to both questions, of course, must be 'both'.

First, graduates enjoy enhanced earnings in most but not all cases. But they also pay more taxes, while not necessarily consuming equally enhanced shares of public services supported by taxation. On average, they are healthier and more law-abiding, even when corrections are made for gender, social class and ethnicity (New Economics Foundation, 2011). More broadly, the impact of higher education is felt not just on the character of individuals (and their life-chances) but also on the tone of society. The UK has become in powerful but intangible ways a graduate society. Next, universities themselves are key institutions within civil society, occupying the space between the state and the market – while, of course, also being part of both. As a result they help to underpin the idea of an open society and to procure public goods of the highest order, such as law, liberty and democracy as well as science and civilisation. But universities are also key organisations within 'clever cities', those urban or suburban sites of creativity and enterprise that generate wealth in a twenty-first-century knowledge economy. Finally, OECD calculations suggest that for every pound (or euro or dollar) of public investment in higher education, three pounds of economic benefit are produced – although it can be counter-argued that only rich economies can afford such investment but also that only developed countries have the social, economic (and maybe political and cultural) arrangements necessary to enable such investment to be realised (OECD, 2012).

Disentangling private benefits and public goods, therefore, will always be difficult (Psacharopoulos, 2009). Economists focus on the balance between them and struggle to calculate their respective proportions. Some argue that public goods constitute the value left when all possible private benefits have been apportioned: in other words, a minimalist interpretation that probably overstates private benefits. Others argue that the inevitable confusion between private benefits and public goods makes strict apportionment too difficult and also that there are private benefits that may need to be curtailed for the public good: a more open, and expansive, interpretation of public goods (Marginson, 2011). The debate among politicians is rather cruder. Its focus is whether private benefits or public goods are the predominant outcome of higher education because of the policy relevance, and ideological resonance, of this single (simplistic?) issue. If private benefits predominate, then students are rightly charged fees; if public goods, the funding of higher education is properly a responsibility of the state. As a result, current ideological fashions may be more influential than any economic calculations (although even economists are not immune from ideological influences). The encroaching hegemony of neo-liberal ideas since the 1980s has contributed to a demonisation of the welfare state and public sector – and, consequently, perhaps also a devaluation, and so an understatement, of public goods.

The problem for both economists and politicians is that the balance between private benefits and public goods is both volatile and variable. It is volatile because calculations of this balance depend crucially on how specified outcomes are defined – and also, an obvious point, because the same outcomes generally both confer private benefits and produce public goods. The balance is variable because, whatever aggregate calculations may produce, the outcomes for specified individuals are very different and also because public outcomes are of variable value to different individuals, social groups, communities, regions or other categories. Only a small number of public goods really satisfy the two standard, and strict, economic tests that are often applied. The first test is 'non-excludability' – in other words, that they can be enjoyed by everyone, which is a test that can be satisfied in many circumstances (at any rate in formal terms), but also in equal measure, a much more difficult test to satisfy. The second test is 'non-rivalrous consumption' – in other words, that their value is not reduced by the number of people who have access to them; most goods are in some important senses positional, even if the relationship between scarcity and value is far from linear (or even predictable).

These difficulties have been compounded by two larger factors. The first is the evolution of the welfare state, preoccupied with social well-being and social justice, into what has been labelled the 'market state', in other words a state that regards its primary function as the promotion of economic growth (which, according to neo-liberal ideology, can only be done by giving freer rein to the market). As a result, the state as provider has tended to be succeeded by the state as regulator. Even when the idea of the market state has not been embraced with as much ideological enthusiasm as it has in England, the state has had to cope with a number of structural challenges – increasing demand, notably the rising cost of 'welfare' (especially pensions) and healthcare; and declining supply, as tax bases have shrunk. This 'hollowing-out' of the state has led to an explosion of privatisation and, less dramatically, outsourcing. Even when public services have not been privatised or outsourced, quasi-market mechanisms have been employed in their delivery. It is against this wider background that the growth of markets in higher education has been encouraged.

The second new factor is a far-reaching change in the organisational culture of universities themselves that is evident on a number of dimensions:

- The rise of the so-called entrepreneurial university
- The increasing emphasis on research impact, and even the popularity of notions of 'mode 2' knowledge (Gibbons *et al.*, 1994)
- The shift from (collegial?) academic self-government to so-called managerialism
- The emergence of consumerist behaviours focused on satisfaction and the 'student experience'
- And intensified competition powerfully promoted by league tables

These cultural changes have tended to emphasise that the effects of higher education are best judged in terms of instrumental outcomes. They have brought higher education closer to the market, in the sense that these outcomes seem to be more readily defined as private benefits than public goods (which, being more difficult to calculate, tend to get downplayed). But the idea of public goods has also shifted as a result of both sets of changes, in the state and in higher education. Not only has it become almost routine for public goods to be produced through markets, there has also been a blurring of once distinct notions of the public and the private (Scott, 2015).

Markets . . . and post-markets?

The question therefore arises of whether, in the light of these changes in the nature of the twenty-first-century (neo-liberal?) state and in the characteristics of higher education institutions and systems, the rationale for predominantly public funding has been eroded to such an extent that some form of market must inevitably be introduced – despite the technical difficulties of distinguishing adequately between private benefits and public goods. This is best answered in two dimensions – first, the characteristics of markets in general; and, second, any more specific conditions that may restrict the development of markets in higher education.

It is important at the start to recognise that there are no perfect markets; all markets are flawed if judged against some ideal theoretical standard. So it is not sufficient for opponents of the marketisation of higher education simply to point out that markets in higher education are bound to be imperfect. So are all markets. However, markets are generally seen as having a number of defining characteristics. Roger Brown himself has set out these characteristics in considerable detail, placing particular emphasis on accurate and transparent information for consumers. Others have identified up to eight essential characteristics, four for the consumers and four for the providers (Jongbloed, 2003). But, to simplify, three are perhaps truly foundational characteristics.

The first is consumer choice. Are potential students able to choose between courses and institutions? This is not as self-evidently a superiority of market systems of higher education as it may appear. It may even be that students are freer to choose within public higher education systems that guarantee access for all successful secondary school graduates. League tables and rankings may also have had the perverse effect of restricting choice because institutions struggle to improve their standing by recruiting 'higher quality' students. It is important not to confuse the increasing paraphernalia of consumer information for enhanced student choice.

The second characteristic of markets is an effective price mechanism. Yet most of the markets that have been created out of formerly public higher education systems, notably in England and Australia, have defined tuition fees not as a true reflection of the cost of higher education but simply as a contribution by students (really, graduates) to that cost. But defining fees in this way as a contribution rather than as a full cost has sharply reduced the incentive, and the case, for charging differential prices – even without taking into account the reputational incentive to charge high fees and the cartel-like instincts that prevail among institutions. The issue is not therefore simply the level of fees but the way in which they have been conceived as student contributions, thus begging the question of how the rest of the cost of higher education is to be funded (and by implication exposing the limits of markets?).

The third characteristic is reasonable access for new providers. But access to the higher education market is – necessarily – severely constrained by two factors. The first factor is the slow historical accretion of reputation that is the basis of the prestige hierarchy among institutions; few newcomer institutions can compete in these terms. Of course, this also applies in commercial markets where some industries are dominated by global high-status companies; for example, Apple and Microsoft in computing or Mercedes Benz and Toyota in automobiles. The second is the need to maintain academic standards, made more insistent by the development of mass higher education systems; arguably quality regimes have become more explicit and intrusive placing greater obstacles in the way of opening up higher education. Regulation in other sectors rarely plays such a powerful blocking role.

So markets always have their limits. In addition, higher education has a number of inherent and more fundamental characteristics that may further inhibit the development of a functioning market. One is that, with very few exceptions, higher education is a one-off experience (or 'purchase') – unlike a car that is changed every few years (or smart phones that may be changed every few months). Although some students go on to take postgraduate courses, generally they do not repeat the cycles of higher education unless they have dropped out or failed. Also, unlike many consumer goods, higher education does not become obsolete and need to be replaced by a newer model or a more technologically sophisticated product. Or, rather, it becomes obsolete in a different sense, as skills and knowledge change (as does the wider socio-economic environment), leading to a permanent need for updating.

Another characteristic is that, especially in its more instrumental modes, higher education is a positional good, its value being defined predominantly in terms of its accessibility and/or scarcity – even if, in its more idealistic modes, a university education is an absolute good in terms of the enlightenment of individual human beings and the transformation of their lives. But its marketability lies largely in its value as a positional good, which is why league tables and brands are so important. 'World-class' translates, potentially at any rate, into the ability to charge higher fees – to heighten prestige (and consumer attractiveness) and also because graduates of elite universities secure a better rate of return on their individual investment in higher education.

A third characteristic is that in higher education the sovereignty of the consumer (student) is necessarily constrained:

- First, students cannot know best because they are junior partners in a complex learning environment (and also joint partners in a collective learning process, if peer-learning is emphasised). So, it follows that their demands cannot be satisfied in a simple, linear way; instead, their needs must be negotiated in a highly reflexive (even dialectical) relationship with their teachers.
- Second, academic qualifications cannot be put 'for sale' (concerns have already been raised by the House of Commons' Public Accounts Committee, among others, about private for-profit institutions recruiting students who are unable to complete their courses – and may indeed have no intention of doing so). And despite the strong correlation between socio-economic status and access to elite universities (which may charge no fees or, in cases where fees are charged, have 'blind' admissions policies that, at any rate formally, ignore the ability to pay), qualifications must be 'earned' by sustained study, and whether students are successful or not is subject to a process of assessment and examination. There are not many markets in which products that consumers have purchased can nevertheless be denied to them. But the ultimate value of the higher education product depends on the fact it must be earned – not simply because standards need to be maintained to maintain its market value, but in an even more important

sense because the effort expended by students is fundamental to the creation of the 'good'.

- Finally, the value of higher education can only be defined over the long haul. That value is constantly being adjusted over the whole lifespan of graduates; it cannot be reduced to the starting salaries of new graduates. But it is notoriously difficult to price goods, the value of which is not only determined over very long time-spans but is also subject to volatile change – as has been frequently demonstrated by large-scale infrastructure projects such as nuclear power. 'Net present values' can be calculated but are subject to so many (arbitrary) assumptions as to be close to meaningless.

- As a result of these constraints, there may be few – if any – examples of properly functioning market systems of higher education. Even in those systems with substantial (and prestigious) private sectors (such as the United States, Japan or Korea), the majority of institutions continue to be public, enrolling the majority of students. In the market experiments that have been undertaken in countries where nearly all institutions were (and generally still are) public, the result has been to create public–private hybrid systems in which students / graduates are, in effect, 'taxed' by being obliged to make increased contributions and (usually a limited number of) private for-profit institutions are allowed access to public funding to which previously only public institutions were entitled.

Although there have been important ways in which higher education has been liberalised, which have provoked principled opposition, the most appropriate conceptual frameworks for describing such liberalisation are perhaps not so much the market as such – but, as has already been argued, the increasing permeability of the public and the private domains; the emergence of an influential new 'third sector' of privatised and outsourced services (not just, or particularly, in higher education); a pragmatic rebalancing of public and private contributions to the cost of higher education as a response to state-mandated 'austerity' (individual contributions have always been substantial in terms of initial income foregone and enhanced future tax contributions); and the renegotiation of the status (formal and informal) of institutions.

Perhaps a better label of these liberalised higher education systems is 'post-market' rather than 'market' systems. True markets require the existence of a clearly defined 'other' – over the past century, the national welfare state. When the market spreads to embrace the bulk of social as well as economic activities, it tends to lose its sharp and distinctive focus and – unwittingly and even paradoxically – provoke its own constraints. This may be especially evident in social, cultural and scientific institutions conceived of (necessarily?) on other principles, such as universities. The more pervasive markets become, the more they generate their own limits.

The reform of English higher education

The reform of English higher education since 2010 has certainly been an ideological 'event'. As has already said, Lord Browne himself – incautiously perhaps – described his report as heralding a 'paradigm shift'. Opponents of the reform have also occasionally indulged in similarly doomsday language (McGettigan, 2013). A number of resistance groups have been established such as the Campaign for the Public University and the Council for the Defence of British Universities, although their target has not been exclusively the alleged marketisation of universities but also the rise of so-called managerialism and increasing surveillance of teaching quality and research performance. So far, their impact has been limited by their failure to develop coherent alternatives to the drift towards marketisation. They are very clear about what they are against; less clear about what they are for.

But it has been more than an ideological clash. As a result of the implementation of the proposals made in the 2011 white paper, England has become an outlier – not simply with regard to the rest of Europe, where the principle of 'free' (in other words, tax-funded higher education) has proved to be remarkably resilient (and in Germany fees charged on some *Länder* have recently been abandoned) – but also the United States, the supposed heartland of market higher education, where tuition fees in even the most celebrated state universities are generally significantly lower than those charged by even less well-regarded English universities. The level of surveillance is also higher than in both the rest of Europe and the United States, most obviously with regard to quality assurance (an almost unknown idea in the US and only now gaining familiarity in the rest of Europe under the label 'quality culture'). However, neither the sharp ideological clashes nor the fact that England is now an (extreme?) outlier prove that a functioning market system of higher education is in the process of being established in England.

If the three tests referred to the last section are applied, the tentative character of the market system established since 2010 becomes clear:

* Student choice has been enhanced – in formal terms. In 2015–2016 there will be no limits on how many students institutions are allowed to admit. But it is far from clear that this will lead to significant changes in the traditional pattern of supply and demand, characterised by a – rough – division between 'selecting' and 'recruiting' universities, wide variations in demand for different subjects and courses and a clearly understood pecking order. The introduction of the National Student Survey, which predated the Browne reforms, and the requirement imposed on institutions in the 2011 white paper to provide so-called key information sets, data on entry standards, success rates and so on, have tended to reinforce rather than to challenge these established characteristics
* There is, as yet, no functioning price mechanism because nearly all institutions charge the maximum allowed – hardly surprising because of the lack of

price sensitivity that is the result of the universal availability of state-funded loans. The (minor) advantages that institutions would gain from charging lower fees are swamped by the (major) disadvantages of reputational loss they might incur (as well as the loss of income that could be used to enhance the student experience and so institutional competitiveness)

• Finally, although a (very) small number of new and alternative – and private – providers have been allowed to enter the higher education market, they continue to be at a disadvantage compared with public institutions in some crucial respects, notably an unrestricted ability to award degrees. Moreover, there is a growing concern about the potential for abuse, in particular students who (perhaps only intermittently – if at all) attend private for-profit institutions often with low academic standards but nevertheless are able to access publicly funded loans to pay their fees. Nor has there been any significant growth in lower-cost local higher education provided by further education colleges

Lord Browne's claims of a paradigm shift, therefore, appear to be unjustified – so far. English higher education is an imperfect market at best. Less may have changed than the ideological *furore* suggests. It is worth remembering that UK higher education has always been a partial market (compared, for example, with the National Health Service) – in the important senses that all institutions are autonomous, public in their values perhaps but not state institutions; and that students have always been free to choose which institution to apply to (although there was – and still is – no guarantee that they would be admitted). The post-2010 reform is perhaps best described not so much in terms of the introduction of high-fees, but of the replacement of (direct) grants to institutions by (indirect) funding through student vouchers (which are only partially repayable because the relatively high repayment threshold and the fixed term of student loans mean that many will never be recovered – the current estimate is that less than 60 per cent will be repaid). The reform has also introduced a more intrusive, if still chaotic, control regime; eligibility criteria for loans must be policed; measures taken to ensure that students, as customers, are given adequate information; rules established for the admission of alternative providers; and much else besides. Unsurprisingly, the reform has provided an extra fillip to managerialism, the major target of many of its critics (Callender and Scott, 2013).

It is possible that the post-2010 reform of English higher education will prove simply to be a staging post on the road to an unambiguously market system. Lord Browne's claim will eventually be vindicated, and Roger Brown's warnings about rampant marketisation will prove to be prescient. But the analysis offered in this chapter suggests that another path is possible. Firstly, private benefits and public goods have become so tangled that they are difficult to separate – not only conceptually but also in policy terms. Secondly, markets have clearly encroached on territory once reserved for the exercise of democratic choice through public policy – but in the process they have had to accept increasing restrictions on their scope, through more intrusive forms of (politicised) regulation, which may end up compromising some of their essential characteristics (ushering in a post-market era?). Finally, although there can no doubt about the deep-structural evolution of English higher education (and most other higher education systems) towards more instrumentally oriented and managerial forms for more than a generation, this has had many strands – which cannot easily be reduced to a single-path of development towards the market. This evolution can also be explained in terms of increasing complexity, heterogeneity, engagement, embeddedness and contextualisation. In short, it may be premature to abandon massification for marketisation as the one-word label to characterise contemporary higher education.

Bibliography

Brown, R. (2009) *The Role of the Market in Higher Education*. Oxford: Higher Education Policy Institute

Brown, R. (ed.) (2011a) *Higher Education and the Market*. London: Routledge

Brown, R. (2011b) *Lessons from America*. Oxford: Higher Education Policy Institute

Brown, R. with Carasso, H. (2013) *Everything for Sale? The Marketisation of UK Higher Education*. London: Routledge and the Society for Research into Higher Education

Callender, C. and Scott, P. (eds) (2013) *Browne and Beyond: Modernizing English Higher Education*. London: Institute of Education Press

Committee on Student Fees and Funding [Browne Report] (2010) *Securing a Sustainable Future for Higher Education*. London: Available at: www.independent. gov/browne-report

Business, Innovation and Skills, Department of [BIS] (2011) *Students at the Heart of the System: White Paper on Higher Education*. London: Department of Business, Innovation and Skills

Gibbons, M., Limoges, C., Nowotny, H., Schwartzman, S., Scott, P. and Trow, M. (1994) *The New Production of Knowledge: The Dynamics of Science and Research in Contemporary Societies*. London: Sage

Jongbloed, B. (2003) Marketisation in higher education: Clark's triangle and the essential ingredients of markets. *Higher Education Quarterly* 57 (2): 110–135

Marginson, S. (1997) *Markets in Higher Education*. London: Allen & Unwin

Marginson, S. (2011) Higher education and the public good. *Higher Education Quarterly* 65 (4): 411–433

McGettigan, A. (2013) *The Great University Gamble: Money, Markets and the Future of Higher Education*. London: Pluto Press

New Economics Foundation (2011) *Degrees of Value: How Universities Benefit Society*. London: New Economics Foundation

Organisation for Economic Cooperation and Development (2012) *Education Indicators in Focus – What Are the Returns on Higher Education for Individuals and Countries?* Paris: OECD

Psacharopoulos, G. (2009) *Returns on Investment in Higher Education: A European Survey* (a contribution to the Higher Education Funding Reform Project). Brussels: European Commission. Available at: www.ec.europa.eu/education/higher education/doc/funding/vol3_en.pdf

Scott, P. (2015) Higher Education, the Public Good and the Public Interest. In O. Filippakou and G. Williams (eds) *Higher Education as a Public Good: Critical Perspectives on Theory, Policy and Practice*. New York: Peter Lang: 41–58

Chapter 2

Paying the price of expansion

Why more for undergraduates in England means less for everyone

Helen Carasso and William Locke

Introduction

As participation in higher education has grown in the United Kingdom (UK) – to the point where it is approaching 50 per cent in England – successive governments have had to address the issue of how to fund the growing costs of teaching and student support at the same time as increasing access and widening participation. While budgetary considerations have inevitably played their part in the incremental increase in maximum full-time undergraduate fees in England from zero in 1997/98 to £9,000 in 2012/13, politicians have also argued that it is right in principle for students to contribute to the cost of their education. This cost-sharing (Johnstone, 2004) has been justified with reference to the personal benefits that individual graduates gain from their degrees. Yet the value of this 'graduate premium' is contested (Thompson and Bekhradnia, 2012) and certainly varies between subjects, institutions and the gender of the student.

Roger Brown has been critical of an increasingly ideological form of policy-making in higher education that has taken hold since the mid-1980s. This has emphasised the economic role of higher education and created a higher education 'market' (Brown, 2008, 2013). It was particularly highlighted by the very limited research evidence employed by the 2010 Browne Report (Browne, 2010), especially when compared with its predecessors, the Dearing and Robbins Reports.

The aim of this chapter is to review the arguments that policy-makers used to justify the significant changes to fees and financial support for UK and European Union (EU) undergraduates at universities in England that were introduced in 1998, 2006 and 2012. We will also compare the political rhetoric with the research evidence that was available at the time to inform the formation of policy and with some of the observable outcomes.

1998: A student contribution is introduced, but the funding gap remains

By the time the Dearing Report (the Report of the National Committee of Inquiry into Higher Education – NCIHE, 1997) was submitted to Parliament in

July 1997, public funding for universities had fallen to 76 per cent of its 1980 value (Watson and Bowden, 1997: 15). University Vice-Chancellors were concerned about their ability to maintain the standards of their institutions' teaching and research. In 1996 they decided collectively that they would introduce a form of 'top-up fees' unilaterally, unless rapid action was taken to increase the resources that were available to their universities (Brown with Carasso, 2013: 82).

It is perhaps therefore not surprising that, on the day that the ten-volume Dearing Report was published, the government made its response in Parliament. The then Secretary of State for Education and Employment, David Blunkett said:

> The [Dearing] committee recognises that we cannot afford further improvement or expansion of higher education on the basis of current funding arrangements. Students should share both the investment and the advantages gained from higher education: rights and responsibilities go hand in hand. The investment of the nation must be balanced by the commitment of the individual: each will gain from the investment made.
>
> [. . .]
>
> We must develop a more efficient system than the present confusion of loans, grants and parental contributions. For lower-income families, instead of the remaining grant, students' living costs will be covered by a maintenance loan of the same value as the current grant and loan package. An additional maintenance loan equivalent to the tuition fee will be available to students from higher-income families. We shall, however, ensure that the poorest students do not have to pay fees. That is the best way of encouraging access to free education for the least well-off. We are equally determined to ensure that there is no increase in parental contributions.
>
> (Hansard, 1997: col. 954)

The main financial measures (which were subsequently to form part of the Teaching and Higher Education Act [1998]) he proposed were:

- The introduction of means-tested fees of up to £1,000 per year (with only index-linked increases on that limit permitted); these were to be paid 'up front' by the undergraduate
- Abolition of means-tested non-repayable grants
- An increase in the sums available through student loans – with favourable repayment terms.

However, as far as undergraduate fees and funding were concerned, the Dearing Committee (NCIHE, 1997) had actually recommended to the government that it should:

- Review the total level of support for student living costs annually, taking into account the movement of both prices and earnings (Recommendation 70)

- Shift the balance of funding, in a planned way, away from block grant towards a system in which funding follows the student [. . .] with a target of distributing at least 60 per cent of total public funding to institutions according to student choice by 2003 (Recommendation 72)
- Introduce, by 1998/9, income contingent terms for the payment of any contribution towards living costs or tuition costs sought from graduates in work (Recommendation 78)
- [. . .] Introduce arrangements for graduates in work to make a flat rate contribution of around 25 per cent of the average cost of higher education tuition, through an income contingent mechanism. [. . .] The contributions made by graduates in this way should be reserved for meeting the needs of higher education (Recommendation 79)

So the report did not suggest that fees should be paid by undergraduates 'up front'; rather, it advocated a move towards a voucher-based system of university funding in which student choice would play a significant role in determining the distribution of public funding within the sector. There was also no proposal to abolish the means-tested non-repayable grant for students from lower-income families. As Watson and Bowden (2007) comment:

> New Labour's first-term policy on higher education [. . .] was structured around Dearing, with the serious modification of his recommendations on fees and student support, which has haunted them ever since. Essentially, the government was too greedy. Ministers took the Dearing recommendation of a student contribution to course costs and ignored what the report said about living costs, especially for poorer students. Simultaneously, they completed a Conservative policy of turning all student grants into loans. [. . .] This precipitate decision has become the Achilles heel of subsequent New Labour policy on higher education.
>
> (Watson and Bowden, 2007: 29)

This 'Achilles heel' was, according to one key policy-maker, principally for two main reasons:

> My view then was that it was too little, the [1998] reform, and that it was flawed in one or two key respects, particularly the up-front nature of the fee that made it very inflexible and secondly the lack of any mechanism or flexibility for increasing it over time, when it was clear that universities were going to need a substantial additional fund of non-state income and, on any credible co-payment basis, this was probably going to involve more student contribution over time.
>
> (Carasso, 2010: 236)

It is therefore not surprising that, within just a few years, the question of undergraduate fees was again on the political agenda.

2006: Top-up fees and the student as consumer

The introduction of a student contribution to fees in 1998 marked a significant shift in the principles behind the funding of studying for an undergraduate degree at English universities. However, the (index-linked) £1,000 was still not enough to compensate for the real-terms decline in public funding for UK/EU students. By 2001–02, it had reached 63 per cent of its 1979–80 value (Watson and Bowden, 2007: 36–37).

During this period (when participation stood at around 40 per cent), the Labour Party had set a target of increasing participation in higher education among young people to 50 per cent by 2010 (Blair, 1999; Labour Party, 2001). However, there was little incentive for universities to increase undergraduate places as teaching was still underfunded, despite the introduction of the £1,000 fee in 1998 (Brown, 2003: 3–4). At the same time, the principle of variable fees was already well established for overseas undergraduates, as it had been in place since 1980, with different levels of fees set not only by individual institutions, but also for different courses at the same institution (UUK, 2001).

It was against this background that the concept of variable undergraduate fees for full-time UK/EU undergraduates at English universities was first discussed in earnest by policy-makers in the early 2000s, as Andrew Adonis, Head of the Prime Minister's Policy Unit under Tony Blair, explained:

> Part of the reason that we laid great store by the variability of the fee and the statutory instrument regime for changing the fee at the time was that we did not want any future government [. . .] to be forced to pass primary legislation every time you wanted to make adjustments to the student finance regime.
>
> And again it was the experience of Australia that led us to think that, if we set up a system on this basis, it would be robust over time. The Australian HECS system had lasted nearly ten years by that time, and our regime had only being going four since Dearing, but it already required one piece of primary legislation. So we were keen that we should have a robust, flexible system that wouldn't require primary legislation every time a change in fee level was contemplated.
>
> (Carasso, 2010: 241–42)

With these considerations in mind, early in 2003, the UK government announced its proposals for revisions to undergraduate fees and funding. However, ministers knew these would be highly contentious:

> It was the Prime Minister's view in 2001 that we couldn't continue to duck [the under-funding of university teaching] if we wanted world-class universities and to expand student numbers. It was that decision, in the knowledge of the fact that any reform would be politically controversial, that put the

issue very firmly on the agenda. If it hadn't been for his personal support for it, there's no way of course that the Education Department alone would have been able to start formulating quite radical policies in a controversial area.

(Carasso, 2010: 240)

They continued to be controversial as the key parliamentary vote approached. Speaking a fortnight before that, the then Prime Minister, Tony Blair said:

It's a big reform and these reforms are always difficult, and if you look back on the history of big social, economic, political reform in the past 20 or 30 years, they have always caused controversy because we're asking people to think anew and there are two elements of argument against us at the moment. One is to say, look University education should be free and therefore the whole concept of fees is wrong. Now I believe it is not fair to put all the burden on the general taxpayer, and I think the country will understand that as you expand higher education places it is fair to ask for the graduate to make a contribution back into the system once they graduate, but we have got to win that argument.

And the second argument is on the variability of the fee and there I think it is important to stress that to force all Universities to charge the same for every course and every University to be treated the same is just not either realistic or fair. There will be 2-year foundation courses that Universities will want to charge less for, than say a 3- or 4-year science or engineering degree, and I think that's perfectly sensible. Or a law degree. And I think to encourage that diversity is a good thing, not a bad thing.

(Blair, 2004)

In practice, the level of opposition that the government faced in Parliament led to a reduction in the maximum permitted fee from £5,000 to £3,000. In spite of this concession to those who were concerned about the extent to which the proposed increase in fees might deter participation in higher education, when the crucial vote was held in the House of Commons on 27 January 2004, it passed by just five votes, even though the government had a majority of 161.

The main points of the resulting Higher Education Act (2004), (which were enacted for full-time UK/EU undergraduates enrolling on a degree course at a university in England from autumn 2006) concerning fees and funding were:

- Maximum annual student contribution to fees increased to £3,000 (with only index-linked annual increases allowed until at least 2010), with deferred liability until the graduate is earning – the amount charged may vary between subjects within institutions, but should not vary within a recruitment cycle;
- Re-introduction of means-tested, non-repayable grants, with eligibility dependent on residual household income (RHI) of a student's family;

- Increase in amount available to students through low-cost loans (0 per cent real rate of interest, only repayable if/when annual income exceeds £15,000, written off after 25 years) to cover fee liability as well as living costs;
- Any university wishing to charge more in fees than the basic amount (£1,200 in 2006 with index-linked annual increases) had to enter into an access agreement with the Office for Fair Access (OFFA) outlining financial support available and other measures in place to promote equality of access to higher education.

The provisions concerning bursaries and access agreements were put in place to address concerns that potential applicants from lower-income backgrounds would be more discouraged than others from taking out student loans. There is some evidence that participation patterns changed following the introduction of the £3,000 fee, in that those from lower socio-economic groups were more likely to apply to a university: near UK; with a low cost of living; or where they expect more opportunities for term-time opportunity (Callender and Jackson, 2008: 426). However, whether because of the financial support that universities were obliged to offer or not, there is no clear evidence that the 2006 increase in fees reduced participation in higher education by some groups more than others.

At the same time, the outcomes of the 2006 changes did not match the expectations of politicians and commentators concerning the fees that would be charged either. These expectations were outlined subsequently by Charles Clarke, who was Secretary of State in 2004, responsible for higher education policy:

> The system of student finance established by this legislation was intended to allow different fees to be charged for different courses at different HEIs, in accordance with their differing quality and value for future life, but in a way which did not carry adverse consequences for those applying to university from poorer backgrounds. The whole repayment system, which removed the upfront payments and established a payback after graduation through the tax system, was designed to achieve this goal.
>
> (Clarke, 2010: 2)

However, in practice, there was little variability in fees charged. All universities charged one fee for all their courses, and in 2006, just four charged less than the maximum permitted £3,000. By the time Charles Clarke was writing in 2010, all universities were charging the maximum fee for all their courses.

However, according to one Vice-Chancellor who, as President of Universities UK, represented the sector in negotiations with the Government in 2003/4, politicians were playing a longer game:

> [. . .] [F]or people like Blair and Andrew Adonis and Charles Clarke this was all part of a bigger strategy to change higher education. I think they did

believe that fees would go up further after a few years when we'd all got used to fees being £3,000. [. . .] So they saw the Higher Education Act as being a historical turning point, but not the end of the story. And that's why they were adamant that the fees had to be variable.

(Carasso, 2010: 241)

Thus further changes were widely expected to follow the next review of undergraduate fees and funding, the Browne Committee.

2012: From cost sharing to cost transfer

The Report of the Independent Review of Higher Education Funding and Student Finance chaired by Lord Browne (Browne, 2010) was a very different exercise from previous reviews of higher education, being largely geared towards assisting the Coalition Government in reducing public expenditure – at least in accounting terms. Based on submissions to the Committee, the Browne Report claimed a consensus around the need for a graduate contribution to the costs of higher education. This, of course, may have just been an acceptance of the status quo and of the likelihood that the next government would have to increase that contribution, rather than a principled agreement to an increased graduate contribution. However, the Report effortlessly slid between this and the assumption that the contribution should cover the *majority* of the costs and, in some cases (in classroom and library-based courses, for example) the full costs of provision (or, even, more than the actual costs).

Two reasons were given in the Report for this: first, that graduates receive more direct benefit from their higher education qualification than the public receives; and second, that higher education study is neither compulsory nor universal – that people choose to go, providing they are sufficiently qualified. We can dismiss the second of these instantly because it is merely an argument for *some* individual contribution, and not necessarily for a majority contribution. The main reason, then, was the claim that the private benefits to the individual are more than 50 per cent higher than the public benefits. The Report cited Organisation for Economic Co-operation and Development (OECD) research to support this view, although it did not identify in which of the hundreds of tables and charts in Education at a Glance (OECD, 2010) its authors found this evidence.

As many have pointed out (Collini, 2012; McGettigan, 2013; Callender and Scott, 2013), the decision to treble tuition fees and slash public funding for teaching was not based on evidence and was a radical mix of neo-liberal ideology and the perceived need to curtail public expenditure. However, it is interesting that Lord Browne still felt the need to refer to sources of evidence that supported his committee's – and the government's – conclusions. However, this evidence is only deployed in order to illustrate the arguments presented. There is no pretence at evidence-based policy-making.

The Report also maintained that, although the 2006 reforms were designed to bring in more private contributions to HE, there had been no increase in the proportion of the private contribution made by students or graduates. It 'illustrated' this with a table from a presentation made to the Committee by the Institute for Fiscal Studies (IFS, 2010) which suggested there was no change in the balance of investments in HE by taxpayers, students, graduates and universities between 2003/04 and 2008/09. However, the IFS used a 'zero sum' model based on a limited sample and a number of assumptions, including no changes in the repayment behaviour of graduates, and this allowed Browne to underplay the significantly increased debt incurred by students following the 2006 reforms. The Report concluded:

> The debate may have changed in favour of changing the balance between public and private contributions to higher education, but the reality has not.
> (Browne, 2010: 21)

However, it then goes on to propose changes to the variables in the existing fees and funding system – the fee level, the interest rate, the salary threshold at which graduates start to pay and the period after which the loan is written off. These variables were to be changed, but not the system itself, and the Coalition Government largely implemented these proposals with a few significant if not fundamental modifications. Working within the legislative framework that had been established by the Higher Education Act (2004), they were able to make these changes incrementally and without primary legislation; this reduced the potential for contentious debates and votes in Parliament, but also resulted in piecemeal changes, rather than a coherent package of reforms.

As others (e.g. Callender and Scott, 2013) have argued, there is much continuity between the 2006 New Labour reforms and the 2012 Coalition Government changes. Also, as we have rapidly discovered, the RAB (Resource Accounting and Budgeting) charge – the eventual cost to the taxpayer of the unpaid loans – has leapt from the government's initial estimate of 30 per cent to over 45 per cent, and so threatens to wipe out any savings it might make. So there is a danger of history appearing to repeat itself (Carpentier, 2012). The government may have wished to transfer the majority of the costs of higher education study to graduates, but its policies will not achieve this, despite ratcheting up their levels of debt.

A final comment on the Browne Report – it did not recommend a cap on tuition fees, at £9,000 or more. This was because it concluded that '[t]here is no robust way of identifying the right maximum level of investment in HE' – that is investment by students and graduates – and so, effectively, the market should determine this. Many, including economists and econometrics experts, fundamentally disagree with this argument, and we will go on to explain why, and what this might mean for fees and funding policies in the future.

'Stealing' the social (and private non-market) benefits of higher education

The analysis on which the Browne Report proposals and the Coalition Government's – and, indeed the preceding New Labour Government's – policies were based does not reflect the true value of higher education to an individual or to society. This is because it is based on investment theory – derived from the finance literature. It draws on a limited range of evidence to calculate the market benefits for individuals, in particular, market earnings and employment benefits. It assumes not just the existence of a market and market behaviour, but the *predominance* of the market and market behaviour, and it uses historical data to predict the future. In contrast, the econometric approach taken in labour economics includes the non-market private and social benefits of higher education and adds these to the calculation of the market benefits, both private and public.

These wider benefits of higher education include the economic and social impacts of an increasingly highly skilled workforce, the generation of new ideas and contributions to social capital. There are also contributions to democratic institutions, human rights, political stability, lower welfare costs, lower health care costs and lower policing and prison costs, for example (Brennan *et al.*, 2013). An economic value can be calculated for all of these, and one of the most sophisticated assessments of this kind is Walter McMahon's *Higher Learning, Greater Good: The Private and Social Benefits of Higher Education* (McMahon, 2009; see also McMahon, 2010). In this book, McMahon identifies and measures the non-market private and social benefits of higher education – here and now, not in the future – using the best data available. He estimates that, together, the private and social non-market benefits are more than half (68 per cent) of the total benefits of higher education. So, it is fair to conclude that the taxpayer should be contributing at least half of the costs of higher education, and that students and graduates should be covering no more than half.

However, the privatisation of higher education, which has resulted in the under-estimation of the social benefits of study, has led to underinvestment in undergraduate and postgraduate education which, in turn, has led to market failure. Fewer qualified students are pursuing higher education study than could, especially part-time, mature and postgraduate. Also, they are increasingly choosing subjects that are perceived as more likely to lead to immediate employment. Yet non-vocational subjects are likely to yield higher non-market private and social benefits, such as creativity, inter-cultural understanding, the development of democratic institutions and the rule of law. The devaluing of these benefits is leading to a long-term skills and knowledge deficit which, in turn, will lead to reductions in overall economic efficiency. It is also diverting universities and colleges towards meeting private needs and away from their broader social purposes, such as widening participation, community engagement and increased public understanding. It will also make it harder to persuade politicians and the public to restore the balance of public and private investment in higher education in the future. Ultimately, the losers will be society and the longer term efficiency of the UK economy.

Let us briefly return to the OECD report that was used by Browne to justify transferring the costs to graduates. If he had read on further, he would have found the following passage. Indeed, many would rather wish he had and then pointed it out to the Coalition Government:

> On average . . . the net public return from an investment in tertiary education is . . . almost three times the amount of public investment in tertiary education across OECD countries, and as such, provides a strong incentive for governments to expand higher education. . . . Public investments in education, particularly at the tertiary level, are rational *even in the face of running a deficit in public finances.*
>
> (OECD, 2010: 145, our emphasis)

Conclusion

The arguments employed by policy-makers to justify introducing fees for under-graduate, full-time study, and then trebling these twice, have been modified on each occasion, reflecting the ideological persuasion and the political and economic challenges of the government in power at the time. Research evidence for these complex and important decisions barely made an appearance and, if it did, it was deployed highly selectively and then sometimes in contradiction with the researchers' own conclusions (Locke, 2009). In 1998, students were required to 'share the investment' in their higher education study with the nation, since their earnings on graduation would rise. In 2006, these unpopular upfront but flat rate fees were to be replaced by increased variable fees repayable on graduation to reflect the differential quality of education between institutions and the variation in value between graduates in different subjects. It quickly became apparent that these would be variable only in name. The 2012 transfer of the majority of the costs of study to graduates was justified on highly questionable 'evidence' that they would gain half as much more direct benefit from their higher education study than the public would receive. As Roger Brown has described it, this is 'policy-based evidence' not evidence-based policy (Brown, 2008; Brown, 2013).

Bibliography

Blair, T. (1999) *Speech at Labour Party Conference*. Bournemouth
Blair, T. (2004) *A future fair for all: Labour's university reforms*. Speech delivered at Church House, Westminster, 14 January 2004
Brennan, J., Durazzi, N. and Séné, T. (2013) *Things we know and don't know about the wider benefits of higher education*. Department for Business, Innovation and Skills: BIS Research Paper 120
Brown, N. (2003) *For What It's Worth*. London: Universities UK

Brown, R. (2008) How do we get more effective policies for higher education? Reflections of a policy-maker. *Higher Education Review* 41 (1): 3–20

Brown, R. (ed.) (2011) *Higher Education and the Market.* London: Routledge

Brown, R. (2013) Evidence-based policy or policy-based evidence? Higher education policies and policy-making 1987–2012. *Perspectives: Policy and Practice in Higher Education* 17 (4): 118–123

Brown, R. with Carasso, H. (2013) *Everything For Sale: The Marketisation of UK Higher Education.* London: Routledge and the Society for Research into Higher Education

Browne, J. (2010) Securing a Sustainable Future for Higher Education. *Report of the Independent Review of Higher Education Funding and Student Finance.* Available at: http://www.independent.gov.uk/browne-report

Callender, C. and Jackson, J. (2005) Does fear of debt deter students from higher education? *Journal of Social Policy* 34 (4): 509–540

Callender, C. and Jackson, J. (2008) Does the fear of debt constrain choice of university and subject of study? *Studies in Higher Education* 33 (4): 405–429

Callender, C. and Scott, P. (eds) (2013) *Browne and Beyond: Modernizing English Higher Education.* London: Institute of Education Press

Carasso, H. (2010) *Implementing the financial provisions of the HE Act (2004) – English universities in a new quasi-market.* DPhil thesis. Available at: http://ora.ox.ac.uk/objects/ora:4584 [accessed 16 November 2014]

Carpentier, V. (2012) Public-private substitution in higher education: Has cost-sharing gone too far? *Higher Education Quarterly* 66 (4): 363–390

Clarke, C. (2010) *Submission to Browne Inquiry into Higher Education Funding.* Available at: http://webarchive.nationalarchives.gov.uk/+/hereview.independent. gov.uk/hereview/2010/03/submissions-to-the-first-call-for-evidence/ [accessed 10 August 2013]

Collini, S. (2012) *What Are Universities For?* Harmondsworth: Penguin

Hansard (1997), HC Deb (1997–98) 298 col. 954. Available at: http://www.publi cations.parliament.uk/pa/cm199798/cmhansrd/vo970723/debtext/70723-22. htm#70723-22_spnew1 [accessed 11 January 2015]

IFS (2010) The impact of the '2006–07 package' of reforms to HE funding. *Presentation was delivered as evidence by IFS at the first public hearing of the Independent Review of Higher Education Funding and Student Finance, chaired by Lord Browne,* by L. Dearden, A. Goodman and G. Wyness. Available at: http://www.ifs.org.uk/ publications/4727 [accessed 16 November 2014]

Johnstone, B. D. (2004) The economics and politics of cost sharing in higher education: comparative perspectives. *Economics of Education Review* 23 (4): 403–410

Labour Party (2001) *Ambitions for Britain: 2001 Labour Party General Election Manifesto.* London: Labour Party

Locke, W. (2009) Reconnecting the research-policy-practice nexus in higher education: 'Evidence-based policy' in practice in national and international contexts. *Higher Education Policy* 22 (2): 119–140

McGettigan, A. (2013) *The Great University Gamble: Money, Markets and the Future of Higher Education.* London: Pluto Press

McMahon, W. (2009) *Higher Learning, Greater Good, The Private and Social Benefits of Higher Education.* Baltimore, Maryland: Johns Hopkins University Press

McMahon, W. (2010) The Private and Social Benefits of Higher Education: The Evidence, Their Value, and Policy Implications. *Advancing Higher Education*. New York: TIAA-CREF. Available at: http://www.philadelphia.edu.jo/centers/iro/The_private_and_social_benefits_of_higher_education.pdf [accessed 21 August 2014]

National Committee of Inquiry into Higher Education (NCIHE) (1997) *Higher Education in the Learning Society*. London: HMSO

OECD (2010) *Education at a Glance*. Paris: Organisation for Economic Co-operation and Development

Teaching and Higher Education Act (1998) London: HMSO

Thompson, J. and Bekhradnia, B. (2012) *The Cost of the Government's Reforms of the Financing of Higher Education*. Oxford: Higher Education Policy Institute

UUK (Universities UK) (2001) *International Student Tuition Fees: Survey Results 2001–2*. London: UUK

Watson, D. and Bowden, R. (1997) *Ends Without Means: The Conservative Stewardship of UK Higher Education 1979–1997*. Brighton: Education Research Centre, University of Brighton

Watson, D. and Bowden, R. (2007) The Fate of the Dearing Recommendations: Policy and Performance in UK Higher Education 1997–2007. In D. Watson and M. Amoah (eds) *The Dearing Report: Ten Years On*. London: Bedford Way Papers, Institute of Education: 6–50

Chapter 3

Choice in the learning market
Tokenistic ritual or democratic education?

Rajani Naidoo

I first met Roger Brown many years ago at an all-male policy event. I was standing there in panic thinking, 'I don't know anybody here. I think I will just leave!' And suddenly Roger was at my side saying 'Oh hello you are not one of the old boys! What a good thing that is!' And many years later at a similar event Roger said to me, 'You do realise you are part of the old boys club now!' I have always remembered this as a cautionary tale. And that links to what is so special about Roger Brown. He of course is not an outsider railing against the system. He is an important and powerful actor: a senior civil servant, a Chief Executive of the Higher Education Quality Council and a Vice-Chancellor . . . but he has always had the courage and the integrity to raise awkward questions, to dig underneath narrow technical accounts of change in higher education and to uncover inconvenient truths. While he is eloquent and concise, he has never been afraid to speak truth to power. And for me that is and will continue to be one of his most important and enduring influences. It is in this spirit that I wish to write this chapter.

One of the most important contributions that Roger Brown has made to studies in higher education is his critical analysis of the development and impact of the marketisation of higher education. Through his corpus of work (Brown with Carasso, 2013), he shows how markets are socially constructed and the consequences for quality and equity. This chapter relates to his work in two ways. First, I present an analysis of the relationship between the state and the market in higher education and show how this leads to a particular type of learning market that re-conceptualises students as consumers, and assumes a number of positive outcomes. Second, I suggest that consumer choice is in many important ways more tokenistic than real and indeed may be seen to work against equity and democracy.

The state-market relationship

The quasi-marketisation of higher education by neo-liberal governments over the past decades has been justified by discourses of globalisation around competition as well as important domestic drivers that have dovetailed with the globalisation discourse (Deem, 2001). The drive towards marketisation is based on the assumption that public higher education systems have become too large and complex for governments to fund on their own, that market competition within and between universities will create more efficient and effective institutions and that management principles derived from the private sector which monitor, measure, compare and judge professional activities will enhance higher education functioning. Marketisation therefore redefines the role of the state and impacts on the roles of public and private actors in higher education systems.

Many accounts of the relationship between the state and the market have asserted that an increase of market co-ordination invariably leads to a reduction in state regulation. However, in the UK, state regulation and quasi-market forces are increasing simultaneously. Furthermore, rather than pulling in different directions, increasing articulation between the two modes of co-ordination occur. State intervention helps establish the conditions for the operation of a quasi-higher-education market by, for example, creating the conditions for a competitive and individualistic ethos amongst students. At the same time, the state mobilises market mechanisms to attain political goals. In this sense, the British state exhibits the characteristics of the 'competitive' state (Cerny, 2005), which is a state that defines its primary objective as one of fostering a competitive national economy. Policies are shaped to promote, control and maximise returns from market forces in international settings while abandoning some of the core discourses and functions of the welfare state. Complex systems are steered from a distance by devolving decision-making down to institutional sub-units while at the same time maintaining strong regulatory, policy and financial management frameworks that restrict the range of choices available to the sub-units (Naidoo, 2008). In this way a particular type of learning market centred around quasi-market competition and state audit and regulation has been developed that positions the student-consumer as a major force for change.

The learning market in higher education

Consumerism as a key motif in policy discourses has arisen in response to criticisms of producer capture, a questioning of the motivations and ethics of academics as well as a desire to make higher education more efficient and responsive to government, business and other stakeholder interests. These discourses have been accompanied by consumer levers that aim to enhance student choice and control over the education process. These include the provision of information on academic courses through performance indicators and key information sets (KIS), student satisfaction surveys, student charters and the institutionalisation of complaint mechanisms. The marketisation of higher education and the re-conceptualisation of students as consumers is expected to impact on universities by altering the nature of rewards and sanctions traditionally operating in higher education and changing behaviour. One assumption behind such policies is that students will utilise such mechanisms to demand high-quality provision and thereby apply pressure to universities to make courses more relevant to the skills they require for the workplace. Low quality will be penalised, and consumer choice will foster competition between universities, resulting in more responsive and higher quality teaching (Naidoo and Jamieson, 2005). It is also assumed that quasi market forces will correct the elitist tendency of higher education and will lead to a more equitable system (Naidoo *et al.*, 2011). In the next sections, I will show that while student choice is positioned as a key element in democratising and equalising higher education with some attendant advantages, at root it is more tokenistic than real. Indeed, I will argue that the reconceptualisation of students in a competitive quasi-market of higher education may in fact further entrench and reproduce widespread systemic inequality.

The problem of choice

My earlier work with colleagues (see Naidoo *et al.*, 2011) has indicated that the reconceptualisation of students as consumers has brought some advantages. Students have greater opportunities than previous generations to choose between courses and universities (Middleton, 2000). Since UK universities are required by statutory bodies to publish information on academic programmes, students have more information on course aims and course content, and greater transparency in relation to criteria and methods for assessment. In addition, performance indicators including throughput rates, academic and social facilities and widening participation measures have been developed by statutory bodies. All of the mechanisms noted above are important levers with a potential to enhance choice and empower students. Mechanisms such as student-satisfaction surveys do not merely give students more information on which to base their choices but the subsequent public availability of such information empowers students to control, and indeed counteract, some elements of the communication process to affect the way in which other consumers perceive individual universities; thus giving them power to challenge and transform higher education.

However, as I have argued previously (Naidoo *et al.*, 2011), the governments' assumptions of student behaviour place great weight on the student-consumer being able to make informed choices. As McCulloch (2009) has noted, students do not necessarily have the tools to retrieve such information and Drummond (2004) warns that the possibility of suboptimal decisions increases in the context of expansion, competition and the rise of marketing activity within the sector. He asserts that this has led to increased information from multiple sources, a high rate of product proliferation and increasing use of imitation strategies with institutions merely mimicking the successful marketing activities of other institutions. While the institutionalisation of complaint mechanisms is welcome, many institutions do not have transfer or exit mechanisms. Students dissatisfied with one course cannot easily move to another course within the same university or to another university. Refunds are also not easily obtained, and this is particularly difficult where higher education is state funded or where students obtain loans from the government which they are expected to repay after graduation.

Furthermore, a crucial difference between higher education and other sectors that has important ramifications for student–university relations is that in the final analysis, institutions have the power to award or withhold a degree based on their judgement of the students' performance. This has important implications for the power relationship between students and faculty, and related issues of empowerment.

More importantly, insights derived from the wider consumption literature indicate that practices of consumerism are highly mediated by the cultural and ideological context of the institution (see Holt, 1995). It is therefore likely that the grafting of a framework derived from the commercial sector that seeks to extend market relations into a sector with a deeply imbedded professional culture may not translate easily into the outcomes intended by policy-makers. By extending the logic of commodity fetishism to higher education (Marx, 1992: 9–40), consumerism works to impose new forms of commodification and their attendant relationships on the inner life of higher education. The pedagogic relationship is construed into one that is dependent on the market transaction of the commodity. It constructs students in the position of consumers of those services and the lecturer as the commodity producer. In this way, Ian Jamieson and I have shown that previously integrated relationships between academics and students are likely to become disaggregated, with each party invested with distinct, if not opposing, interests (Naidoo and Jamieson, 2005). What is missing from such a conceptualisation is the fundamental importance of the relational and collaborative aspects of learning and teaching, including a high level of trust. Students need to trust expert authority at key points in the educational process, and academics need to understand the needs, interests and experiences of students. However, the threat of student litigation and complaints, together with requirements to comply with extensive external monitoring procedures may encourage academics to opt for 'safe teaching', which is locked into a transmission mode where pre-specified content can be passed on to the student and assessed in a conventional manner. More importantly, the reduction of the pedagogic relationship into a commodity relationship may crowd out intrinsic motivation as well as the pure joy and pleasure of teaching.

Choice and inequality

I have joined with Roger Brown in challenging the myth that market forces and student consumers will correct the elitism of higher education, and we show that consumerism in no way addresses systemic inequities but instead compounds inequality.

Consumerism constructs an idealised version of the good student: the 'good' student is perceived as one that compares the market and shops around to ensure they receive the best value-for-money (Naidoo and Williams, 2014). However, numerous studies show that the inherited cultural capital of students and their families result in differential access to the resources required to negotiate contextual and institutional mechanisms of choice (Hemsley-Brown, 1999). Those with dominant cultural capital possess an understanding of the implicit and explicit rules that accompany the process of choice and can negotiate through these procedures, including identifying the hierarchy of institutions and the social and economic implications of this hierarchy (Brown and Scase, 1994; Pugsy, 1998). Working class families and certain ethnic minority groups are less likely to successfully negotiate choice mechanisms in comparison to their middle class peers (Reay *et al.*, 2005). King *et al.* (2008) for example have shown that league tables are not a crucial component of the decision-making of applicants who are mature, vocationally oriented or from less advantaged background. In addition, the socialisation of students from socially disadvantaged backgrounds often results in processes of self-exclusion from high status universities. The feeling that they will not fit in overrides other calculative processes and judgements (Reay *et al.*, 2001; Allen, 2002).

Second, the penetration of market forces on a national system of higher education that is already stratified by status and wealth has little positive impact on equity. Elite universities do not compete on a level playing field as they are able to capitalise on the past cachet, which includes strong reputation, track records in research, intergenerational social capital and reserves of wealth (Meadmore, 1998). In addition, such universities are compelled to constrain expansion in order to maintain and maximise their positional status (Marginson, 2006). More worryingly, the competitive pressures introduced in quasi-market systems apply pressures on all universities to achieve a type of productivity that is measured by outputs such as the entry qualifications of students, their progression rates and the quality and quantity of research. These pressures militate against equity as students from disadvantaged social backgrounds on average achieve lower school-leaving scores, which in turn adversely affects a university's position in league tables. In addition, elite research-focused universities perceive such students to be time-intensive as they may need extra support to achieve academic success, thus reducing the time available for research and posing a threat to the university's research performance (Naidoo, 2000). The introduction of measures to ensure that universities that charge the maximum tuition fee engage in widening participation provides few counter-incentives to the powerful incentives and sanctions associated with research performance and status. This leads to dysfunctional effects for the whole system of higher education: research-intensive universities in general do not participate in widening participation in any significant manner, while teaching-intensive universities are penalised, rather than rewarded for doing so. Thus choice and competition in a marketised higher education environment positions the most vulnerable students in society as collateral damage.

Choice and democracy

As noted in a recent paper with Geoff Whitty (Naidoo and Whitty, 2013), consumerism links to particular notions of 'student voice'. It has been perceived by other commentators as a tokenistic gesture towards consumerism (Rudduck, 2004) and has been dismissed as a process of managerial co-option. Numerous researchers have questioned the presumed link between students acting as consumers with greater choice and democracy. Sabri (2011) has referred to the 'sacralisation of the consumer' and argues that students are deprived of agency at the same time as apparently giving them voice (Sabri, 2011: 658). The crucial insight that neo-liberal governance offers more choice and less democracy as there is little opportunity to influence the fundamental nature of provision has been well made by Finlayson (2004). Klemencic (2010) has persuasively argued that the ethos of individual self-interest leads to higher education institutions being unable to act as sites of citizenship. More fundamentally, choice as an endemic feature of contemporary life may produce more anxiety than happiness (Schwartz, 2005). According to Gilbert (2008: 557–558), drawing on, amongst others Sennett (2000) and Bauman (2001), we are being offered a bewildering number of life choices that force us to micromanage our lives to such an extent that it 'makes it impossible to concentrate on wider social and political issues and in effect undermines the bases for any coherent forms of community through which genuinely democratic power could be exercised' (Gilbert, 2008: 557–558).

Some ways forward

Given the discussion above, I want to turn now to some ways forward in thinking about policy, practice and further research. We know from empirical evidence and the work of Pierre Bourdieu that higher education has always been elitist, that inequality is produced not by individual higher education institutions but by the system-wide actions of a stratified system acting in concert and that teaching continues to be low status in many research intensive universities. To move beyond the simple choice between student consumerism and the student as a powerless apprentice, I have explored together with colleagues (See Naidoo *et al.*, 2011; Naidoo and Whitty, 2013) some possibilities in the democratisation of student learning. We have noted that co-creation, when appropriately re-contextualised to pedagogical relations in higher education, represents a more dialogical model that no longer merely privileges the university's vision of education but provides resources that foster the creation of specific innovative forms of student participation. In this way, the problems encountered by a model based on the notion of a passive and instrumental student consumer can be replaced by the notion of an engaged and co-creative learner. From this perspective, students will be configured as uniquely skilled participants who must be given the opportunity to share their knowledge and make significant inputs to the learning and teaching process. This also requires a new understanding of the role of teaching faculty. At the same time it is important to understand the limits of co-creation, the points in the process where the relationship cannot be equal, that students do not always have to be satisfied but also challenged (see Gibbs, 2014) and the balance between student choice and input, particularly where professional expertise must override student input (see Young, 2008).

The phrase 'the student experience' is very much in vogue now. However, the discourse of the student experience as presently constituted is hollow because, as Sabri (2011) notes, it homogenises the student experience, and as John Brennan and colleagues have shown (Brennan *et al.,* 2010) there is not one but many student experiences. My experience of one of the most elite universities in England and a post-1992 London university has revealed to me that the student experience could not have been more different in the two institutions. Government policy and funding in effect penalised the post-1992 university for carrying out its mission. I could see first-hand how the lack of resources impacted on the student experience, despite deeply committed and highly skilled teachers. The student experience is also of course not bounded within the university walls but extends into the everyday lives of students. And here too the difference could not be starker. My students in the post-1992 institution were mainly time-poor, single mothers working full time in low-waged labour who were subjected to racism as soon as they left university. Two issues arise here. The first is how to take the important principles of education that arise out of a historically elitist education system and implement these in a mass and unequal higher education system. In other words, how do we transform higher education as a system to respond to the needs of all students rather than expecting disadvantaged students who are in the majority in our society to adapt to universities that were designed to keep them out in the first place? The second issue that we need to focus on is how to link research on higher education more closely to transformations occurring elsewhere in society. In the UK we are witnessing the development of a highly precarious labour market. There is more outsourcing and more automation. It is predicted that this will result in less demand for highly skilled graduates (Brown *et al.,* 2014). The greatest demand will be for what Castells (2001) has called 'generic workers' – that is low-skilled low-paid workers who are treated as exchangeable and disposable. In analysing how human welfare has been undermined by the intersecting logics of human capital and national security, Means (2014: 724) refers to Judt's warning that we are moving to an 'eviscerated' society where the thick mesh of social interactions and public goods encapsulated in the principles of social democracy and the welfare state is being reduced to a minimum (Judt, 2010: 118). The challenge for educators and university administrators, following Barnett (2013), is how to re-imagine the university in this context: how do we assess the very real barriers that are in place, how do we open up to new possibilities linked to individual and group aspirations and how do we influence not just higher education in the present but the future trajectories of our societies?

I wish to conclude by stating that first we need to assess in a sober and self-reflective manner the extent to which pre-marketised higher education has contributed to democracy. Studies on the role of universities have indicated that universities play multiple roles, sometimes contributing to the transformation of societies and at other times reproducing unequal relations in society and often doing both simultaneously (Brennan and Naidoo, 2006). Research and policy therefore need to identify which of the major functions of higher education should be publicly funded and protected. At the same time, it is essential for academics, students and managers to oppose market fundamentalism and the neo-liberal drive to impose the logic of the commodity on every possible common good and social relation (Rifkin, 2000), particularly when such commodification is seen to be destructive of the public good, ethical social relations and social justice. Bourdieu (1998) has referred to neo-liberalism as a 'doxa' that operates at all levels of society, from individual perceptions and practices to state policy, as if it were the objective truth. More crucially, the positioning of this doxa as an objective truth prevents policy-makers and researchers from thinking about strategies that have worked in the past and others that could work in the future. It is thus vital to emphasise that there is at present a lack of evidence to support the assumption that a higher education market will lead to the development of quality or equity. We need theoretical and empirical research that challenges this doxa and protects higher education from the most corrosive effects of commodification while steering higher education towards complementing the distribution of private benefits with a contribution to the public good.

Bibliography

Allen, D.E. (2002) Toward a theory of consumer choice as socio-historically shaped practical experience: the Fits-Like-a-Glove (FLAG) framework. *Journal of Consumer Research* 28 (4): 515–532

Barnett, R. (2013) *Imagining the University*. London: Routledge

Bauman, Z. (2001) *The Individualized Society*. Cambridge: Polity Press

Bourdieu, P. (1988) *Homo Academicus*. Cambridge: Polity Press

Brennan, J., Edmunds, R., Houston, M., Jary, D., Lebeau, Y., Osbourne, M. and Richardson, J. (2010) *Improving What Is Learned at University: An Exploration of the Social and Organisational Diversity of University Education*. London: Routledge

Brennan, J. and Naidoo, R. (2006) Managing Contradictory Functions: The Role of Universities in Societies Undergoing Radical Social Transformation. In G. Neave (ed.) *Knowledge, Power and Dissent: Critical Perspectives on Higher Education and Research in Knowledge Society*. Paris: UNESCO Publishing

Brown, P., Lauder, H. and Ashton, D. (2014) *The Global Auction*. China: Human Science and Technology Press

Brown, P. and Scase, R. (1994) *Higher Education and Corporate Realities: Class, Culture and the Decline of Graduate Careers*. London: UCL Press

Brown, R. with Carasso, H. (2013) *Everything for Sale? The Marketisation of UK Higher Education*. London: Routledge and the Society for Research into Higher Education

Castells, M. (2001) Information Technology and Global Development. In J. Muller, N. Cloete, and S. Badat (eds) *Challenges of Globalisation: South African Debates with Manuel Castells*. Cape Town: Maskew Miller/Longman

Cerny, Philip G. (2005) Political Globalization and the Competition State. In R. Stubbs and G.R.D. Underhill (eds) *Political Economy and the Changing Global Order*. Canada: Oxford University Press: 376–386

Deem, R. (2001) Globalisation, new managerialism, academic capitalism and entrepreneuralism in universities: is the local dimension still important? *Comparative Education* 37 (1): 7–20

Drummond, G. (2004) *Consumer Confusion Reduction Strategies in Education*. Buckingham: Open University Press

Finlayson, A. (2004) *Making Sense of New Labour*. London: Lawrence and Wishart

Gibbs, P. (2014) Happiness and education: troubling students for their own contentment. *Time and Society*. Online publication. Available at: http://tas.sagepub.com/content/early/2014/12/12/0961463X14561780.full.pdf+html

Gilbert, J. (2008) Against the commodification of everything. *Cultural Studies* 22 (5): 551–566

Hemsley-Brown, J. (1999) College choice: perceptions and priorities. *Educational Management and Administration* 27 (1): 85–98

Holt, D. B. (1995) How consumers consume: a typology of consumption practices. *Journal of Consumer Research* 22: 1–16

Judt, T. (2010) *Ill Fares the Land*. New York: Penguin Press

King, R., Locke, W., Puncher, M., Richardson, J., and Verbik, L. (2008) *Counting what is measured or measuring what counts? League tables and their impact on higher education institutions in England*. Report to HEFCE by the Centre for Higher Education Research and Information (CHERI). Open University and Hobsons Research

Klemencic, M. (2010) Higher Education for Democratic Citizenship. In E. Froment, J. Kohler, L. Purser and L. Wilson (eds) *EUA Bologna Handbook: Making Bologna*. Berlin: RAABE Academic Publishers: 1–26

Marginson, S. (2006) Dynamics of national and global competition in higher education. *Higher Education* 52: 1–39

Marx, K. (1992) *Capital*. In C.J. Arthur (ed.) *Marx's Capital: A Student Edition*. London: Lawrence & Wishart: 39–40

Meadmore, D. (1998) Changing the culture: the governance of the Australian premillennial university. *International Studies in Sociology of Education* 8 (1): 27–45

Means, A. J. (2014) Beyond the poverty of national security: toward a critical human security perspective in educational policy. *Journal of Education Policy* 29 (6): 719–741

McCulloch, A. (2009) The student as co-producer: learning from public administration about the student–university relationship. *Studies in Higher Education* 34 (4): 171–183

Middleton, C. (2000) Models of state and market in the modernisation of higher education. *British Journal of Sociology of Education* 21 (4): 537–554

Morley, L. (2004) *Theorising Quality in Higher Education*. London: IOE Press

Naidoo, R. (2000) The 'Third Way' to widening participation and maintaining quality in higher education: lessons from the United Kingdom. *Journal of Educational Enquiry* 1 (2): 24–38

Naidoo, R. (2008) Building or Eroding Intellectual Capital? Student Consumerism as Cultural Force in the Context of Knowledge Economy. In J. Valimaa and O-H. Ylijoki (eds) *Cultural Perspectives in Higher Education*. Netherlands: Springer

Naidoo, R. and Jamieson, I. M. (2005) Empowering participants or corroding learning? Towards a research agenda on the impact of student consumerism in higher education. *Journal of Education Policy* 20 (3): 267–281

Naidoo, R., Shankar. A. and Ekant, V. (2011) The consumerist turn in higher education: policy aspirations and outcomes. *Journal of Marketing Management* 11/12: 1142–1162

Naidoo, R. and Whitty, G. (2013) Students as consumers: marketising or democratising learning. *International Journal of Chinese Education* 2: 212–240

Naidoo, R. and Williams, J. (published online 2014) The neo-liberal regime in English higher education: charters, consumers and the erosion of the public good. *Critical Studies in Education*. DOI: 10.1080/17508487.2014.939098

Pugsy, L. (1998) Throwing your brains at it: higher education, markets and choice. *International Studies in Sociology of Education* 8 (1): 71–92

Reay, D., David, M. E. and Ball, S. (2005) *Degrees of Choice: Social Class, Race and Gender in Higher Education*. Stoke-on-Trent: Trentham Books

Reay, D., Davies, J. David, M., and Ball, S. J. (2001) Choices of degree or degrees of choice? Class, 'race' and the higher education choice process. *Sociology* 35 (4): 855–874

Rifkin, J. (2000) *The Age of Access: The New Culture of Hypercapitalism, Where All of Life Is a Paid-For Experience*. Los Angeles, CA: Tarcher

Rudduck, J. (2004) The innovation bazaar: determining priorities, building coherence: the case of student voice. Keynote address. *UCET Annual Conference*. Hinckley, November

Sabri, D. (2011) What's wrong with 'the student experience? *Discourse* 32 (5): 657–667

Schwartz, B. (2005) *The Paradox of Choice: Why Less Is More*. New York: HarperCollins

Sennett, R. (2000) *The Corrosion of Character: The Personal Consequences of Work in the New Capitalism*. New York: W. W. Norton

Young, M. (2008) *Bringing Knowledge Back In: From Social Constructivism to Social Realism in the Sociology of Education*. London: Routledge

Chapter 4

Marketing and marketisation

What went wrong, and how can we put it right?

Rob Cuthbert

Introduction

In *Everything for Sale? The Marketisation of UK Higher Education*, Brown with Carasso (2013), show how marketisation has narrowed the way higher education (HE) is valued, pushing policy-making too far into a cost-benefit analysis in which money is the only currency that counts. In contrast, marketing in UK HE was first espoused (Cuthbert, 1980a) as a useful perspective partly because it offered new ways to embed academic and educational values in HE management. Marketing rapidly became an explicit responsibility of HE managers during the 1980s. The negative connotations of marketisation emerged later as part of new public management, and the spread of managerialism, debasing the debate and leading to an unduly sweeping disavowal of 'the market' by many in HE who should know better. In this chapter, I will review the development of marketing ideas and marketisation policies in UK HE. By restoring the differentiation between marketing as management perspective and marketisation as political ideology we can rediscover the value of marketing in sustaining rather than damaging academic values. This reconstructs ideas about 'students as customers' and 'the student experience' and suggests ways of changing how HE is valued by future policy-makers.

Why marketing was needed

Marketing and competition between institutions have always existed, but the marketing perspective remained mostly unnoticed until the 1980s, when the expansion of postsecondary education stretched budgetary and political control mechanisms to a breaking point. Until then, academic authority had been unquestioned in UK HE governance. The national university funding body, the University Grants Committee (UGC), was dominated by academics, and the locally-controlled non-university institutions experienced little external academic regulation or control over costs. Consequently long periods of bottom-up academic dominance were punctuated by budget crises with financial cuts applied from the top down (Cuthbert, 1980b, 1981).

After major spending cuts in 1981, the UGC protected spending per student, thus restricting numbers, whereas non-university HE expanded, despite reductions in spending per student. Worldwide HE expansion in the 1980s was shaped in the UK through three postsecondary sectors: universities; polytechnics and HE colleges; and further education (FE) colleges mostly providing lower-level courses. This created competition at the margins between the sectors and promoted diffusion of new management practices, first within one sector and then between sectors.

The first article proposing a marketing perspective in UK HE was my 1979 Coombe Lodge Information Bank paper, leading to a 1980 article (Cuthbert, 1980a). Beginning with an apology for addressing such a 'disreputable activity', it argued that education management should learn from marketing in other domains. Narrow access in an elite HE system meant that the supply of students was never questioned; marketeers called this the 'product concept'. Even as HE expanded, institutions rarely went beyond the idea (the 'selling concept') that courses might need to be promoted for full recruitment. Beyond HE, marketing texts (Kotler, 1976) argued instead for the marketing concept, focusing on customers – 'find a need and fill it'. But the customer was not always right, leading to the societal marketing concept – 'a management orientation aimed at generating customer satisfaction and long-run consumer and public welfare as the key to satisfying organisational goals and responsibilities' (Kotler, 1976: 18) – marketing with added corporate social responsibility.

My 1980 article argued for societal marketing, rather than 'the prevailing management orientation . . . which sees the product, the course, as paramount and the problem as one of finding customers in sufficient numbers to make the course viable' (Cuthbert, 1980a: 533). At that time, the US was perhaps the only country where HE marketing was widely recognised. Even there the selling concept probably dominated, albeit tempered with some concern for affordability and diversity. In the UK it was FE, rather than HE, where marketing first became established. FE colleges were used to engage with local communities and design programmes in response to need. Colleges' receptiveness, the promotion of marketing through a national Staff College and government pressure for change (Cuthbert, 1987) meant that by the mid-1980s most FE colleges had a member of their senior management team with explicit responsibility for marketing.

Pressures for managerial change in HE took longer and were more strongly resisted. Three national reports (Jarratt, 1985; Croham, 1987; National Advisory Body, 1987) paved the way, but change, when it came, was not only broader but was widely seen as opposing academic values rather than incorporating them.

New public management

The growing cost of HE was part of the broader problem of the growth, affordability and accountability of public services. The preferred solution in most countries was new public management, emphasising specification of outputs, performance measurement to improve management and business practices such as contracts for service, increased competition between HE providers and a quasi-market framing students as customers (Dill, 1998).

The transition from elite to universal HE made changes in HE funding inevitable. First came spending cuts and a squeeze on funding per student. HE for the first time became electorally significant, but difficult. Student demand grew despite spending restrictions; in 1997 and again in 2010, an outgoing government connived with the opposition party to establish an inquiry straddling a general election (Dearing, 1997; Browne Report, 2010). Each time the incoming government raised tuition fees to transfer some of the costs of HE from the state to the student, although it is a moot point whether the conservative-liberal coalition government in the UK has in fact achieved any reduction in public funding, despite the decision to triple fees to £9,000 in 2010 (Bekhradnia and Thompson, 2013).

The argument that the best guarantee of academic quality was institutional and academic autonomy could no longer satisfy governments facing significant costs and demanding greater accountability. HE became merely one example of attempts to rein in the power of the professions, under Thatcherism in the UK and parallel ideological changes in many other countries. Michael Power criticised the first phase of new public management in *The Audit Society* (1999), and in *The Risk Management of Everything* (2004) argued that external surveillance through audit was being supplanted by internalised controls through risk cultures in which individuals became their own agents of surveillance. This seemed sadly true in HE, where for most institutions the pressures of survival induced compliance, glaringly apparent in the feeble acceptance by the vice-chancellors' body, Universities UK, of the £9,000 fee level, fearing that the alternative was huge cuts in total HE spending.

Everything for sale?

The crucial step was introducing tuition fees, creating the appearance of a market. Instead of students being treated as customers for some (strictly limited) purposes (Cuthbert, 2010), students became constructed as primarily or only consumers. This attitude became political orthodoxy through Browne's (Browne Report, 2010) election-straddling review, which stated baldly that HE is too complex for government to control: it must be left to the market to decide what quality is, so that informed student choice could drive up quality.

This at least had the virtue of being transparent about its intellectual poverty. But the US 'academic arms race' had already shown that institutions compete for students with almost anything *except* academic quality – better sports facilities (and, in the US, more successful sports teams), better student residential accommodation and so on. The limitations of rankings as any kind of measure of quality have been repeatedly demonstrated (Kehm and Stensaker, 2009). 'The student experience' has become a central focus for many institutions but, instead of taking a suitably long view of the student's best interests, universities have – in the UK as in the US – invested in student accommodation, new buildings and expanded marketing departments. Universities compete on the basis of prestige and reputation, gained predominantly through research rather than teaching. Academics needing little encouragement to focus on research for career advancement were indulged by institutions that allowed them either to avoid teaching altogether or at best to satisfice, with the gaps filled variously by 'teaching only' staff, or part-timers and adjuncts on short-term contracts. Global academic culture was as much to blame as university management.

The supposed empowerment of the student consumer was supported in several ways. In the UK there was more and better information for prospective students. Institutions came under fire in a series of academic analyses and reports. In the US, right wing critics such as Bloom (1987) and Arum and Roksa (2011) blamed massification; left wing critics such as Slaughter and Leslie (1997) blamed academic capitalism, but very few academics questioned global academic culture. In the UK, successive reports by the Higher Education Policy Institute (HEPI) (www.hepi.ac.uk) on student experience in the UK criticised the variability in contact hours within and between disciplines and institutions. HEPI in effect suggested that some, if not most, UK students needed to work harder. The decline in hours worked per week over decades is also noted by Palfreyman and Tapper (2014: 136).

Many students seek part-time employment to finance their studies, and many others plan to enjoy what they see as a student lifestyle without much regard to cost (Harrison *et al.*, 2013), trusting that future income will somehow repay the debt they build up. There is no conspiracy, but there is a line of least resistance, with government, institutions, academics and students colluding in what some people represent as a spiralling decline of expectations about the performance needed to achieve a good degree. This might be better seen as the large-scale acceptance of what probably always existed for marginally performing students. In an elite system, the small numbers of such students did not constitute a threat to systemic integrity. In a universal system, the mainstreaming of what used to be marginal performance poses fundamental challenges to the meaning, purpose and benefits of HE, as Roger Brown's critique shows.

Palfreyman and Tapper (2014) talk of *The Rise of the Regulated Market*, but regulation is only a small part of the solution. Market mechanisms are inadequate to deal with problems of values (Ouchi, 1980). If universities' shortcomings are addressed only, or primarily, through the market there will be serious distortion. Students will address the things most easily measured, such as contact hours, rather than the complex but more important issues of student engagement and workload and the accessibility of academics and learning support. Market-driven careers encourage academics to value research more than teaching, the discipline more than the institution, and cosmopolitan mobility more than local stability. Managers in market-driven institutions chase short-term revenue rather than long-term academic integrity. And governments can 'let the market decide' rather than face politically difficult and complex choices.

Technological change always makes a difference, not least in making knowledge more accessible in different ways. If technology could drive fundamental change in HE then we would expect market forces to make it happen. But the technology of HE remains stubbornly, perhaps inevitably, the same at its core – inquiry-driven people encouraging students to develop individually in ways that cannot be pre-specified, even though in important respects the processes and outcomes should be. The paradox at the heart of HE is the need to specify learning outcomes so that students can transcend them.

In the US, with longer experience of a market mentality, students vary in the extent to which they embrace the role of customer. Business students are most likely to take the view that 'I've paid, so I deserve a good degree', humanities students least likely (Obermiller *et al.,* 2005). Students themselves are largely reluctant to behave as customers, showing an instinctive understanding of what is best for them in the long term.

Academics, too, resist the idea of the market determining their relationships with students. Academics who see teaching and research as indivisible parts of their academic practice are frustrated by the commodification of higher learning, because learning is in every case an individual construct, assembled through a partnership between student, academics and institution. Commodification promotes deprofessionalisation, which drives down academic standards, standards become simply what you can get away with, instead of being the best that is achievable in the circumstances.

Markets emphasise control through regulation, depending on objective information about prices. But price and product in HE defy specification in many important respects, short-term and long-term, because the ultimate claim is that universities change lives and life courses (Watson and Slowey, 2003; Watson, 2009). Universities are better construed as institutions with a common academic culture, emphasising regulation through shared values.

What is to be done?

To talk about a tension between educational values and marketing values is wrong-headed. There is no necessary tension between the two: marketing as first proposed in HE was actually intended to restore traditional academic values, as a corrective to 'producer capture' through societal marketing. But there *is* a conflict between marketisation and academic quality and values. Marketisation suggests the customer knows best, whereas academic values suggest that although students may have the best idea about students' best interests, academics will have better ideas on what counts as knowledge so far, and no-one can actually know best about what might happen in the long term. Furthermore, resources are always limited, and people always want more than can be afforded.

Should different standards prevail in different parts of the system? Selective universities, where market forces are least likely to intrude, are those most in demand from the social and financial elite. This is not just because HE is a social filter, but because the kind of HE offered by the US Ivy League, the UK Russell Group, the Australian Group of 8 and their analogues is valued most highly for its own sake. In this respect the obsession of politicians with diversity of access to elite institutions is perhaps justified, as a counter to the reproduction of social elites. But the only solution which will work in a democratic society with a universal HE system is for *all* of HE to have its head in the clouds and its feet on the ground. This means HE that serves the needs of society by generating diverse and unpredictable outcomes in the long run, while meeting short-term student and public demands for accountability, employability and student satisfaction.

How might this come about? Market forces to 'drive up quality' do not work; the global competition for students does not work and threats to the long-term competitiveness of national economies will probably take too long to work. The only workable solution is academic and institutional self-improvement.

Market forces do not work, if that means relying on the profit motive in a marketised system. The growth of private and for-profit institutions (run as a business to generate profit) is perhaps the most notable feature of global HE in the last 10 years. Some private institutions have an honourable history, not least in the US Ivy League, and in some countries they drive national expansion. UK universities have both private and public features. Whether institutions are ostensibly 'public' but regulated, or private but not-for-profit (not publicly supported, but not constituted as a business), matters less than whether long-term corporate and social responsibility is given sufficient weight. But for-profit HE distorts competition between institutions, by extracting profits, dividends and inflated executive salaries, but also by shifting effort towards marketing and selling, to the detriment of academic operations. The US has realised that for-profit HE has been too much at the expense of the government through federal grants, and at the expense of students recruited to programmes with poor prospects for future employment to repay student debt.

Another notable feature of global HE is the emergence of new national systems in the Far East and Middle East. These systems, especially in China, could leapfrog older systems, but seem more likely to reinforce inappropriate values and regulation than to replace them. We still do not know the long-term impact of mass graduation rates in the general population, with graduates being half or more of the whole population of working age. It remains to be seen whether this will have a democratising, liberating or even socially transformational effect, and this in a sense is a large-scale test of how HE prepares its graduates.

The long-term competitiveness of national economies may become an issue, if marketised HE fails on its own terms to help sustain economic viability. But the causal connections are complex and unclear, and the lags involved in forming any judgement about HE success will militate against such considerations becoming significant. A side issue, but one which becomes increasingly important, is that as the prestige of HE declines in a universal system, and as the non-financial rewards of academic life are increasingly circumscribed, people good enough to be academics will vote with their feet. Those once willing to take lower salaries because they valued academic autonomy will increasingly find fewer non-financial compensations in the audit society, even in HE. The slide in academic standards is accelerated as there are fewer people left to defend academic values against compliance, league table management and managerial fear of failure.

There have of course been numerous attempts to launch a defence of academic values and standards, but these largely fail on two counts. First, they are reactive and oppositional. They see the challenge in the terms in which it is framed – marketisation in which anything or everything is for sale. By opposing it in these terms they are unable to change the terms of the policy debate about HE. The second reason why these defences are inadequate is that for the most part they are dominated by elite organisations aiming to uphold elite values.

We are indeed living through *The Rise of the Regulated Market* (Palfreyman and Tapper, 2014), but the transfer of almost all funding of teaching from government grants to tuition fees offers opportunities as well as threats. The key opportunity is that no-one in HE wants everything to be for sale – not students, not academics and not managers. People in HE want HE to be as life-changing as David Watson (2009) has described. Former HE Minister David Willetts, who oversaw the transition to £9,000 annual fees, was probably right when he said that in future we will look back and wonder how we got research and teaching so out of kilter. But he was wrong that market forces would drive up academic quality (Willetts, 2013). Students should indeed be central, but only academics themselves can drive up academic quality, supported by the right kind of institutional management.

We must put an end to the unnatural separation of teaching and research in how we think about academic practice. This means (Cuthbert, 2008) a significant change in how we think about what we do, so that issues of academic freedom, purpose and context become central. We need to rethink the whole academic enterprise in these terms, so that we can learn to live by a consistent set of academic values and make them work better in practice. This means changing the academic culture through key mechanisms like academic promotion processes. New public management encourages a managerialist ideology that sets managers above what is managed, but management is no more than a necessary means to making HE work properly. The danger is that it can alienate the managed rather than be their natural support.

What we need to do is create within each institution an academic culture which recognises that the heart of the system is learning, which staff and students do together. That is why protecting institutional cultures is so important. And that means giving them enough autonomy – not insulating them from the external environment, but enabling them to make strategic choices that protect academic values.

In this, managers also have a crucial role. I have argued elsewhere (Cuthbert, 2011) that managerialism is a consequence of managerial failure to tackle the challenge of institutional evaluation. For people in HE, academics and managers, piecemeal social engineering may be the best approach, doing good in small particulars. Thus, for example, institutions may choose to opt out of league tables and ranking systems, holding on to academic values in the face of external pressures for anti-academic compliance. Grand theories are almost certainly impractical; subversive approaches may be better. Marketing, but not marketisation, can help: 'a management orientation aimed at generating customer satisfaction and long-run consumer and public welfare as the key to satisfying organisational goals and responsibilities' (Kotler, 1976: 18).

Bibliography

Arum, R. and Roksa, J. (2011) *Academically Adrift: Limited Learning on College Campuses.* Chicago: University of Chicago Press

Bekhradnia, B. and Thompson, J. (2013) *The cost of the government's reforms of the financing of higher education: an update* Oxford: HEPI: Available at: http://www.hepi.ac.uk/2013/12/17/the-cost-of-the-governments-reforms-of-the-financing-of-higher education-an-update/ [accessed 14 November 2014]

Bloom, A. (1987) *The Closing of the American Mind: How Higher Education Has Failed Democracy and Impoverished the Souls of Today's Students.* New York: Simon and Schuster

Brown, R. with Carasso, H. (2013) *Everything for Sale? The Marketisation of UK Higher Education.* London: Routledge and the Society for Research into Higher Education

Browne Report (2010) *Securing a Sustainable Future for Higher Education.* Available at: https://www.gov.uk/government/uploads/system/uploads/attachment_data/file/31999/10–1208-securing-sustainable-higher education-browne-report.pdf [accessed 14 November 2014]

Croham, Lord (1987) *Review of the University Grants Committee.* London: HMSO

Cuthbert, R. (1980a) The marketing function in education management. *Coombe Lodge Reports* 12 (11): 520–533

Cuthbert, R. (1980b) Costs and quality in higher education. *Higher Education Review* Summer 1980: 57–61

Cuthbert, R. (1981) Quality control in higher education: two ideologies and their correlates. In T. Bone and H. A. Ramsey (eds) *Quality control in education?* Special issue of *Educational Administration* 9 (2) 1981: 87–91

Cuthbert, R. (1987) Efficiency and the Marketing Mechanism in Further and Higher Education. In H. Thomas and T. Simkins (eds) *Economics and Education Management.* Basingstoke, Hants: Falmer Press: 164–175

Cuthbert, R. (2008) Beyond the student experience: rethinking higher education for the 21st century. Keynote opening speech. The Higher Education Academy Annual Conference. Harrogate, 1–3 July 2008. Available at: https://www.academia.edu/14852205/Beyond_the_student_experience_rethinking_higher_education_for_the_21st_Century [accessed 10 August 2015]

Cuthbert, R. (2010) Students as customers? *Higher Education Review* 42 (3): 3–25

Cuthbert, R. (2011) Failing the Challenge of Institutional Evaluation: How and Why Managerialism Flourishes. In M. Saunders, R. Bamber and P. Trowler (eds) *Reconceptualising Evaluation in Higher Education: The Practice Turn.* Maidenhead: Society for Research into Higher Education and the Open University Press/McGraw-Hill: 133–138

Dearing Report (1997) *Higher Education in the Learning Society.* London: HMSO

Dill, D. (1998) Evaluating the 'Evaluative State': implications for research in higher education. *European Journal of Education* 33 (3): 361–377

Harrison, N., Chudry, F., Waller, R. and Hatt, S. (published online 2013) Towards a typology of debt attitudes among contemporary young UK undergraduates. *Journal of Further and Higher Education* 39 (1): 85–107. Available at: http://www.tandfonline.com/doi/full/10.1080/0309877X.2013.778966#abstract [accessed 12 August 2015]

Jarratt, A. (1985) *Report of the Steering Committee for Efficiency Studies.* London: CVCP

Kehm, B. M. and Stensaker, B. (eds) (2009) *University Rankings, Diversity and the New Landscape of Higher Education.* Rotterdam/Boston/Taipei: Sense Publishers

Kotler, P. (1976) *Marketing Management.* New Jersey: Prentice-Hall, 3rd edition

National Advisory Body (1987) *Management for a Purpose. Report of the Good Management Practice Working Group.* London: National Advisory Body for Public Sector Higher Education

Obermiller, C., Fleenor, P. and Raven, P. (2005) Students as customers or products: perceptions and preferences of faculty and students. *Marketing Education Review* 15 (2): 27–36

Ouchi, W. G. (1980) Markets, bureaucracies and clans. *Administrative Science Quarterly* 25 (1): 129–141

Palfreyman, D. and Tapper, T. (2014) *Reshaping the University: The Rise of the Regulated Market.* Oxford: Oxford University Press

Power, M. (1999) *The Audit Society: Rituals of Verification.* Oxford: Oxford University Press

Power, M. (2004) *The Risk Management of Everything: Rethinking the Politics of Uncertainty.* London: Demos

Slaughter, S. and Leslie, L. L. (1997) *Academic Capitalism: Politics, Policies and the Entrepreneurial University.* Baltimore, MD: Johns Hopkins University Press

Watson, D. (2009) *The Question of Morale: Managing Happiness and Unhappiness in University Life.* Maidenhead: McGraw-Hill/Open University Press

Watson, D. and Slowey, M. (2003) *Higher Education and the Lifecourse.* Buckingham: Open University Press and Society for Research into Higher Education

Willetts, D. (2013) *Robbins Revisited: Bigger and Better Higher Education.* London: Social Market Foundation

Chapter 5

Scotland and the higher education market

Tony Bruce

Introduction

In *Everything for Sale? The Marketisation of UK Higher Education*, Roger Brown with Helen Carasso (2013) analyse the development of a competitive regime that has its origins in the introduction of full cost fees for overseas students in 1980. Although this study covers the evolution of higher education in the four countries of the UK, the focus is on England where there has been a 'textbook case of a transition from a "non-market" to a market-based system' (Brown with Carasso, 2013). The principal features of the new arrangements in England include controlled competition on price with tuition fees covering a high proportion of the cost and low barriers to market entry with many competing suppliers.

This chapter reviews recent developments in Scotland where the transition to a more market-based system as part of UK-wide developments was interrupted by the process of devolution from 1999. From that point, successive Scottish administrations have focused on developing higher education as a public service within the constraints of the wider UK and international market in which Scotland operates. In examining how Scottish higher education has evolved since 1999, it is useful to review the main policy changes in light of Brown's framework of market and non-market models. He suggests that a pure non-market model would have the following characteristics:

- Institutional status – independent but with little ability to determine prices
- Competition – high barriers to market entry with few suppliers
- Price – teaching funded mainly through grants to institutions; no or purely nominal tuition fees
- Information – limited information about price, quality or availability
- Regulation – protects standards and constrains competition
- Quality – usually determined through a combination of state and academic self-regulation

This chapter will consider the extent to which the features of a non-market-based system have been adopted in Scotland – particularly those relating to institutional status, price, competition and quality. It will then assess the degree of policy convergence or divergence with England and will conclude with some comments on whether Scotland has developed an effective, efficient and fair system, avoiding some of the limitations of the market identified by Roger Brown.

Devolution process

The main aim of the devolution of legislative powers to Scotland (and to Wales and Northern Ireland) in 1999 was the preservation of the United Kingdom as a unitary state by responding to pressures for self-government, which had intensified from the late 1980s. The intention was to preserve the status quo by accommodating change, but the devolution process has actually had the effect of intensifying demands for further constitutional change, leading to the Scottish independence referendum in September 2014.

Under the Scotland Act 1998, responsibility for higher education was transferred to the Scottish Parliament, which can legislate in all matters except those expressly reserved to Westminster. These include the research councils and social security, which provides financial support to some students. Although legislative devolution has had a relatively short history, the Scottish Office was responsible for higher education from its creation in 1885 apart from the funding of Scottish universities, which was a UK responsibility from 1919 to 1992. Administrative devolution was extended by the Further and Higher Education Act 1992, a seminal legislative text that abolished the binary line and established separate territorial funding councils for England, Scotland and Wales.

By 1992 Scottish higher education had a number of distinctive features – notably 4-year degrees; higher participation rates among young people; and a more significant role for further education colleges in providing higher education – but in other respects it was little different to the English system. Scottish universities are strongly influenced by the wider UK and international market in which they operate for the recruitment of students and research funding. The dominance of England (with more than 83 per cent of total UK student numbers in 2012/13) means that policy changes introduced there, particularly in relation to fees and funding, will inevitably demand a Scottish response because of their effect on cross-border student flows and other impacts. Although English and Scottish domiciled students display little mobility in proportionate terms, in absolute terms England contributed more than one-eighth of the students studying in Scotland in 2012/13.

Apart from these cross-border student flows, UK higher education also remains a single market for the recruitment of academic and professional staff and provides access to other resources. For example, Scotland participates in the UK-wide quality assurance system (with national variations), student admission arrangements, pay bargaining, pensions provision and data collection. The need to compete successfully for international students is another pressure for policy convergence as is participation in the European Higher Education Area (www.ehea.info). The UK-wide assessment and funding of research is another important external influence on how Scotland organises in order to compete successfully. Funding through the research councils remains a non-devolved function and Scotland allocates its own research funds based on quality ratings generated by voluntary participation in the UK research ranking exercise, presently known as the Research Excellence Framework. As a result, institutions have consistently pressed the case for the Scottish government to take the impact of the wider UK and international market fully into account in developing national higher education policies.

However, there are a number of specific Scottish issues. As in the rest of the UK, Scottish policy is also being shaped by a decline in the 18-year-old population over the next 10 years, but it will be more significantly affected than England. The need to improve the performance of the Scottish economy is a major political priority (Raffe, 2013). The proportion of employees with higher level skills should be increased, and the role of higher education in research and development needs to be enhanced. Finally, the government has given priority to the role of the state in promoting national identity, economic self-determination and cultural awareness, with higher education being expected to play a significant part in this process (Scottish Government, 2013).

Scottish higher education strategy

Scottish higher education policy has been developed through a series of enquiries and reports since 1999, building on the distinctive features of Scottish education that developed in earlier periods. As noted by Trench (2008) and Bruce (2012), the following are the most important features of the new Scottish system:

- A less market-oriented approach than has been evident in England
- A reliance on public funding and a rejection of the principle of a student contribution
- A focus on lifelong learning with a more integrated approach to the post-16 sector
- The higher priority given to widening access
- Less selectivity in research funding until recently, although improving research performance has been a priority, primarily by developing collaborative research pools between institutions
- A much greater focus on enhancement in the quality assurance process than in other parts of the UK

Since the Scottish National Party (SNP) formed a minority government in 2007, the future of higher education has been under review, with the aim of developing a 'unique Scottish solution'. A Scottish government white paper (2011) described its vision for post-16 education which:

> [. . .] plays a central role in improving people's life chances, delivering the best outcomes for learners; which supports and develops a world-class research capacity; and which maximises its contribution to sustainable economic growth for Scotland.
>
> (Scottish Government, 2011: 5)

Although there was a strong emphasis on the economic role of higher education in the White Paper, priority was also given to it as a civilising force that 'provides cultural energy and leadership at home and abroad' (Scottish Government, 2011: 9). According to a ministerial statement, Scotland would retain a distinctive approach to university funding and any shift in the funding of higher education from the state to the student as in the other countries of the UK was firmly rejected.

The government described a post-16 education system in which the different parts were connected so that learners could easily move between them with the aim being 'to drive forward our nation's economy both at home and abroad' (Scottish Government, 2011: 6). This included integrating the planning of the curriculum and widening the number of students with the qualifications necessary to progress to university. All 16–19 year olds would have a place in post-16 education and training. Using a catchphrase also adopted in England in very different circumstances (in the UK Government's Higher Education White Paper, 2011), learners in Scotland would be at 'the heart of the system' and be in a position to take informed decisions in the knowledge of their future labour market opportunities.

A Scottish government white paper (2011) set out proposals that would be the subject of legislation in 2013 and reaffirmed the dominant role of the state in higher education funding. Public funding would no longer be distributed by the funding council solely on the basis of a formula. It would be supplemented by a more strategic approach to the funding of teaching – based on the introduction of 'outcome agreements' (which describe what universities plan to deliver in return for their public funding) – so that it facilitated the implementation of government plans. These plans included giving increased priority to widening access where progress since devolution had been limited. While the government recognised that the key to widening access lay in transforming the life chances of children and their families, universities would be required to broaden their approach to the selection of prospective students.

Evidence of a more interventionist Scottish approach was also provided by the government's conclusion, as expressed in a 2011 white paper that there was a need to restructure the post-16 sector through greater collaboration or merger. There was 'too much duplication and unnecessary competition within colleges and regional universities' (Scottish Government, 2011: 43) and some consolidation of the university sector was needed. The current structure 'is not encouraging the sectors to make the rapid changes that we think are needed' (Scottish Government, 2011: 43) and, according to the government, responsibility for it can no longer be left in the hands of the universities. It was proposed that the funding council should be given a power to review the number and pattern of institutions and that ministers should have the power to require governing bodies to work with the council to implement recommendations arising from a review.

Tuition fees

The most significant policy change in Scottish higher education since 1999 has been the abolition of tuition fees for full-time Scottish and EU undergraduate students. In 1999, up-front tuition fees for full-time students were charged at all UK universities under the Teaching and Higher Education Act 1998, which ended free tuition and replaced maintenance grants by loans with income-contingent repayments. One of the first actions of the new Scottish Executive was to establish an enquiry under Andrew (now Sir Andrew) Cubie into the funding of higher education, which, as previously mentioned, was a devolved matter under the Scotland Act 1998. The review recommended the abolition of upfront student fees for Scottish domiciled students studying in Scotland and their replacement by a graduate endowment scheme. The Executive agreed to abolish these fees and replace it with an endowment scheme: under the terms of the new scheme, Scottish graduates were to pay back £2,000 with repayments starting once their earnings had reached £10,000 a year.

The creation of the Scottish graduate endowment – together with associated changes to student maintenance – represented the first significant variation from UK-wide higher education funding arrangements and introduced the first complexities into the devolved system which have been its hallmark ever since. Under the new arrangements introduced in 2001, students from the rest of the UK studying in Scotland would continue to be liable for the same upfront fee (£1,075 in 2001/02) that apply elsewhere, but would not be required to pay the endowment.

In 2006 in England, the fixed upfront tuition fee was replaced by a variable fee of up to £3,000 a year, for which payment was deferred until after graduation. It was introduced to address the problem of underinvestment in universities. Graduates would be required to contribute to the cost of their education once their earnings reached £15,000 a year, and a subsidised loan scheme with income-contingent repayments was introduced with the increased fee. Variable fees were also introduced in Wales and Northern Ireland, but the graduate endowment continued in Scotland. The fixed fee charged to students from the rest of the UK studying in Scotland was retained, but was increased to £1,700 a year (£2,700 for medical courses) from 2006; it was also combined with a public loan with income-contingent repayments. These increases were a response to fears that English applicants to Scottish universities would increase dramatically if no action were taken, forcing Scottish domiciled students out at the application stage. The adoption of the new fee was also a response to concerns about an emerging funding gap with England. The principle of free full-time higher education has wider political support in Scotland than elsewhere in the UK, and it was re-established when the SNP-led government abolished the graduate endowment from 2008.

The Scottish Government responded to the UK decision in 2010 to raise the fee cap in England to £9,000 a year from 2012 by allowing Scottish institutions to set their own tuition fees for students from the rest of the UK at a rate no higher than the fee cap. But free higher education for full-time undergraduate Scottish students studying in Scotland would continue. This policy, based on residence, 'recognises the need to maintain the current mix of students from different parts of the UK in Scottish universities' (Scottish Government, 2013: 199) and to ensure that Scottish domiciled students had the opportunity to study in Scotland. It also reflected the need to secure additional funding for Scottish universities in order to reduce the resultant funding gap with England. Apart from determining undergraduate fees for students from the rest of the UK, Scottish universities also set the fee levels for all part-time and postgraduate students. They also set their own fee levels for international students and compete with other institutions in a global market.

Structure of the sector

Until 2007 no major concerns were expressed in Scotland about the structure of the sector, and attention was focused on increasing research collaboration rather than encouraging mergers between institutions. The government has given more priority to ensuring that higher education is available in underserved areas, and this has resulted in the creation of new provisions. The question of the structure of the Scottish sector has, however, been raised in earnest since 2007. The government's conclusion was that there was room for some consolidation as there was too much duplication and unnecessary competition. It argued that very often different colleges and universities were competing for the same students while similar programmes were being run by institutions within a few miles of each other.

As a result of these pressures, the government was no longer willing to leave decisions on the structure of higher education and what was delivered solely to individual universities. Under the Post-16 Education (Scotland) Act 2013 (Section 17), the Scottish Funding Council may, with the consent of ministers, 'review the extent to which fundable further education or fundable higher education is being provided by post-16 education bodies in a coherent manner' (www.legislation.gov.uk/asp/2013/12/crossheading/review-of-further-and-higher education/enacted), but there is no public information on how this is being progressed.

Governance

Since its creation in 1992 the funding council model has operated on a broadly similar basis in England and Scotland, but radical changes are now being made. Following the move to a more market-based system from 2012, it is intended that the Higher Education Funding Council for England (HEFCE) will have stronger and wider regulatory functions as well as having residual funding responsibilities. In Scotland, strong political pressures have led to a modified remit for the funding council so that it can intervene more directly in support of national objectives.

The first significant change came in 2005 when the separate funding councils for further and higher education were merged as the Scottish Funding Council (SFC). In 2011, the Scottish government raised fundamental questions about the future role of the SFC and whether its allocation mechanisms were too conservative, protecting institutional stability rather than incentivising creativity or flexibility. The intention was that it would be given a new role of 'leading and supporting change on a number of fronts'.

As a result, the SFC has increasingly been regarded as an arm of government, with a strategic role in the sector, and this trend has been underlined by statutory changes, increasingly prescriptive ministerial guidance and modifications to its funding methodology. The funding council's role has also been affected by the government's practice of engaging directly with the sector through formal and informal contacts. The outcome agreement, which was introduced in 2012, is the principal mechanism by which universities are individually required to demonstrate that they are fulfilling Scottish government priorities. It bears close similarities to the mission-based funding method that Roger Brown has long advocated. The agreements for 2013 included targets related to widening access, the learner journey, research, knowledge exchange, graduate skills and environmental sustainability. Progress against the targets is monitored, and future funding can be reduced if performance is unsatisfactory.

The Scottish Government also initiated a separate review of university governance, which reported early in 2012. It made wide-ranging recommendations that included transferring the Privy Council's role in regulating Scottish universities (as explained below) to Scotland, enacting a statute for the sector that sets out the key principles of governance and management and establishing a stakeholder forum. These principles were adopted in a quite prescriptive *Scottish Code for Good Higher Education Governance,* published in 2013.

Quality assurance

As part of its UK-wide regulatory role, the Privy Council (a branch of the UK government) is responsible for the award of university title and degree-awarding powers, and the arguments for maintaining the status quo have prevailed so far. In considering applications for degree-awarding powers in Scotland, the Privy

Council has sought advice from the responsible Scottish minister in accordance with practice elsewhere in the UK.

In Scotland, applications for university title are considered under criteria approved in 1999 (which, before 2004, were applicable to all parts of the United Kingdom). In 2004 it was decided in England and Wales to change the criteria for the award of university title so that it was no longer necessary for an institution first to have secured research degree-awarding powers.

These changes were the first indication that the UK government was to take a more liberal approach to degree-awarding powers and university title than has been evident in Scotland. As a result of the new approach, five private providers in England now have degree-awarding powers, and three have university titles. Following the changes adopted in 2012, private providers will have access to HEFCE funding as well as student support. However, in Scotland, existing restrictions on market entry remain in place, and there are no plans to change them.

Scotland – as in the rest of the UK – subscribes to the principle that universities have the main responsibility for ensuring that quality and standards are maintained and that they should be independently overseen by the Quality Assurance Agency (QAA). All universities use a common set of tools to underpin their work in maintaining quality and standards. The legislation creating the funding councils in 1992 included a specific obligation to ensure that provision is made by each council for assessing the quality of the provision it funds. In 1997, the QAA was created as a UK-wide independent body funded by universities and funding council contracts, which require it to devise and apply quality assurance methods. Scotland continues to support the need for comparable UK standards based on institutional review and has endorsed the view that quality assurance at the subject level should be the responsibility of the universities.

Clear differences of approach have nevertheless developed between England and Scotland, and their contracts with the QAA require it to adopt different approaches. After 2001, quality assurance in Scotland began to move in the direction of quality enhancement, and enhancement-led institutional review was promulgated in 2003. The planned move to risk-based quality assurance in England from 2017, as a result of the changes adopted in 2012, is likely to increase the differences in approach between the two countries. However, following HEFCE's announcement in October 2014, Scotland will be reviewing its quality assessment arrangements in parallel with England, and it will be some time before the outcome can be assessed.

Conclusion

As it has developed since 2007, Scottish higher education now offers a distinct alternative to the market-based models being adopted in England, Australia and some other countries. Although there has been a mix of policy convergence and divergence with the rest of the UK since devolution, the most distinctive change in Scotland has, of course, been the adoption of free higher education for full-time home undergraduates. In other respects policy conservatism was in evidence in Scotland until 2007 when it gave way to strong political pressure for change. Reform has been driven by demographic and financial pressures as well as the need to improve economic performance. There is a positive view of higher education's potential contribution to economic development, but also a belief that performance needs to be enhanced in order to maximise impact and secure greater value for money in a period of economic stringency. The increasing divergence in policy between England and Scotland builds upon marked historical differences in the education systems of the two countries, which were a product of the earlier period of administrative devolution.

Scotland has shown little appetite for the market-based reforms adopted in England, and while acknowledging the need to maintain the autonomy of universities, it seems to be moving in some respects in the direction of a more traditional European model of higher education with a more direct role for central government. There is an emphasis on lifelong learning, more coherent pathways for learners from schools and colleges to university, the need for the rationalisation of provision, and enhanced research performance. Higher education is seen primarily as serving economic and social objectives even more than is the case in England, and this focus is shaping how the Scottish government secures the changes in the sector that it is seeking. There is a real possibility that the autonomy of Scottish universities will be eroded and a risk that their relationship to government may soon be similar to that of the further education colleges or to the polytechnics in England and Wales before incorporation. It is too early to assess the potential impact of these wide-ranging changes, but they raise important questions that will need to be addressed in due course.

There is no doubt that Scotland has retained many of the features of the non-market model identified by Roger Brown, although it includes some elements of a market-based system, including the setting of some tuition fees, provision of consumer information and aspects of the (UK-wide) quality assurance arrangements. But has Scotland found a better balance between market and non-market approaches than has been evident in England? Brown argued that competition would adversely affect participation in higher education partly because the increasing stratification of institutions would present a further barrier to students from lower socio-economic groups. It is too early to reach a conclusion on this issue but it is evident there have been no significant differences in the rate of improvement in socio-economic participation between England and Scotland despite the priority that Scotland has given to widening access in recent years. Free tuition has not encouraged a greater proportion of students from poorer backgrounds to enter higher education, but significant fee levels do not seem to have discouraged them.

Brown also associates market-based policies with reduced expenditure per student, leading to increased efficiency but a reduction in the quality of education experienced by most students. These funding pressures have also been evident in Scotland where, as in England, student numbers have increased more rapidly than funding during the past decade. The introduction of variable fees in England in 2012 produced a funding gap which the Scottish government has closed for the time being by charging students from the rest of the UK higher fees, increasing public investment and taking steps to enhance sector efficiency, which appear to have made an impact. In the longer term, however, there are questions about the sustainability of free higher education, particularly in a post-referendum Scotland with its own tax-raising powers but where the public subsidies from Whitehall through the Barnett formula may no longer be available.

Bibliography

Brown, R. with Carasso, H. (2013) *Everything for Sale? The Marketisation of UK Higher Education*. London: Routledge and the Society for Research into Higher Education

Bruce, T. (2012) *Universities and Constitutional Change in the UK: The Impact of Devolution on the Higher Education Sector*. Oxford: HEPI (Higher Education Policy Institute)

Raffe, D. (2013) *Devolution and Higher Education: What Next?* London: Leadership Foundation for Higher Education

Scottish Government (2011) *Putting Learners at the Centre: Delivering our Ambitions for Post-16 Education*. Edinburgh: White Paper

Scottish Government (2013) *Scotland's Future: Your Guide to an Independent Scotland*. Edinburgh: White Paper

Trench, A. (2008) *Devolution and Higher Education: Impact and Future Trends*. London: Universities UK

UK Government (2011) *Higher Education: Students at the Heart of the System*. London: Department for Business, Innovation and Skills

Part II

Students in a marketised environment

Chapter 6

Contractualising the student experience through university charters

Joanna Williams

Student charters, now ubiquitous in UK higher education, emerged in their most recent form as a result of successive national government policies enacted since the 2010 *Review of Higher Education Funding and Student Finance* (*The Browne Review*), which led to an increase in tuition fees paid by students from 2012. Every higher education institution (HEI) in England is now required to have a student charter, or partnership agreement that details the minimum level of service students can expect from their university and, in return, what will be expected from them. As such, charters have become important institutional documents with two key functions: they simultaneously market a university to potential students and they manage the expectations of current students.

My critical analysis of student charters focuses upon their use as marketing documents and the impact they have in commodifying higher education into a product and constructing students as consumers. This draws extensively upon Roger Brown's research into the marketisation of higher education, in particular *Higher Education and the Market* (Brown with Carasso, 2011b) and *Everything for Sale? The Marketisation of UK Higher Education* (2013). I argue that although by no means uniquely responsible for the positioning of higher education as a product, and the student as consumer, charters are a key vehicle for presenting the relationship between students, academics and their university as one of customer service. In this way, charters contribute towards the commodification of higher education.

The imposition of a service agreement and the gradual transformation of the relationship between lecturer and student to one of service provider and service user may contribute towards a culture of intellectual passivity within higher education. The lowering of the legal age of majority in 1970, from 21 to 18, and the consequent lapsing of universities' responsibilities *in loco parentis*, established universities as adult spaces in which students aspired to make autonomous decisions about their own learning. In formally setting out mutual expectations, there is a risk that for some students, fulfilling the terms of the agreement comes to replace more active engagement with their learning. Charters may be experienced by some students as infantilising. An assumption that students will determine for themselves the nature and extent of their engagement with the university is replaced by a written agreement detailing how such decisions have been made for them by others within the institution.

The policy context

Institutional student charters have become a recent fixture in the marketised landscape of the post-tuition-fees university, particularly in the UK. However, the concept of the student charter predates the introduction of fees paid by individuals and can be seen as contributing towards the creation of the student as consumer, rather than just responding to its existence. In 1993, the British government's Department for Education (DfE) published an English Charter for Higher Education, *Higher Quality and Choice*. This was just one of in a series of 'citizen's charters' introduced at this time. The then Conservative government saw charters as a means of promoting the services provided by the state for minimal financial outlay. Such charters contributed to a process of renegotiating the relationship between state and citizen to that of customer and service provider (see Williams, 2013).

There was little opposition to the 1993 Charter as it emerged into a receptive higher education climate. Some HEIs, particularly in England and Australia, had already introduced charters, variously called 'student agreements' or 'student contracts', that primarily focused upon identifying institutional and individual student rights and responsibilities (Aldridge and Rowley, 1998: 32). Specific justifications for their introduction varied: Beeson (1998) describes the decision to introduce a 'charter of student rights and responsibilities' at Deakin University in Australia in 1994 as having 'developed from a component of quality improvement' (Beeson, 1998: 17).

Two key trends drove an interest in charters at this time. The first was a growing awareness of the potential for litigation, which led to some university managers becoming increasingly concerned that implicit agreements with students needed to be formalised in order to better protect institutions. Although an institution's 'prospectus, handbook and regulations' had once been considered sufficient to determine an implicit contract with students (Gaffney-Rhys and Jones, 2010: 712), the introduction of charters, it was argued, simply formalised and drew students' attention to the status quo (Aldridge and Rowley, 1998: 35; Kaye, Bickel and Birtwistle, 2006:113). The emergent notion of higher education as a 'right' helped legitimise claimants taking cases of alleged institutional negligence to court. This 'rights-culture', which has been suggested as one of the means of constructing the student as consumer, is premised on the image of education as a service to be consumed rather than an activity in which to participate (Kaye, Bickel and Birtwistle, 2006: 87).

The second trend that led to interest in charters in 1993 was an increase in the numbers of students overall and so-called 'non-traditional' students in particular, as a result of policies designed to widen participation, that turned the attention of some universities to pedagogical approaches for supporting student learning.

It was argued that assumptions relating to course aims, assessment criteria and teaching processes needed to be made increasingly explicit to students (Scott, 1999: 199). At the same time, it has also been suggested that charters were instrumental in allowing universities to be 'reinvented' in the context of a 'disaggregated and individualised wider community' (Rochford, 2008: 41).

Higher Quality and Choice set some important precedents that continue in today's institutional charters. A key aim of the document was to make 'everyone more aware of what is provided for the large amount of public money that goes into higher education' (DfE, 1993: 1). This began to establish HE as a *quid pro quo* between government and HEIs. In return for public money, universities were expected to respond 'to the needs and demands of customers' (DfE, 1993: 1). Here we see the first example of a British government policy document applying the label 'customer' to students. This acted as significant step in moving HE away from informal arrangements negotiated between staff, students and universities and towards a more explicit sense of academics as service providers and students as customers.

Higher Quality and Choice not only told students how universities would meet their demands but, importantly, it determined expectations for them, particularly in relation to their education. The charter informed students, 'You should know in advance how your course will be taught and assessed' (DfE, 1993: 12). This removes opportunities for lecturers to be spontaneous in approach and suggests that HE is less a process of ongoing negotiation than something that can be known and quantified in advance.

Despite growing awareness that students were adopting a 'consumerist approach to higher education' (Gaffney-Rhys and Jones, 2010: 711), the national student charter was only gradually replaced by institutional-specific documents. By 2007 nine British universities had formal student agreements in place, with a further seventeen considering such a move (Gaffney-Rhys and Jones, 2010: 711). One reason suggested for the slow uptake of charters was that within institutions there was little coherent sense as to where responsibility for their production lay. This lack of clarity was indicative of the uncertainty as to whether the authors of charters were to be the arbitrators of student complaints or the people with corporate responsibility for the quality of the student experience (Aldridge and Rowley, 1998: 31).

Following the 2006 increase in tuition fees, the number of English universities with student charters grew rapidly. In 2010, the British Conservative-Liberal Democrat coalition government launched the *Student Charter Group*, a working party tasked with exploring 'current best practice in the use of Student Charters and other student agreements' (Student Charter Group, 2011: 3). Of the English HEIs that responded to this consultation, fifty-two already had charters in place. The group's *Final Report* recommended that every English HEI have a student charter for two distinct purposes: first, to provide information to help steer the choices of prospective students, and second, to provide 'information for students when they are starting a course – and during the course – so they know what they can expect and what is expected of them' (Student Charter Group, 2011: 3). The 2011 national HE policy document *Students at the Heart of the System* endorsed 'the Group's recommendation that each institution should have a student charter, or similar high level statement, to set out the mutual expectations of universities and students' (BIS, 2011: 33)

Charters within a marketised HE sector

The two main uses of student charters, as outlined in the *Final Report* demonstrate the extent to which such documents are intended to be a marketing tool. The underlying assumption behind the recommendation is that markets drive up quality. As Roger Brown notes, '[i]deologically, there is a strong belief on the part of many governments and policy-makers that market competition makes institutions more efficient and responsive to stakeholders' (Brown, 2011a: 18). The currency of the higher education marketplace is information: 'consumers use the available information to select the product that is most suitable for them' (Brown, 2011a: 15), and charters provide one form in which such information can be accessed and compared by target customers.

One problem with using student charters in this way is that, as Brown suggests, 'the theory of markets assumes either a reasonably homogenous product or the capacity of purchasers to distinguish effectively between different products. Neither assumption applies to higher education' (Brown, 2011b: 10). When student charters from very different HEIs are compared, the similarities between each document are apparent. All tend to describe, using general, non-quantifiable language, what the university, students and the students' union at each institution 'undertakes to' or 'is committed to' do. Such statements appear as short sentences broken up into bullet points or placed in numbered lists.

The extent of the similarities between documents should come as little surprise. Deliberately opaque language may be a tactical means of universities avoiding anything that is potentially legally binding (Gaffney-Rhys and Jones, 2010: 718). It masks the fact that charters cannot encompass specific 'promises': the fact that one charter is to apply to all students whatever their personal circumstances and no matter which subject they are studying precludes detailed assertions. The document produced by the University of Birmingham begins with the statement:

> The student charter sets out the general principles of the partnership between students, the University of Birmingham and the Guild of Students. It applies to all registered students of the university following taught or research programmes, whether studying on or off campus.

It needs to be very general indeed to apply equally to over 27,000 individual students.

Furthermore, the role such documents are expected to play within a higher education market incentivises homogeneity. While it is in the interests of each institution to present themselves in the best light possible, no one institution wants to appear to stand out from the rest of the market to too great an extent. Brown with Carasso note that:

> [One of] the aims of successive governments has been to increase consumer – student, employer and research funder – choice. It is therefore somewhat ironic that there has at the same time been some reduction in institutional diversity.
>
> (Brown, 2013: 40)

The *Final Report of the Student Charter Group* suggests charters are a response to 'major changes to the higher education funding system' (Student Charter Group, 2011: 4) which, it acknowledges, 'have the potential to alter the relationship between universities and students' (Student Charter Group, 2011:4). The report claims that charters can usefully 'establish clear mutual expectations, and help monitor the student experience and how relationships are working' (Student Charter Group, 2011: 4). This suggests a further reason for the similarity between institutional charters: the role they play in managing the expectations of current students. It is assumed that charters convey significant messages about how institutions wish to be viewed by their customers (Aldridge and Rowley, 1998: 30) and in the subsequent shaping of students' expectations, compose 'an essential element of the socialisation process' (Hill, 1995: 15).

Universities may see charters as a way to manage students' expectations 'in order to align them as closely as possible with what can be delivered by way of service quality' (Sander *et al.*, 2000: 309). This would further limit variation as few institutions are likely to want to commit to substantially more or less than their competitors. One incentive for universities to formally monitor and manage expectations is the importance given to student satisfaction ratings that help determine an institution's league table position. The logic of this is that it is preferable for students to have low expectations which can be easily met rather than high expectations which may leave them disappointed.

Hill explains that:

> [S]ervice consumers who have achieved a high level of organisational socialisation should have more accurate expectations regarding the service transaction than might otherwise have been the case.
>
> (Hill, 1995: 15)

Scott suggests there is 'a natural tendency for customers to reconcile expectations with experience, even if this means lowering expectations' (Scott, 1999: 198). This suggests that the longer students remain in higher education, the lower their expectations will be and importantly, that this is to be welcomed by universities who can then score more highly on student satisfaction rankings. Knowing the expectations of students in advance is important for lecturers if their role is conceived primarily as that of service provider. They can then ensure that unrealistic expectations (of a high quality learning experience) can be 'managed to a more appropriate or realistic level' (Sander *et al.*, 2000: 311).

The Sheffield Hallam University charter can be seen as typical in its claims to embody the institution's:

> [C]ommitment to delivering a high quality student experience and sets out the expectations and responsibilities we have for our community of students and staff. [. . .] The charter is not a contractual document but it forms the basis for the relationship between staff and students with the aim of improving the student experience.

The repeated focus upon the student experience suggests charters have become incorporated into institutional quality assurance processes, as the prime motivation for their existence is managing students' expectations so as to achieve customer satisfaction. The University of East London, for example, uses its charter to commit to offering students, 'a welcoming, polite and professional service at all times'. Beeson (1998) describes Deakin University's charter as contributing to the 'overall quality assurance programme by highlighting the university's commitment to its students' (Beeson, 1998: 18). In the next section I will explore the impact of such documents upon what it means to be a student today.

Passive learners

As can be expected, all institutional charters place a significant emphasis upon the students' learning experience. However, teaching and learning necessarily vary greatly according to discipline and an individual student's prior educational attainment. The teaching needs of a final year biochemist will be different from those of a first year historian. Student charters set out conditions for learning in HE that, in attempting to be equally as applicable to all students, end up being very general. Lancaster University's charter, for example, tells students they can expect, 'to experience a variety of approaches to learning, teaching and assessment'. While this is undoubtedly true, it is perhaps more obvious than helpful. Most charters do little more than make students aware of the opportunities available for them to access. The University of Kent, for example, commits to 'providing access to library and IT facilities' and 'providing access to activities which will enhance students' graduate prospects, skills development and well-being'.

The 'one-size-fits-all' charter assumes that the learning experiences of individual students can be 'literally the same or identical' (Rochford, 2008: 44), but the nature of education is that it is experienced entirely individually and comes with no guarantees. Virtually all charters expect students to commit to regular attendance, meeting assessment deadlines and some form of active engagement or participation in learning opportunities. Yet doing all of these things still provides no indication that learning will occur. If charters create an unrealistic expectation that identical learning outcomes will be achieved by all students then when these outcomes cannot be met the temptation is for institutions to further specify a new contract with more precise terms. This may result in an unachievable endeavour to create 'a new, concrete benchmark against which observable and concrete outcomes can be measured' (Rochford, 2008: 47).

Attempts at providing a more precise indication of what students will learn are often dependent upon outcomes being transparent, known in advance and replicable for large numbers of students. Loughborough University's charter, for example, claims students will be provided with 'details of programme regulations, specifications and modes of programme delivery'. Birmingham University commits to ensure all students, '[c]an learn within a framework that facilitates their active learning and helps them achieve the outcomes of their programme of study'. Meanwhile, the University of East Anglia claims students will 'study within a structure which is governed by clearly articulated and easily accessible policies, procedures and regulations'. This emphasis on specifications, regulations and procedures alienates students from the subject content of their chosen degree course. Furthermore, it suggests that learning in higher education can be reduced to a passive process of following instructions rather that a deeper level of intellectual engagement. Attempts at producing a standardised service can result in the 'McDonaldization' of higher education (Hayes and Wynyard, 2002).

Ultimately, charters can create an impression that '[i]t is simply the responsibility of the teacher or instructor to make sure that the student is educated' (Kaye, Bickle and Birtwistle, 2006: 97–98), and all the student must do is demonstrate certain specified behaviours such as attendance and meeting deadlines. Students at Cardiff are told they can expect the university to 'provide an inspiring and enriching educational experience' but the nature of what is experienced as inspiring is very individual, and what is 'enriching' depends very much on a student's prior educational experiences. The nature of education means it cannot be reduced to simple rights and responsibilities (Beeson, 1998: 19); for example, if a student does not learn from a lecture it is unclear whether this is the responsibility of the individual student, the lecturer or the university. As learning is an individual process, with each student starting from, and arriving at, a different intellectual point, it is impossible to determine what each individual may learn from any one experience (Gibbs, 2009: 32) and the quality of education depends 'not only on the performance of the service provider's personnel, but also on the performance of the consumer' (Hill, 1995: 11).

Undermining trust

Many charters rightly emphasise the importance for students of belonging to a learning community and of partnership between staff and students. Positive relationships with academics, considered crucial to a student's learning, are often premised upon trust. For real learning to take place students need to trust their lecturer when they are pushed beyond their intellectual comfort zone. Prior to the introduction of charters, relationships between students and universities were perceived as being based primarily upon trust in an unwritten psychological and moral contract (Aldridge and Rowley, 1998: 35). The specific nature of trust as a quality is such that attempts to legislate it into existence are often counterproductive.

It may be the case that charters, through constructing the academic as service provider, actually serve to undermine the trust between student and lecturer. As relationships become increasingly formalised and predetermined a 'contractualisation' of the student experience occurs. The instruction in the *Final Report of the Student Charter Group* that '[c]harters should be signed off by Vice-Chancellors and Students' Union's Presidents' (Student Charter Group, 2011: 8) removes individual academics from the process of negotiating expectations and relationships with their students. Sabri suggests that the presumed interests of a generic student are 'set in opposition to the vested interests of knave-like academics' (Sabri, 2011: 657).

The existence of institutional charters circumvents the need for individual academics to negotiate specific relationships with their own students. Expectations are determined at an institutional level rather than with individual lecturers. At the University of Essex students and academics learn, '[o]ur Student Charter has been jointly developed by the University of Essex and the University of Essex Students' Union'. Similarly, at the University of Gloucestershire, '[t]he Student Charter is reviewed and approved annually by both University Council and Academic Board'. Such faceless and monolithic bodies as 'the university', 'the academic board' and even 'the students' union' risk distancing students and academics alike from individual relationships.

Morley (2003) suggests that when students are 'asked to trust the measures, rather than the professionals delivering the service, then education comes to be delivered defensively' (Morley, 2003: 84). This 'cascade of contracts' approach to higher education moves beyond marketing and quality assurance to have a detrimental impact upon the whole idea of a university community (Rochford, 2008: 50) as there is an assumed conflict of interest between student and lecturer that 'inexorably erodes the relationship of trust [. . .] on which the academic enterprise is founded' (Furedi, 2009: 2). Ironically, an excessive focus on procedures can lead to the learning needs of individual students being overlooked.

The tendency for universities to negotiate with a generalised concept of a typical student means the overwhelming majority of students at each institution have little say in determining the individual relationships they form with academics. This misses the fundamental point that so much of higher education takes place through relationships between academic and student. Charters re-interpret the role of the student as less concerned with individual intellectual commitments and more about fulfilling a set of predetermined responsibilities. The good students are no longer the ones who are sufficiently engaged with their chosen subject that their pursuit of knowledge takes them into terrain perhaps even unfamiliar to that of their lecturers. Instead, the good students are those who comply with predetermined regulations. This creates a culture of intellectual passivity.

Infantilising or empowering?

The nature of the charter is that students are (or appear to be) given rights in return for the fulfilment of certain responsibilities, although the exact nature of the relationship between such rights and responsibilities can be contentious (Beeson, 1998: 19). This provision of rights and responsibilities suggests an attempt by institutions to socialise students, and charters can act as codes of conduct (Aldridge and Rowley, 1998: 32). The University of Sheffield's charter commits students to 'respect staff, students, and our environment and see myself as part of the wider University and local community, recognising that my actions affect those living with and around me'. At the University of Kent, students are similarly committed to 'respectfulness' and 'treating all people equally'. On the one hand, this can be seen as the university exercising its duty of care to students collectively and also safeguarding members of the local community. However, when seen in the context of marketisation, such statements take on a new dynamic. At Canterbury Christ Church University students undertake to 'be proud ambassadors for the University and the Students' Union and represent them in a manner that best promotes their respective reputations in the local community and elsewhere'. This shifts behaviour regulation away from protecting local communities and towards recruiting students into marketing mechanisms. Local institutional reputation becomes a concern with growing the customer base.

In return for behaviour regulation, charters are seen as empowering students through the provision of better customer information. *Students at the Heart of the System* claims that '[s]tudent charters and student feedback will take on a new importance to empower students whilst at university' (BIS, 2011: 6). Yet the notion that, as young adults, students can be empowered by an institution, or more specifically by a promise contained in a document, rather than taking control of their own educational experience, reduces the concept of empowerment to a service level agreement (Morley, 2003: 84). Sabri suggests that arguing against student empowerment, or the dominance of the student voice, is akin to challenging the 'sacralisation of the consumer' (Sabri, 2011: 658) which has taken place as the status of students as fee-payers has become elevated within institutions. Gibbs (2009) argues that far from empowering students (and disempowering academics) charters 'reproduce practices of oppression and exploitation' within the university (2009: 34) as the language used reinforces the authority of the institution over students. Sheffield Hallam University's charter tells students, 'We expect you to . . .' and Nottingham Trent University similarly informs students 'You are expected to . . .'. Despite the use of pronouns in this discourse, the personalised nature of charters is illusory as no individual students formally sign-up to such documents other than by taking up their university place. Charters can infantilise students by removing opportunities for them to negotiate individual responsibility, behaviour, relationships and learning while expecting them to passively follow predetermined commitments.

Conclusions

As universities attempt to use charters as both a marketing device for new students and a means of setting the expectations of existing students, there is a risk that, in the process, the nature of higher education is undermined. It can be argued that charters have given students some power to negotiate the terms of their education and in particular for them to ensure they receive value for money with the payment of higher tuition fees. However, while students may gain some rights, for example to better and more timely feedback on assessed work, this comes with a shift away from student identity to that of consumer and a corresponding repositioning of the academic as service provider. Delight in being a student is sacrificed to an instrumental focus upon complying with specified regulations in order to ensure a return on the tuition-fee investment.

Bibliography

Aldridge, S. and Rowley, J. (1998) Students' Charters: an evaluation and reflection. *Quality in Higher Education* 4 (1): 27–36

Beeson, G. (1998) A Student Charter as a component of quality improvement in higher education. *Quality in Higher Education* 4 (1): 17–25

BIS (2011) *Students at the Heart of the System.* London: The Stationery Office

Brown, R. (2011a) The March of the Market. In M. Molesworth, R. Scullion, and E. Nixon (eds) *The Marketisation of Higher Education and the Student as Consumer.* London: Routledge: 11–25

Brown, R. (2011b) *Higher Education and the Market.* London: Routledge

Brown, R. with Carasso, H. (2013) *Everything for Sale? The Marketisation of UK Higher Education.* London: Routledge and the Society for Research into Higher Education

Browne, J. (2010) *Securing a Sustainable Future for Higher Education.* London: The Stationery Office

DfE (1993) *Higher Quality and Choice: The Charter for Higher Education.* London: DfE Citizen's Charter

Furedi, F. (2009) 'Now is the age of the discontented'. *Times Higher Education,* (04/06/09)

Gaffney-Rhys, R. and Jones, J. (2010) Issues surrounding the introduction of formal student contracts. *Assessment and Evaluation in Higher Education* 35 (6): 711–725

Gibbs, P. (2009) Learning agreements and work based higher education. *Research in Post-Compulsory Education* 14 (1): 31–41

Hayes, D. and Wynyard, R. (eds) (2002) *The McDonaldization of Higher Education.* London: Greenwood Press

Hill, F.M. (1995) Managing service quality in higher education: the role of the student as primary consumer. *Quality Assurance in Education* 3 (3): 3–21

Kaye, T., Bickel, R.D. and Birtwistle, T. (2006) Criticising the image of the student as consumer: examining legal trends and administrative responses in the US and UK. *Education and the Law* 18 (2/3): 85–129

Morley, L. (2003) Reconstructing students as consumers: power and assimilation? In M. Slowey and D. Watson (eds) *Higher Education and the Lifecourse.* London: SRHE and Open University Press: 79–92

Rochford, F. (2008) The contested product of a university education. *Journal of Higher Education Policy and Management* 30 (1): 41–52

Sabri, D. (2011) What's wrong with 'the student experience'? *Discourse: Studies in the Cultural Politics of Education* 32 (5): 657–667

Sander, P., Stevenson, K., King, M. and Coates, D. (2000) University students' expectations of teaching. *Studies in Higher Education* 25 (3): 309–323

Scott, S.V. (1999) The academic as service provider: is the customer 'always right'? *Journal of Higher Education Policy and Management* 21 (2): 193–202

Student Charter Group (2011) *Final Report of the Student Charter Group.* London: The Stationery Office

Williams, J. (2013) *Consuming Higher Education: Why Learning Can't Be Bought.* London: Bloomsbury

Institutional charters

Canterbury Christ Church University: http://www.canterbury.ac.uk/sup port/student-support-and-guidance/Partnership-Agreement.pdf (accessed 29/01/15).

Cardiff University: http://www.cardiff.ac.uk/for/current/student-charter/ index.html (accessed 29/01/15).

Lancaster University: http://www.lancaster.ac.uk/current-students/student-charter/ (accessed 29/01/15).

Loughborough University: http://www.lboro.ac.uk/students/charter/ (accessed 29/01/15).

Nottingham Trent University: http://www.ntu.ac.uk/current_students/docum ent_uploads/87328.pdf?utm_medium=short_url&utm_campaign=student charter&utm_term=IM&utm_source=short_url (accessed 29/01/15).

Sheffield Hallam University: http://www.shu.ac.uk/university/overview/gover nance/studentcharter/message.html (accessed 29/01/15).

University of Birmingham: http://www.birmingham.ac.uk/undergraduate/bir mingham/student-charter.aspx (accessed 29/01/15).

University of East Anglia: http://www.uea.ac.uk/calendar/section3/regs(gen)/ the-student-charter/The+Student+Charter (accessed 29/01/15).

University of East London: http://www.uel.ac.uk/wwwmedia/uelwebsite/con tentassets/documents/studentlife/studentcharter.pdf (accessed 29/01/15).

University of Essex: http://www.essex.ac.uk/students/experience/charter/ (accessed 29/01/15).

University of Gloucestershire: http://www.glos.ac.uk/supporting/Student Charter/Pages/default.aspx (accessed 29/01/15).

University of Kent: http://www.kent.ac.uk/regulations/Student%20Charter% 202013.pdf (accessed 29/01/15).

University of Sheffield: https://www.sheffield.ac.uk/ssid/ourcommitment/ charter (accessed 29/01/15).

Chapter 7

UK universities as a single entity

Striking a balance between public and private needs

Bernard Longden

Converging interests

This chapter challenges the ubiquitous faith in league tables and calls into question their ability to capture the richness and complexity of UK universities. It discusses their limitations as a tool to help students, and their parents, choose a university place. There is concern in the UK that when the general public is faced with random lists of universities, they rank them as if they were a single entity with shared missions, history and contexts.

In his work on the markets, Roger Brown has clearly stated the limitations of such rankings:

> [. . .] [L]eague tables lead inexorably to the conclusion that the best judge of quality, and the best safeguard of quality, is the market. This is both untrue and damaging. It is untrue because, as with any other complex activity, the only proper judges of quality are the professionals involved, in this case academics (clearly, student comments and views should be an important factor in making those judgments, but ultimately the only proper judgments about the value of an essay or a qualification are those of qualified academic staff). It is damaging because the emphasis upon markets and rankings can provide an excuse for members of the academy to neglect their professional obligations in this respect.
>
> (Brown, 2006: 38)

Whilst Brown and I argue from two distinct perspectives, we have both strived to find alternative models that could legitimate rational comparisons between universities. Brown's perspective comes from his criticism of claims by league table publishers that relate ranking to quality. My own perspective is based on the inappropriate manipulation and interpretation of data, giving rise to the false premise that an institution can be reduced to a number, which can then be treated as a meaningful measure.

Sharing Roger Brown's distaste for league tables, it seemed logical that our collaboration, as colleagues at Liverpool Hope University should focus on seeking alternative ways to account for the student experience in UK universities. We considered the possibility of using a tool emulating the Carnegie Classification, which has served the United States well for over 40 years. The US classificatory system acknowledges institutional diversity through a descriptive analysis derived from institutional data but still enables clustering of universities to be performed.

We asked whether the UK might use a similar model and whether it would enable more meaningful comparisons between universities. The challenge was to provide a well-informed and fearless critique of the growing enchantment with and dependence on university ranking and league tables. As Brown noted, the market increasingly forms part of the UK higher education narrative carrying with it the risk to the commitment of providing access to higher education for all able to benefit from it while, at the same time, balancing the institutional tension between research and teaching.

Reflecting on the 'league tables' world

These questions reflect our respective research hinterlands and writings. Roger Brown is a prolific author with a long professional career as a policy advisor, challenger and implementer. His focus has culminated in a widely respected set of publications questioning the impact and influence of the market on higher education. He argues that league tables are having a profound influence on institutions, leading many to apply flawed policies (Brown, 2011). The worldwide marketisation (Brown, 2010) of higher education creates increased demand for information about universities and colleges and what they offer. Institutional rankings and league tables are attempts to meet that need.

But amongst the many limitations of such approaches is the fundamental principle that league tables treat all institutions as having the same mission – international research universities are grouped together with former colleges of technology, diversified teacher training institutions and urban former polytechnics (for a recent discussion see Kelm and Stensaker, 2009). My own work on student experience and performance indicators has critiqued the methodological inadequacy of university rankings and the selection and use of performance measures (Longden, 2011).

Brown's and my own interest in the inadequacy of university league tables, and our reluctant acceptance that university rankings are unlikely to go away, drew us to approach the issue by breaking ranks and offering an alternative construction. We were of the opinion that this might open up a debate that would benefit the sector.

It is important, at this stage, that the positionalities of both Roger Brown and myself, as author, be declared. We both acknowledge our interest in the area of university ranking, and this arises, in some part, from working at institutions that, despite fulfilling a valued role nationally, would not claim to be perceived as 'best in show'. Indeed, Roger Brown challenged a reporter who was heavily involved in developing *The Times* 'League Tables', asking if his newspaper would ever publish a table showing an institution like Southampton Solent coming out top. His refreshing honest answer [Brown continues] was 'no' (Brown, 2006: 33).

Take a bad song and make it better

In *Perspectives,* Brown's paper *League Tables: Do We Have to Live with Them?* starts with a quote from an earlier paper by Yorke and Longden (2005) that stated that:

> 'League tables' are here to stay. The vested interests behind them will not pass up an opportunity to boost the circulation of their publications. The practical response is for the higher education sector to engage with the compilers and, in (almost) the words of Lennon and McCartney's *Hey Jude*, to take a bad song and make it better.
>
> (Yorke and Longden, 2005: 22)

Hey Jude, coined by Mantz Yorke, captured our attempt then, and my interest now, to open a discussion challenging the existing protocol for generating league tables and claim that they are flawed. Yet in the absence of anything better, the higher education community is prepared to perpetuate those errors. Peter Scott (maybe with a degree of derision) proposed swamping the number of league tables available by diluting their influence and introducing numerous methodologies, stating that 'by striving for serial exactitude across an ever wider range of domains, fuzziness may be achieved' (Scott, 2013: 126).

Thinking-up alternative classifications: learning from Carnegie

What is the best way to present a listing of all universities' results? Should they be sorted into an alphabetical list? Would a chronological list be more appropriate? Mc Cormick and Zhao (2005: 53) argue that an intuitive response is to make sense of the list by aggregating, sorting and clustering the data. Indeed the way most make sense of data involves reducing the number of data points to as few as possible by creating concepts that hold specific attributes, allowing us to have a minimal demand on our memory. However, classification tends to be a retrospective process based on observations of past performance.

A contemporary example of grouping and clustering would be the categories developed by the American sociologist Martin Trow. He is credited with being the first scholar to describe the transition in higher education from élite, to mass, to universal student participation in a seminal paper written in 1973 for the Organisation for Economic Cooperation and Development (Trow, 1973). In the UK, once a single-funded higher education system was introduced with the removal of the binary divide, it became possible to make direct comparisons between all individual members of higher education providers. The next step was inevitable – the creation of league tables.

In the US, prior to 1970, no external classification system capable of being based on a reliable protocol to differentiate the diverse range of higher education providers was available. This limited the Federal Government's ability to devise policies based on validated evidence. The Federal Government sought assistance from the Carnegie Foundation to resolve the problem, and Clark Kerr was appointed to head the Carnegie Commission to develop a universal US scheme. It was not surprising that the scheme he proposed reflected the mission differentiation scheme that Kerr had developed in the 1960s as part of the California higher education master plan (University of California, 1960).

The Carnegie Foundation (Carnegie Commission on Higher Education, 1971) provided a mechanism for differentiating the diverse institutions by grouping roughly comparable institutions to meaningful, analytical manageable categories. Each category would be sufficiently homogenous in relation to the function of the institution, and to the profiles of students and academic staff. The central motif for the classification might be summed up as 'what they did, who they taught and in what setting'. This motif had great appeal in seeking an alternative to the hegemony of self-interest shown by universities, where they manage and control the release of data to ensure a positive image of their university.

Currently, in the UK, universities tend to select which group of universities they wish to be seen to belong to – through a mechanism whereby they apply to join their chosen group. This way of labelling institutions has led to a situation where most prestigious institutions find themselves in the same group, whilst those institutions that cannot join the elite group are left to flounder forming *ad hoc* groupings based on less prestigious criteria.

The prototype alternative cluster suggested in this chapter could be used for any of the statutory reports where performance metrics are published. The central criticism of the existing use of league tables remains: until commercial publishers acknowledge institutional diversity of mission, history and context in their representation of institutional data, they will continue to reinforce existing elitism within the university sector.

The classification currently operating in the US is provided in Table 7.1 from the Carnegie website (Carnegie Classification Website, 2014).

Roger Brown and I set about developing some possible alternatives adapted from the Carnegie Classification but reflecting the UK context. The prototype solution was presented at the Oslo meeting of the Consortium of Higher Education Research (CHER) in 2010. The paper, entitled *Classifying Universities: An Initial Attempt at Providing a Theoretically Sound Basis for Classifying Universities,* hints at the tentative nature of our proposition. While we did not seek publication, the ideas embedded in the paper retain relevance and offer a challenge to the status quo.

Table 7.1 Current classification used by the Carnegie Foundation to group higher education providers in the US (Carnegie Classification Website, 2014)

Associate's colleges	Includes institutions where all degrees are at the associate's level, or where bachelor's degrees account for less than 10 per cent of all undergraduate degrees. Excludes institutions eligible for classification as tribal colleges or special focus institutions.
Doctorate-granting universities	Includes institutions that awarded at least 20 research doctoral degrees during the update year (excluding doctoral-level degrees that qualify recipients for entry into professional practice, such as the JD, MD, PharmD, DPT, etc.). Excludes special focus institutions and tribal colleges.
Master's colleges and universities	Generally includes institutions that awarded at least 50 master's degrees and fewer than 20 doctoral degrees during the update year. Excludes special focus institutions and tribal colleges.
Baccalaureate colleges	Includes institutions where baccalaureate degrees represent at least 10 per cent of all undergraduate degrees and where fewer than 50 master's degrees or 20 doctoral degrees were awarded during the update year. (Some institutions above the master's degree threshold are also included). Excludes special focus institutions and tribal colleges.
Special focus institutions	Institutions awarding baccalaureate or higher-level degrees where a high concentration of degrees (above 75%) is in a single field or set of related fields. Excludes tribal colleges.
Tribal colleges	Colleges and universities that are members of the American Indian Higher Education Consortium, as identified in IPEDS 1. Institutional characteristics.

Evolving an alternative to league tables

Principles

The central principle is that the classification should reflect an attempt to identify publicly available and robust data sufficiently stable, and persisting over time, while ensuring easy access of the data so that comparisons can be made.

The thesis underpinning our CHER paper was that markets need information; rankings group diverse universities together irrespective of their mission, their context or their reputation; those tables are used by the market. An alternative solution might be benchmarking, which has been used informally for several decades enabling direct comparisons to be made between universities. The universities creating a benchmark with other universities tend to have similar missions, contexts and profiles. Metrics used in any classification system, we argued, needed to satisfy simple criteria, i.e.:

* Be quantitative in nature – thus reducing the risk of bias
* Use easy measures – so they would form part of existing data sets

- Be directly evidenced measures – therefore accessible without complex protocols
- Data should be transparent – likely to be part of existing public datasets
- Data should be accessible by all – so form part of a published dataset

Method

All the data used was obtained from the Higher Education Statistics Agency (HESA), thus ensuring a level of confidence with their validity and reliability that could be secured from accessing the universities data directly.

The data was presented without further manipulation or adjustment except for a process of standardising nominal data to conform to a 'z score standardisation', ensuring large numerical differences between metrics, such as institutional size, were normalised.

Cluster analysis was used. This statistical technique is designed specifically to identify homogeneous objects and is widely used in marketing, business, psychology and in biological taxonomy. Cluster analysis groups universities, in this case, so that universities within a same cluster offer more similarities between each other than with universities in other clusters. A dendrogram produced by SPSS was used to decide how many clusters should reasonably be retained. From our analysis of universities, the cluster analysis suggested that three would provide an acceptable solution, based on the number of institutions contained in each cluster. It is important to keep in mind that cluster analysis will always produce clusters as that is the design of the SPSS programme. It is therefore important to ensure that the strength of the linkage between two metrics is considered carefully.

Selecting appropriate metrics

The following dimensions were used to arrive at a set of valid metrics:

1   *External esteem* provides an indicator of the perceived standing that the university holds among potential undergraduate students. The metric has been obtained from the HESA data which reports the percentage of applications accepted compared to the number that applied; so the lower the number, the higher the esteem. It is possible that this metric, for some universities, might be a lower value than would reasonably be expected because a student might choose not to apply to a university where the chances of being accepted are slim.

2   *University size and complexity* offers a metric that differentiates universities based on curriculum, level of provision (postgraduate, undergraduate) number of teaching sites and type of teaching delivery (face-to-face, web-based). The student population, comprising both student numbers and student demographics, provides a measure of university complexity and diversity of

provision. An alternative approach was to use net income to the university as a metric that reflected the size and complexity of universities; however, this was not chosen because of the difficulty in accessing reliable data.

3   *Research intensity* is diverse within the UK higher education sector. In this instance, it was calculated from the ratio of research income over the total income (R + T) of the university.

4   The focus of teaching is another dimension of university activity. *Teaching intensity* has been measured through the ratio of students to staff. During the development of a working model it was found that this metric contributed very little to the clustering process and was dropped from the final models as it was too variable across departments and faculties within one institution to be offered as a measure between institutions and subjects.

5   *Widening access* forms another dimension that the authors considered to be a metric that might differentiate institutions. This metric has been extracted from the data held by HESA on equity – the commitment to attracting and admitting students from a wide range of societal backgrounds. This measure is determined from institutional data submitted to HESA from the student data set based on family employment. The correlation between employment and socio-economic standing is strongly contested.

6   The final metric extracted from the finance record held by HESA, considers the *viability* of the university as expressed by the number of days a university could survive without an injection of funds.

The process ensured that each university had a number of metrics attributed to it; the resultant matrix consisted of the following metrics:

Table 7.2 Metrics adopted for the cluster analysis

Metric	Detail	Selected metrics
Charter	Length of time since receiving university charter	selected
Institutional esteem	Data derived from ratio of acceptances compared to applications	
Institutional size as measured by student numbers	Reported undergraduate student numbers reported to HESA	
Public research funding	R/R+T – ratio of research income compared to total funding income	selected
Public teaching funding	T/T+R – ratio of teaching funding compared to total funding income	selected
Widening access	Socio-economic measure derived from HESA data	selected
Financial viability	Cash reserved data derived from funding councils	

The metrics selected reflected our view of the nature of a university – it is by its very nature bound to be a subjective call and other metrics could have equally been justified, such as any combination of metrics provided in Table 7.2. It is an interesting proposition to consider if increasing the number of metrics would improve the separation of universities into clusters. Again this is a subjective judgement that needs careful consideration before settling on a specific number. Table 7.2 sets out the list of those metrics finally selected to create clusters.

Justification for this methodology

A three-cluster solution was provided. It is possible to merge clusters that are close together (where the distance between two clusters has the smallest value). The clusters have been developed based upon an interpretation of what the authors perceive as the main characteristics of a university within the context of location, time and policy. It is acknowledged that these metrics are open to alternative interpretation, however, it has not been the purpose of this paper to produce a definitive classification of UK university provision, but to initiate a discussion that produces a classification based on sound metrics is preferable to the present situation in the UK where all the universities are clustered together into a single heterogeneous mass.

We adopted a simpler approach, focussing on a smaller number of variables as described. The three shades of grey in Figure 7.1 represent the three-cluster solution produced from the cluster analysis protocol. In each case, a five-metric input (see Table 7.2 for metrics selected) has been selected with three clusters discernible. A striking finding was the importance of longevity in determining an institution's standing in the development of a classification protocol. Concepts contributing to the longevity of an institution are reputation and prestige; these ensure the maintenance of the status quo.

What are the benefits of promoting an alternative classification system to the ones currently used in ranking and league tables? There are at least three justifications that can be advanced:

1   Decrease in the subjectivity that is evident in the current schemes where the interests of the publishers are strong and where the prestige institutions promote certain metrics to their own advantage.
2   Increase the transparency in such a way that, given the criteria, institutions can identify with the classification group or cluster without further manipulation of the metrics.
3   Focus on metrics that relate directly to what is taught, to whom and within what mission context.

To avoid ossification, a regular re-assessment of the metrics would be carried-out by an external agency to adjust for changes in the institutional metrics that decrease or increase the homogeneity of the classification group or cluster.

There is no point in rehearsing the illogical and negative moral position taken when constructing and using league tables and rankings. Roger Brown has provided a line-by-line critique of each of the defences made by those promoting rankings, dismissing them in a decisive surgical fashion with the ultimate claim that 'none of their defences hold water' (Brown, 2006: 35).

A positive stance towards ranking and league tables, influenced by Darwinian evolutionary theory, has been the basis of this chapter. This theory is predicated upon the consequence of change. The theory offers three responses to any change: *tolerating* the change, *avoiding* the change by migration or *adapting* to the change. I have put the case for adapting to the change; seeking a better way to appreciate the diversity of UK universities.

The proposed way forward represents a compromise between the misguided beliefs that a single number can be generated for such a complex system as higher education and the need to make rational and valid comparisons between institutions. There are at least three interested parties: the students wishing to make a wise purchase of their undergraduate course; the institutions wishing to monitor their own progress in relation to comparable institutions; and the government, even though the influence of the state may have decreased in recent years.

Results

Figure 7.1 has been generated with quantitative analysis software (SPSS) for the production of clusters. The correlation of all the universities against their

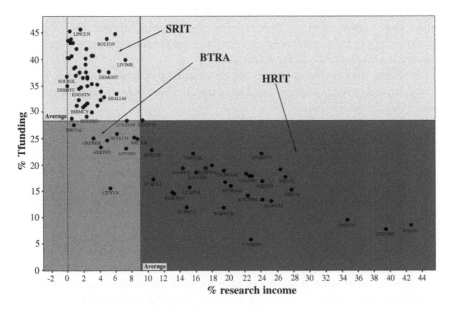

Figure 7.1 Distribution of institutions using a five-metric input and resultant three-cluster solution comparing % teaching income against % research income

percentage research and teaching totals have been separated into three groups depending on the length of time each has held a university charter. This separation into clusters has been achieved through the methodology described above. Each of the clusters can be ascribed a descriptive title reflecting the nature of the cluster:

Group 1   Scholarship and research-informed teaching (SRIT)
Group 2   Balance between teaching and research activity (BTRA)
Group 3   High intensity research activity alongside teaching (HIRT)

If this classification were developed along lines similar to the Carnegie Classification, a final classification would include two more categories:

Group 4   Specialist independent institutions and private providers
Group 5   Further education funded institutions offering undergraduate teaching

Recent work by Boliver (personal communication with publication pending) on 127 English higher education providers resulted in a four-cluster solution. Her analysis was based on five dimensions: research activity, teaching quality, economic resources, academic selectivity and socioeconomic student mix. A similar selection of criteria had been adopted in the CHER paper. A comparison between the two sets of clusters (one by Boliver and the other from the CHER paper) show remarkable similarities.

Implications

What are the implications of moving towards a cluster analysis solution? There are four possible implications of moving to a different system of classification. They are

1   A decreased dependence of the commercially produced ranking tables with their associated issues and dangers. Salmi (2013: 237) has compiled a graph of the percentage dependencies (government, agencies and media) that different regions across the globe use in the production of their world ranking tables (see Figure 7.2). It is clear from the graph that Western Europe has the greatest dependency on media

The proposed classification ensures appropriate metrics are used to ensure measures between institutions with comparable missions and provision. The use of the single number as a measure of the quality, reputation or worth of institutions needs to be constantly challenged. This is a remorseless process of undermining the dominant perception that the single number representing an institution has reliability and validity.

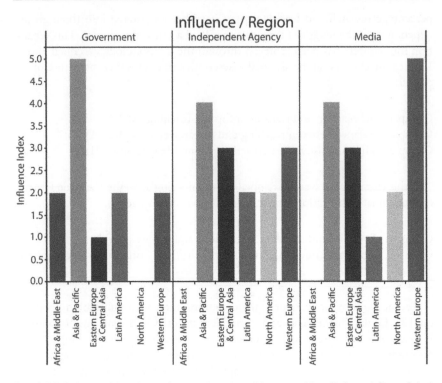

Figure 7.2 Relative dependency for production of league tables (Adapted from Salmi, 2013: 237)

2   The benefit of enabling institutions of similar missions to compare themselves in a realistic context, promoting benchmarking to provide constant monitoring at the institutional level.

3   The emphasis on the difference between clusters such that a hierarchical relationship between clusters is avoided.

4   The proposal to use a Carnegie type approach would reduce institutional pressure to adapt to a consequence of the ranking tables for the drive to 'race to the top'. None of the rankings is perfect; none of the evaluation systems is absolutely foolproof. Limits exist. University rankings merely provide reference information, which should not become a university goal to pursue

Developing institutional clusters is offered as a means of addressing the interests of the state, students, and institutions. Although there is a dearth of agencies in a position to broker the agenda in a fair and neutral manner, there are agencies, for example HESA and UCAS, that are capable of providing a level of independence to satisfy the needs of the public.

And finally

In answer to Roger Brown's paper *League Tables: Do We Have to Live with Them?* I am inclined to proffer the response 'Yes'. The market has invested too much in their production and an unfortunate level of dependence on them has become evident. This is not to say that I support them or encourage them – I don't.

I concur with Roger Brown and share his bottom line, and trust the alternative proposed in this chapter might gain credence:

> . . . I believe, quite genuinely, that if we continue to acknowledge them [league tables] we shall seriously damage the quality of what we can offer.
>
> (Brown, 2006: 37)

Bibliography

Boliver, V. (27th December 2014) Personal communication with Vikki Boliver commenting on her paper 'Are there distinctive clusters of higher and lower status universities in the UK?' (under review)

Brown, R. (2006) League tables: do we have to live with them? *Perspectives: Policy and Practice in Higher Education* 10: 33–38

Brown, R. (ed.) (2010) *Higher Education and the Market.* London and New York: Routledge

Brown, R. (ed.) (2011) *Higher Education and the Market.* London: Routledge

Brown, R. and Longden, B. (2010) Classifying Universities: An Initial Attempt at Providing a Theoretically Sound Basis for Classifying Universities. In Consortium of Higher Education Research (CHER) (ed.) *Effects of Higher Education Reforms.* Oslo: Oslo University (unpublished)

Carnegie Classification Website (2014) www.carnegiefoundation.org/classification [Accessed November 2014]

Carnegie Commission on Higher Education (1971) *New Students and New Places: Policies for the Future Growth and Development of American Higher Education.* New York: McGraw-Hill

Kelm, B. M. and Stensaker, B. (eds) (2009) *University Rankings, Diversity, and the New Landscape of Higher Eduction.* Rotterdam: Sense Publications

Longden, B. (2011) Ranking Indicators and Weights. In J. C. Shin, R. Toutkoushian and S. Marginson (eds) *Ranking, Reputation and Quality of Higher Education.* Netherlands: Springer: 73–104

Mc Cormick, A. C. and Zhao, C.-M. (2005) Rethinking and Reframing the Carnegie Classification. *Change* 37: 50–57

Salmi, J. (2013) If Ranking Is the Disease, Is Bench-Marking the Cure? In P. T. M. Marope, P. J. Wells and E. Hazelkorn (eds) *Rankings and Accountability in Higher Education.* Paris: United Nations Educational, Scientific and Cultural Organization: 235–255

Scott, P. (2013) Ranking Higher Education Institutions: a critical perspective. In P.T.M. Marope, P. J. Wells and E. Hazelkorn (eds) *Rankings and Accountability in Higher Education*. Paris: United Nations Educational, Scientific and Cultural Organization: 113–127

Trow, M. (1973) *Problems in the Transition from Élite to Mass Higher Education*: Berkeley, CA: Carnegie Commission on Higher Education

University of California. (1960). A Master Plan for Higher Education in California 1960–1975. Available at http://www.ucop.edu/acadinit/mastplan/MasterPlan 1960.pdf [accessed 11 August 2015]

Yorke, M. and Longden, B. (2005) *Significant Figures: Performance Indicators and 'League Tables'*. London: Standing Conference of Principals

Chapter 8

Some considerations on higher education as a 'post-experience good'

Morgan White

One of the keys to a cohesive and healthy society is having a reasonable level of trust between its members. Higher education exemplifies the importance of trust, in this instance, the importance of trust in those in authority, in this case academic teachers. The marketisation of higher education damages relations of trust with those in authority. Higher education is a form of credence good where trust and authority are central. An overly instrumentalised higher education dissolves trust and therefore precludes the student's acquisition of authority.

There is a moral problem with conceiving higher education in economistic terms. The tendency to see higher education as a good to be distributed through a market mechanism leads to attempts to provide more information to consumers and levelling out power differentials between buyers and sellers in the market. This is problematic if we want to hold on to the idea that academics carry legitimate authority and therefore necessarily hold more power than students. Hannah Arendt argued that education fundamentally concerns passing authority from one generation to another in order that the next generation carries the capability of making the world anew for itself (Arendt, 1993a,b). In this perspective, many policies associated with a marketised higher education system undermine educational purposes. Throughout this chapter, I am referring to general tendencies, rather than any absolute claim that academic authority has gone, or that trust no longer exists.

Instrumental value in the market for education

Roger Brown describes higher education not as a 'search good' where value can be determined prior to consumption, nor as an 'experience good' where value is determined as the good is consumed, but as a 'post-experience good':

> [H]igher education is actually a '*post*-experience good', the effects of which may not appear for many years and may not even be traceable to a particular educational experience. [. . .] Because higher education is an intangible product, and because it involves a judgement-based, customized solution,

as in any professional service, it is not always clear to either the teacher or the student what the outcome will be.

(Brown, 2011: 24)

Marketisation is intended to inject dynamism into universities, to make them responsive to demanding customers (see BIS, 2014), but Brown points out that this post-experience feature of higher education renders quality indicators problematic. Proxies for price signals tend to spread misinformation. Individuals cannot easily value education because of information asymmetry between producers (the universities) and consumers (the students). The difficulty with valuing the good of higher education, for Roger Brown, is that its true worth can only be grasped many years later. Policy-makers, furthermore, tend to see the solution to market failure in informational terms (opening out information to potential customers in the market). Ironing out information is insufficient, however, because such informational policy solutions actually serve to screen out the moral dimension of education (that it necessarily involves authority, trust and commitments).

State higher education policies are often justified in terms of instrumental value such as increasing productivity, but such a stance involves a category mistake. When we regard education as 'adding economic value' to persons through education, we miss a fundamentally important moral role that education takes on: the transfer of authority, understood as a capacity to act in public and make the world. There are, however, instrumental benefits that diminish alongside declining legitimate authority: teachers, colleges and universities play a vital role in identifying students with talent and potential. The students' grades are a reflection of educators' judgements about the students. Students, their families, their future employers are put in a position of trust towards the educators' judgements. Or, consider the possibility that higher education supports the public sphere. Universities' first duty is to the public and developing competent persons capable of acting in the public sphere (Smith, 2010). Democratic states should trust universities to carry out this role to sustain the democratic legitimacy of the state. However, instrumental higher education dilutes the authority of academic teachers. This reduces the possibility that students acquire their own authority through their education. Reduced authority in students diminishes the public sphere, and an atrophied public sphere harms the legitimacy of the democratic state. An economistic understanding of education brings political problems.

Policies associated with marketisation of higher education transform a public institution (fundamentally concerned with sustaining the world) into a largely private one (fundamentally concerned with economic necessity). In the process, trust and authority evaporate in the heat of policies intended to correct for market failure, because construing education in terms of a market involves an economic understanding of the good being traded. This involves functional reliance (for instance, a degree will increase my labour value) rather than moral trust involving educational commitment (for instance, recognising that my professor can help show me how to analyse and criticise a complex argument). Remember that trust involves commitments and promises between persons. These might be expressed formally, as in taking a vow, but more often rest on tacit background assumptions.

Information asymmetry

Market failure is often caused by asymmetrical information between producers and consumers. Akerlof (1970) sets out the problem in relation to second-hand cars where the quality of the good on offer is subject to uncertainty, where buyers use some sort of market statistic to judge the quality of prospective purchases. This generates:

> [I]ncentive for sellers to market poor quality merchandise since the returns for good quality accrue mainly to the entire group whose statistic is affected rather than to the individual seller. As a result there tends to be a reduction in the average quality of goods and also in the size of the market.
>
> (Akerlof, 1970: 488)

For example, some universities might promote themselves by making exaggerated claims about 'the student experience' or future employment prospects. This may cause the market to degrade as low quality merchandise crowds out good quality offerings. Roger Brown's identification of higher education as a post-experience good is in part a recognition that education, as a relational good, is highly differentiated between different individuals undergoing different experiences with different effects at different points over the course of a lifetime. In other words, the contextual nature of learning means that information symmetry in the education market is not even a theoretical possibility because the same course at the same institution may well be experienced differently by different students in different circumstances.

Credence goods, trust and authority

In the economics of information, post-experience goods are also sometimes referred to as 'credence goods' (Darby and Karni, 1973). Dulleck, Kerschbamer and Sutter explain that:

> Repair services, medical treatments, the provision of software programmes, or a taxi ride in an unknown city are prime examples of what is known as a credence good in the economics literature. Generally speaking, credence goods have the characteristic that though consumers can observe the utility they derive from the good *ex post*, they cannot judge whether the type or quality of the good they have received is the *ex ante* needed one. Moreover, consumers may even *ex post* be unable to observe which type or quality they actually received. An expert seller, however, is able to identify the type or

quality that fits a consumer's needs by performing a diagnosis. He can then provide the right quality and charge for it, or he can exploit the information asymmetry by defrauding the consumer.

(Dulleck, Kerschbamer and Sutter, 2011: 526)

The notion of a credence good adds another dimension to the concept of the post-experience good. If the consumer of a higher education can estimate the utility (however this is defined by the consumer) of that higher education, she may still struggle to grasp whether that higher education was what she needed before she began to study. Moreover, she may well be unsure of the quality of her higher education even at the end of life. A decision to consume a credence good involves both trust and reliance. While trust is a moral quality, involving making a commitment, reliance is merely a functional concept. We often rely on inanimate objects but do not trust them. Trust and reliance involve different reactions. As Hawley explains:

Our reactions to misplaced trust differ from our reactions to misplaced reliance. Suppose I trust you to look after a precious glass vase, yet you carelessly break it. I may feel betrayed and angry; recriminations will be in order. I may demand an apology. Suppose instead that I rely on a shelf to support the vase, yet the shelf collapses, breaking the vase. I will be disappointed, perhaps upset, but it would be inappropriate to feel betrayed by the shelf, or to demand an apology from it.

(Hawley, 2014: 2)

There are different sorts of credence goods. Sometimes credibility relates mainly to the functional aspects of a good and involves the recipient of the good relying on it to function appropriately. At other times, however, credibility relates mainly to trust and a moral commitment between the consumer and producer. The way we understand a good relates to our purposes and the purposes we associate with the good. Fair trade coffee or organic pork products carry a 'kitemark' that represents a set of standards involved in the production of the good through a vertical supply chain. The consumer of the credence good trusts in the meaning of the kitemark, and the observation of standards set by the authority of the institution represented by the kitemark. Advanced division of labour renders the consumer relatively powerless to determine production standards of the various inputs at each stage of production, so the consumer places trust in the authority of the kite mark. The university might be considered similarly. The status of university designation acts as a badge of quality assurance and indicates an institution has been granted its own degree-awarding powers where university lecturers hold authority to teach.

Zdenko Kodelja (2013) argues that authority always involves trust. Authority, on a standard analysis, takes two forms: epistemic and deontic authority, also sometimes expressed as 'an authority' and 'in authority'. R. S. Peters argued that epistemic authority, being an authority, grounds deontic authority, being in an authoritative post (Peters, R. S. and Winch, P., 1967). For Kodelja:

> What makes the professor a *de facto* epistemic authority is not his or her knowledge, but rather the students' belief [in the professor's knowledge]. However, they would not believe if they knew that the professor did not have the knowledge they supposed.
>
> (Kodelja, 2013: 323)

In other words, the university teacher's authority over students rests upon recognition of that authority by those students. The teacher holds authority to the extent that she is trusted by the student. This relationship between authority and trust is familiar to readers of Locke's liberal social contract theory. According to Locke, in civil society the overarching good is the common good, but the uncertainty involved in political life can sometimes mean that political authority fails to sustain the common good. Locke turns to the notion of fiduciary trust as a model for ruling. Here citizens should remain vigilant towards those they trust in authority. Emily Nacol says, of Locke's liberal idea of trust, that:

> The trust model is appropriately open and flexible, but this elasticity contains the potential both for profitable political relations and for profound betrayal. That is, a trust can be either a means of security and benefit or a source of insecurity and loss; it always holds the seeds of both, as risks do.
>
> (Nacol, 2011: 581)

For Locke, citizens take on a role whereby they are required to exercise judgement over whether their trust is being honoured by the trustee state. At the heart of Locke's social contract lies risk: agents in the state of nature enter into an agreement to give up their natural rights in exchange for civil rights on the understanding that the government will support the common good. The source of the authority of the state is therefore the will of trusting, consenting citizens, but their trust and consent is always and everywhere provisional. Similarly, in higher education the authority of the academic is fallible and provisional. A functional, instrumental conception of the university as an investment good will undercut academic authority if the university or parts of the higher education system come to be regarded in dysfunctional terms (such as degrees not leading to 'graduate jobs').

Trust and authority dissipate as risk management has been incorporated into a bureaucratic ethic associated with the modern office. It should come as no surprise that talk of obedience problems and discipline in school (and even university) classrooms has risen as the authority of teachers transformed into a bureaucratic system (see Weber, 1991). Gradually, education, especially higher education, is losing its moral dimension, crowded out by value-free market norms.

Trust, Katherine Hawley (2014) argues, is a moral quality, involving more than mere reliance. Trust involves commitments and promises (though commitments can also arise out of conventions and social norms), when trust fails, betrayal is involved. Moreover, Hawley finds it analytically helpful to examine the concept of trust in opposition to distrust and non-reliance. An increasingly transactional relation between students, teachers and universities has altered relations in terms of trust and authority. In effect, new arrangements for higher education finance (such as a £9,000 annual tuition fee ceiling in England) generate a situation where trust becomes distrust, and academic authority withers. The imposition of high-level fees, alongside quality indicators, and students as partners all serve to alter academic relations. To be sure, there may well be other ways to analyse this phenomenon, but we can claim it is likely that the credence good is no longer imbued with credibility of the appropriate sort. In other words, higher education makes vague promises of increased future income, the student relies on this, yet if this does not materialise then the consumer of a higher education can no longer rely on her degree to boost income.

For Hawley (2014), distrust is the result of situations which involve a moral commitment yet lack reliability. It becomes clear that conceiving of higher education in economistic terms also raises the possibility of distrust towards this higher education. The social rules and conventions involved in the interpretation of what it means to study at a university are altered. Universities are generating, for instance, expectations (which consumers should expect to rely upon) that students are being prepared for professional work. The shift from trust to reliance undermines legitimate authority, or possibly, for some (students and academics, or even employers), brings a sense of betrayal. To give one example: a predominant policy response to this situation is to encourage universities to engage in practices that support 'student partnership'. However, it seems to me that there may be a real danger that this partnership takes place at a formal policy level rather than organically embedded into the meaning of belonging to the university as a student. Hawley argues that distrust is:

> nonreliance plus a tendency to resentment, a tendency to judge the distrustee negatively, or tendency to think that an apology is warranted: distrust is something like disappointed trust, though perhaps not preceded by an episode of trust

> (Hawley, 2014: 9)

It is 'appropriate to trust or distrust someone to do something only if that person has an explicit or implicit commitment to doing it.' (Hawley, 2014: 9). This means that trust involves reliance plus some extra sense of commitment.

Hawley argues that the appropriateness of relations of trust or distrust hinges on an explicit or implicit commitment from the trustee towards the trusting:

> To trust someone to do something is to believe that she has a commitment to doing it, and to rely on her to meet that commitment. To distrust

someone to do something is to believe that she has a commitment to doing it, and yet not rely upon her to meet that commitment.

(Hawley, 2014:10)

Authority of the university teacher

The university teacher's authority turns on recognition of the teacher's commitment and purposes. It is likely that the university teacher understands her commitment in epistemic terms or in terms of attitude towards developing a sense of intellectual curiosity and even love for a particular subject. The student, however, is encouraged by higher education policies and practices to understand the university teacher's commitment on a different horizon of skill development in preparation for paid employment. The bureaucratic manager is keen to understand the academic's commitment in terms of targets, various league table positions and research evaluation scores. This turns moral into prudential action.

We should notice that the student who distrusts his teacher might distrust a particular attitude in his teacher: 'Perhaps', Hawley writes, 'expecting the distrustee to have an interest in frustrating our interests' (Hawley, 2014: 6). But, she points out, such negative expectations are not necessary for distrust: we would distrust a liar or a cheat even if he held no interest in frustrating our interests. Hawley's point is that motive-based accounts of trust in general cannot cope with the concept of distrust. It is worth pausing to reflect on her analysis. The idea of students as consumers, armed with information about previous students' satisfaction levels, and the powers to influence course content and the form of assessments, places the student and the academic teacher in opposition. The market model of consumers and producers encourages the student to adopt a non-reliant or even distrustful stance towards the teacher and to regard the academic's interest as distinct from the student's interest, or uncouples the academic's ethical self-understanding from an understanding of the purpose of the university. In other words, a non-moral, thin, functional conception of higher education precludes trust and therefore precludes the recognition of authority, which in turn renders impossible an acquisition of authority by students through education.

Less thoughtful student-consumers might rely on their tutors and lecturers to hand over the learning materials required to pass the qualification, but such reliance actually turns a potentially authoritative educational relationship into a power relationship. Credence goods, like organic meat, or windscreen glass are substantively different from a higher education. While kitemarked windscreen glass involves reliance that the glass will shatter relatively safely in an accident, a university education ought to involve a trusting commitment between students, academics and the university itself. However, the lifeworldly horizon of the university appears in different ways to policy-makers, senior managers, future employers, students and academics. Whether this is something new is not the focus of this argument, but it is likely that if universities no longer inspire trust to the same extent, then there will be increasingly fractional interests within the institution.

The instrumentalised climate involving high-fees, 'employability' and 'students as partners' helps to generate an attitude from many students, administrators and academic teachers that students are, indeed, justified in regarding themselves as consumers, or lecturers are justified in simply delivering a body of knowledge. Student partnership, from a consumer perspective, can be understood in terms of an increase in student power, but a diminution in trust and authority. The practices and policies involved in a marketised higher education system are indeed transformative, but not in educational terms. Educational authority becomes power in the labour market, trust becomes distrust, commitment to diligent study evaporates and reliance on support from the *alma mater* turns into a functional reliance on the academic teacher to provide knowledge and skills as a steppingstone to a particular degree class and career.

Authority and power

Moral relations of trust and authority are all too easily transformed in an overly instrumentalised higher education into strategic relations of power and distrust. For example, formalised student voice and engagement to help design curriculum, or determine modes of assessment, or inclusive representation (without providing appropriate support and training) imposes student engagement from outside the teacher-student relationship. The outside imposition, unless done in a way that takes pains to protect the authority of the academic teacher, undermines relations of authority and trust between students and their teachers. Educational commitments (a tacit background contract between teacher and student) between students and teachers reduce, damaging the legitimacy of the teacher's authority. Authority, without recognition (from the student) becomes mere power, and the purpose of the process of higher education is no longer the gradual development of authority through studying, but the acquisition of power to be wielded in the labour market. Relations of trust and authority degrade in a culture of instrumentalism, and this degradation can be seen as a fundamental inefficiency and a misdirected waste of time and effort. Onora O'Neill makes much the same point about trust in conditions of transparency. Where outcomes and targets are tracked, the incentive to game the outcomes increases, trust reduces and authority diminishes (O'Neill, 2002).

Whether the academic teacher holds authority, depends on the understanding of relative commitments to moral integrity between the trustees in authority and those who hope to acquire that authority. The fundamental problem with the National Student Survey, student partnership, employability and league table position is that these cultivate divergent interests and commitments in the different participants in higher education. The result is a tension between intellectual trust at the normative level alongside instrumental distrust on the empirical level, where the latter frequently trumps the former.

The difficulty, however, with the potentially authority-conferring concept of the moral credence good, is that the individual student is in no position to value the development of her authority, since authority concerns recognition from others. The university's commitment was once to protect students and academics from outside influences in order that they served the public good. However, a marketised higher education treats higher education as an object to be privately valued and consumed, invested or brandished on a CV. This is not a consumer good (of the search, experience or post-experience variety). Rather, higher education is, at the normative level, a public good which supports a critical, inquiring public ethos necessary for meaningful authority in a strong democracy. This analysis suggests that to conceive of higher education as a post-experience good still concedes too much to advocates of a particularly conspicuous form of consumption.

Bibliography

Akerlof, G.A. (1970) The market for 'lemons': quality, uncertainty, and the market mechanism. *Quarterly Journal of Economics* 84 (3): 488–500

Arendt, H. (1993a) The Crisis in Education. In H. Arendt *Between Past and Future*. London: Penguin: 173–196

Arendt, H. (1993b) What Is Authority? In H. Arendt *Between Past and Future*. London: Penguin: 91–142

BIS (2014) *Improving the Student Learning Experience: a national assessment*. BIS Research Paper 169. Available at: https://www.gov.uk/government/uploads/system/uploads/attachment_data/file/311288/bis-14-700-improving-the-student-learning-experience.pdf [accessed 17 September 2014]

Brown, R. (2011) *Higher Education and the Market*. London: Routledge

Darby, M. and Karni, E. (1973) Free competition and the optimal amount of fraud. *Journal of Law and Economics* 16 (1): 67–88

Dulleck, U., Kerschbamer, R. and Sutter M. (2011) The economics of credence goods: an experiment on the role of liability, verifiability, reputation, and competition. *American Economic Review* 101 (2): 526–555

Hawley, K. (2014) Trust, distrust and commitment. *Nous* 48 (1): 1–20

Kodelja, Z. (2013) Authority, the autonomy of the university, and neo-liberal politics. *Educational Theory* 63 (3): 317–330

Nacol, E.C. (2011) The risks of political authority: trust, knowledge and political agency in Locke's *Second Treatise*. *Political Studies* 59: 580–595

O'Neill, O. (2002) *A Question of Trust*. Cambridge: Cambridge University Press

Peters, R. S. and Winch, P. (1967) Authority. In A. Quinton (ed.) *Political Philosophy*. Oxford: Oxford University Press: 83–111

Smith, W.D. (2010) *Public Universities and the Public Sphere*. New York: Palgrave Macmillan

Weber, M. (1991) Bureaucracy. In H. H. Gerth and C. Wright Mills (eds) *From Max Weber: Essays in Sociology*. London: Routledge

Chapter 9

The 'unravelling' of English higher education

Patrick Ainley

Introduction

This chapter reflects on the lack of resistance to the introduction of market regimes to English higher education. Roger Brown, as well as being an eminent and respected scholar, has also been actively committed at all stages of his career as administrator and academic to progressive social democratic politics, especially of education. He has persistently warned about, analysed, criticised and organised against such an advance of market ideology and mechanisms in universities. Indeed, one of his most recent papers (Brown, 2013) comprehensively indicts the new post-2010 regime for its failure 'to assure financial stability, raise quality and enhance social mobility'. However, despite Brown's and others' best efforts, there has been remarkably little resistance and perhaps this needs explaining in order to understand the current situation in England. This explanation reaches beyond the higher education system itself to acknowledge changes in the social, political and economic contexts in which higher education is embrocated that may partly account for the lack of coherent and sustained reaction from higher education staff and students. In conclusion, this chapter also points towards more adequate responses in the future.

The 'unravelling' of English higher education

'At the heart of the problem,' writes Gary Rolfe (2013: 71), 'is the unravelling (quite literally the dis-integration) of the university'. Perhaps, it was the rapidity of the realisation that – rather than 'unravelling' – we (staff and students) had been 'stitched up' that accounts for the lack of any immediate reaction. Particularly as that realisation followed a millennial zenith of hubris and self-delusion amongst a generation of academics, by then in positions of influence if not power, whose own experiences as the first in their families to enter higher education led them to feel that higher education could transform society in the way they often felt their own lives had once been transformed. Simultaneously, new communications technology seemed to open new worlds of information if not knowledge to universal access and limitless possibility. UK New Labour Prime Minister, Tony Blair's policy of widening participation to high education was also very popular – with parents at least, especially those who had not themselves attended higher education. It was presented in the same way that the former Prime Minister Thatcher had previously encouraged and subsidised opportunities for everyone to buy their own home as symbolising access to 'a better life tantalizingly out of reach', as Selina Todd (2014: 316) puts it in a chapter of her popular history on Old Labour's previous reform of secondary education. But part of the unravelled situation in which the universities suddenly found themselves at the turn of the twenty-first century was that this apparent professionalising of the proletariat actually disguised a proletarianisation of the professions – academics notable amongst them – now increasingly reduced towards the conditions of waged labour.

The new market-state (Bobbitt, 2002) that has replaced the post-war welfare state imposes 'disorganised dissent' (Vickerstaff and Ainley, 1994) through its operating principle of 'centralised decentralisation' in which responsibility if not power is contracted out to individual agents and institutions to meet targets (Ainley, 2000). As mere 'deliverers of services', academics have no explanation for their situation beyond what Terry Eagleton called 'a vague opposition to the present political set-up, linked to an intense pessimism about the hope of any alternative' (Eagleton, 1991: 165). Consequently, the two main campaigning groups, the Council for the Defence of British Universities and the Campaign for a Public University, appear to have failed so far to gain much purchase amongst the mass of academic staff.

The main lecturers' and academic staff's union, the University and College Union (UCU) in the UK is misguidedly campaigning to save further and higher education for 'the knowledge economy'. Along with traditional disciplinary subject associations, it sometimes fights effective rear-guard actions against some particularly flagrant management abuse, e.g. to cut pensions at older universities, to move still more staff onto zero-hours contracts or move towards privatisation of services. But there is no overall strategy for an effective defence of further education and higher education. In principle, the UCU is united with the National Union of Students in demanding reductions in university fees; but it is uncertain how (or whether) this would be effected. Since academics are now directly dependent on their universities' income, in the new funding regime, if fees were reduced to £6,000 as the UK opposition Labour Party is proposing – the money would have to be made up from elsewhere to maintain things as they are, and it is not clear where that would be. If the Conservatives are returned to government they may lift the current £9,000 limit on fees. As a result, 'top' universities will charge more, leaving less strong universities in an impossible position, thus fragmenting the remnants of what was until recently a more or less coherent system of further and higher education provision in the UK.

Lost Generation?

The *Fight Back* (Hancox, 2011) in the student *Springtime* (Solomon and Palmieri, 2011), when large student demonstrations were met by an aggressive police response, reacted briefly if spectacularly 'from the perspective', as Matthew Cheeseman (2011) wrote, 'of a left that does not believe in formal organization [but] . . . imagines itself as modern-day Levellers incarnated by the horizontal, connective powers of the internet'. In an immediate reaction to the urban riots that followed the student demonstrations (Ainley and Allen, 2011) Martin Allen and I pointed out that even though this was the second confrontation of youth with police, following the winter 2010/ spring 2011 student protests, the student protestors represented a very different constituency:

> The student protestors can be defined as middle- or 'aspirational' working-class. They've played by the rules and worked hard at school but quickly became politicised in response to the way university is being put beyond their reach and that of their younger brothers and sisters. Despite government and opposition promises, they realise their generation will be the first to be worse off than their parents. Even if many will eventually find work, in many cases it will not be anywhere near commensurate with their hard earned qualifications.
>
> [. . .]
>
> On the other hand, the urban rioters [. . .] have become marginal to society [. . .] There have been opportunities for these two groups to come together – FE students joined the HE student protests against fees and to demand the restoration of Educational Maintenance Allowances – but it's difficult to imagine them ever being united for long.
>
> (Ainley and Allen, 2011)

Three years later, UK Skills Minister in the Department of Business Innovation and Skills, Matthew Hancock (2014), declared that, in order to 'rebalance' school-leaver destinations in the UK, with the age of participation (in school, college or training) rising to 18 in 2015, 'university or apprenticeship will be the new norm' for all 18+ year-olds. This possibility was also raised by the Labour leader Ed Miliband's promise to the 23 September 2014 Labour Party Conference to 'ensure as many school leavers go on apprenticeships as go to university' (quoted in Allen, 2014a). Since about 40 per cent of 18–21 year-olds are students (60 per cent of them female) but only c.8 per cent apprentices (again the majority of them female), this clearly is not going to happen (Allen, 2014b: 7). Nevertheless, higher education students have acclimatised themselves to paying high fees mainly because of the lack of any other alternative to access the secure and semi-professional employment they still aspire to and to avoid the subsidised job-placement that most apprenticeships represent.

Raising fees across the sector did not contribute to rebalancing Hancock's new norm by reducing student numbers, as originally intended (see Allen and Ainley, 2013). Nor did it hone student choice to increase interest and motivation, as arguably, it has dulled it to the extent that study is regarded by many students as merely another imposition to be gone through with a routine compunction. It has shifted student choice towards courses that appear to hold more secure employment outcomes, but these are often illusory. It has also added an estimated 9 per cent to the deficit that the UK government's austerity policies were supposed to reduce. In this sense, the UK government has lost what McGettigan (2013) called *The Great University Gamble* since it has admitted it does not expect to recover more than a third of what will add-up to £330 billion unpaid loans by 2046 when outstanding balances begin to be written-off. This voucherised system in which students carry the funding that institutions compete to attract has failed to create the market that both New Labour and Coalition governments intended in higher education as all institutions charge near the maximum, regardless of the social hierarchy inherent in UK higher education institutions.

Yet, under these funding arrangements, science and technology are in danger of being drawn, at one end, into academic-industrial-medical complexes, through their increasingly close relations with large pharmaceutical corporations; this, at the same time as, at the other end, various links with schools, further education community colleges and training schemes have been set up by universities to widen participation to more routine undergraduate science courses. While Bourdieu and Passeron (1979) noted 'enrolment in Science faculties seems to be less related to social origin' (Bourdieu and Passeron, 1979: 8) than in other university departments, they added that 'the teaching of culture (even scientific culture), implicitly presupposes a body of knowledge, skills, and, above all, modes of expression which constitute the heritage of the cultivated classes' (Bourdieu and Passeron, 1979: 21).

Women in higher education

To these class dynamics there is, in addition, an important gender dimension in the choices made by young women who are not evenly spread across subjects. They have, however, entered territories previously seen as male bastions and have for some time represented some 70 per cent of the student population in medicine and law; and they are also generally better qualified to apply to university than their brothers (Leathwood and Read, 2009: 97). They are also possibly more motivated to live away from their parental home for the 3 or 4 years before they have – predictably for the majority – to return there. This is one of the reasons why the anticipated uptake of students studying close to home has not so far materialised to improve recruitment at local universities. There are also fewer other employment opportunities open to young women locally than to young men (Brinkley *et al.,* 2013). For these and probably other reasons, young women are applying to and graduating from higher education in larger numbers than ever before, but – often after numerous internships (the graduate equivalent of an apprenticeship) – do not often secure full-time employment outside of the service, retail and office jobs that are stereotypically female occupations (Young Women's Trust, 2014).

Women are therefore in the vanguard of the *Lost Generation* (Ainley and Allen, 2010) or the precariat that Standing (2011) sees growing in parallel with the declining middle and working classes. Instead of Standing's scheme, Ainley and Allen (2010) advance that the growth of services and use of new technology have contributed to automate, de-skill, downsize and outsource – in brief, unravel – formerly professional employment. There is no longer any floor for the traditionally non-manual middle-class to stand on, above a traditionally manually working working-class, large parts of which have been reduced to a reserve army of labour. Those in the middle are therefore running up a down escalator of inflating qualifications, desperate not to fall into the so-called underclass beneath. This adds to the hysteria surrounding a fetishised education, which, like Freud's 'return of the repressed', manifests real but unacknowledged conflicts as irrational symptoms. Along with housing, policing and other areas of policy, education has played a large part in this reconstitution of social class in England (Ainley, 2013). In these circumstances is it possible to 'reboot Robbins' in the way that Labour's Shadow Minister for Universities, Science and Skills, Liam Byrne (2014) has proposed?

Rebooting Robbins in *the second machine age*

The Second Machine Age by Erik Brynjolfsson and Andrew McAfee (2014) describes how digitising technology is automating mental labour just as the first industrial revolution de-skilled manual labour. Like Dickens' Mr. Panks, the authors condemn what they see as the negative pessimism of their more traditional academic colleagues, who perpetually worry about being trapped in Foucault's version of Weber's iron cage.

This is at least refreshing but is anything to be made of it in relation to higher education? Liam Byrne, Labour Shadow Higher Education spokesperson, clearly thinks so. Just like former Prime Ministers Blair and Brown, Byrne tells us everyone can win the global *Race to the Top* (Byrne, 2014: 28). Indeed, there is only one way to do so: 'To build a bigger knowledge economy with more high skill jobs and fewer low skill, low wage jobs' (Byrne, 2014: 29). This requires 'a different sort of higher education system' that should promote scientific growth in 'globally excellent shared science platforms – aka "universities"|' (Byrne, 2014: 35). But, unless related to economic reform to end austerity and the continued slide into low-wage, low-skill employment, these proposals risk repeating the failures to rebuild a vocational route to replace the industrial apprenticeships lost in the 1970s, but this time at a tertiary level of learning. Especially as Byrne's colleague, Shadow Education Minister, Tristram Hunt, has proposed a technical baccalaureate for the half of school students who don't make it onto the academic route, rebranding further education colleges as 'Institutes of Technical Education' with new part-time, 2-year 'technical degrees'. This bipartism could bring back secondary technical schools and polytechnics.

However, Byrne's proposals at least allow some possibility of higher education recovering itself in connection with further education by replacing market-driven expansion with regional partnerships to end the 'ferocious' competition, as he describes it (Byrne, 2014: 69), between universities, colleges and private providers encouraged by the UK government. This is because Byrne has connected them to the need for devolution of the new market-state revealed by the Scottish referendum. Apart from Scotland and Wales though, which are national regions, there are no natural regions in England like those in mainland Europe, and they will not be constituted by 'US-style directly-elected mayors with cabinets', which Peter Latham (2011) describes as 'the optimal internal management arrangement for privatised local government services' (Latham, 2011: 2). This however increases unravelling and ends what semblance there ever was to a coherent system of further education and higher education in the UK. I5 leads to a state of affairs where, as Byrne says, 'the work-based degree route has simply collapsed' (Byrne, 2014: 72). Drawing upon Spours and Hodgson's 2012 'unified and eco-system vision', as well as on MacFarlane's recommendations for tertiary colleges that could unite sixth forms and FE (see Simmons, 2013), Byrne affirms that 'an integrated system is possible' (Byrne, 2014: 74). Such a system could make real contributions in education, training and research alongside local and regional government-led economic regeneration. It would require an administrator of Roger Brown's determination and genius to make it happen though.

Conclusion

The problem remains that, while schools, colleges and universities claim to make their graduates employable, education cannot guarantee employment. So, fundamentally the perception of the problem needs to change: from being one where young people are seen as having to be prepared for employability by earlier and earlier specialisation for vocations that may not exist. Instead, the starting point should be a common general but not academic schooling to 18, giving entitlement to progression for citizens as:

> Fully developed individuals, fit for a variety of labours, ready to face any change of production and to whom the different social functions they perform, are but so many modes of giving free scope to their own natural and acquired powers.
>
> (Marx, 1971: 494)

This implies confronting the possibilities of flexibility but avoiding the current situation in which there are more people in the workforce, but many are paid little for unregulated employment. Of course, this would require an alternative economic framework but not necessarily 'the right to work' with which most of the traditional trades union 'labour movement' continues to operate in a post-war collectivised model of the labour market. Instead, a general education to high school graduation linked to the assumption of citizenship at 18 means learning about work but not just learning to work.

An expectation of, and an entitlement to, local / regional adult further and higher continuing education should be integral to school leaving, just as it is (or was) for US high school graduates. There, as in mainland European countries and Scotland, many home students are likely to be living at home. Such an entitlement should be the aim, even if not everyone wants to progress to higher education immediately. It should give the adult students who have been lost to higher education chances of again participating. For universities, paradoxically, such an approach would mean re-finding the vocational nature of the higher education preserved by the most prestigious subjects at the most elite institutions, as in the original vocations of law and medicine. Importantly, this includes an academic vocation dedicated to learning critically from the past with research and scholarship affording change in the future. Undergraduates can contribute to that continuing cultural conversation, giving them a sense that many have lost of what higher education is supposed to be about.

Bibliography

Ainley, P. (2000) *What Has happened to the Welfare State? The Example of Education.* Socialist History Working Paper 5. London: London Socialist Historians' Group

Ainley, P. (2013) Education and the Reconstitution of Social Class in England. In R. Simmons and R. Thompson (eds) *Research in Post-Compulsory Education* 18 (1–2): 46–60

Ainley, P. and Allen, M. (2011) *Most young people did not riot but can the lost generations find their way?* Available at: http://radicaled.wordpress.com/2011/08/14

Ainley, P. and Allen, M. (2010) *Lost Generation? New Strategies for Youth and Education.* London: Continuum

Allen, M. (2014a) *Postscript to Another Great Training Robbery.* London: Radicaled

Allen, M. (2014b) *Another Great Training Robbery or a Real Alternative for Young People? Apprenticeships at the Start of the 21st Century.* London: Radicaled

Allen, M. and Ainley, P. (2013) *The Great Reversal, Young People, Education and Employment in a Moribund Economy.* London: Radicaled

Bobbitt, P. (2002) *The Shield of Achilles: War, Peace and the Course of History.* London: Allen Lane

Bourdieu, P. and Passeron, J-C. (1979) *The Inheritors: French Students and their Relation to Culture* (trans R. Nice). Chicago: University of Chicago Press

Brinkley, I., Jones, K. and Lee, N. (2013) *The Gender Jobs Split, How Young Men and Women Experience the Labour Market.* London: TUC Touchstone Publication

Brown, R. (2013) *England's New Market Based System of Student Education: An Initial Report.* Berkeley: University of California Center for Studies in Higher Education Research and Occasional Paper Series: CSHE 7 (13)

Brynjolfsson, E. and McAfee, A. (2014) *The Second Machine Age: Work, Progress, and Prosperity in a Time of Brilliant Technologies.* New York: Norton

Byrne, L. (2014) *Robbins Rebooted: How We Earn Our Way in the Second Machine Age.* London: The Social Market Foundation

Cheeseman, M. (2011) Book review of Solomon and Palmieri 'Springtime: The New Student Rebellions' and Hancox 'Fight Back'. *Studies in Higher Education* 36 (6): 737–740

Eagleton, T. (1991) *Ideology: An Introduction*. London: Verso

Hancock, M. (2014) *Speech on world class apprenticeships*. London: Department of Business Industry and Skills press release 08/12/2014

Hancox, D. (ed.) (2011) *Fight Back! A Reader On The Winter Of Protest*. London: OpenDemocracy

Latham, P. (2011) *The State and Local Government: Towards a New Basis for 'Local Democracy' and the Defeat of Big Business Control*. Croydon: Manifesto Press

Leathwood, C. and Read, B. (2009) *Gender and the Changing Face of Higher Education, a Feminized Future?* Maidenhead: Open University Press and the Society for Research into Higher Education

Marx, K. (1971) *Capital: A Critical Analysis of Capitalist Production* (trans. S. Moore and E. Aveling, ed. F. Engels). London: Allen and Unwin

McGettigan, A. (2013) *The Great University Gamble: Money, Markets and the Future of Higher Education*. London: Pluto

Rolfe, G. (2013) *The University on Dissent: Scholarship in the Corporate University*. London: Routledge with the Society for Research into Higher Education

Simmons, R. (2013) 'Sorry to have kept you waiting so long, Mr. Mcfarlane': Further Education after the Coalition. In M. Allen and P. Ainley (eds) *Education Beyond the Coalition, Reclaiming the Agenda*. London: Radicaled: 82–105

Solomon, C. and Palmieri, T. (eds) (2011) *Springtime: The New Student Rebellions*. London: Verso

Spours, K. and Hodgson, A. (2012) *Towards a Universal Upper Secondary Education System in England: A Unified and Ecosystem Vision*. London: Institute of Education

Standing, G. (2011) *The Precariat: The New Dangerous Class*. London: Bloomsbury

Todd, S. (2014) *The People: The Rise and Fall of the Working Class 1910–2010*. London: Murray

Vickerstaff, S. and Ainley, P. (1994) Centralised decentralisation: education and training in the contract state. *Management Research News* 17 (7, 8 and 9): 22–24

Young Women's Trust (2014) *Totally Wasted? The Crisis of Young Women's Worklessness*. London: YWT

Part III

Regulating a marketised sector

Chapter 10

Regulating risk in the higher education state

Implications for policy and research

Roger King

Introduction

Roger Brown has written trenchantly on marketisation and regulation in higher education and this chapter focuses and elaborates on these themes. Particularly, it examines the import of private sector models of governance and external quality assurance arrangements for universities and colleges, especially the utilisation of risk tools and techniques. As with Roger Brown's work, it offers a critique of risk-based regulation as a model for external quality assurance. Rather, concepts of uncertainty and resilience are suggested as offering more fruitful and effective ways forward, particularly if quality assurance is to be strongly buttressed by quality enhancement and the promotion of collective staff buy-in for improvement at the local level.

Regulation and non-state models

In recent years in the UK (and elsewhere), state regulation gradually has co-opted more non-state bodies into its operating mechanisms. As Roger Brown has noted regularly, more broadly within the state since the 1990s within many countries, there has been a move from public ownership and top-down control from the centre, to more private organisations operating in competitive markets. This has not resulted so much in less regulation but in state regulation becoming more fragmentary. Rather than being exercised almost solely from within government departments, regulation in a sector these days may include among its institutional forms more specialist state agencies, independent regulatory bodies and governmentally licensed (or 'enforced') self-regulation.

Although in part, such developments reflect increasing scholarly and policy critiques of the efficiency and effectiveness of 'command-and-control' state models, outsourcing, decentralisation and 'contracting out' to the private sector also have become mechanisms with wider governance implications. Reintegration of apparently more inchoate regulatory processes, and inclusion of both state and non-state actors, takes place in networks of various kinds where boundaries and accountabilities are less clear-cut than before.

In the UK higher education sector, at least, regulatory 'contracting out' to the private sector has been less problematic than it would be in some other sectors, not least as there is a strong and traditional emphasis in universities as being 'private' self-governing communities themselves. But the incorporation of such notions as academic freedom into more formalised regulatory cultures, nonetheless has shaped notions of individual and institutional autonomy so that they assume rather different and more organisational contemporary forms than traditionally. Institutions have become more corporatised and managerialist and, as a consequence, academic communities now are much more controlled by university executives. On the surface, at least, higher education institutions in England, at least, look more like private sector organisations than before and institutional rather than individual autonomy is now more the norm.

This adoption of private sector models by the state is exemplified by its use of traditional risk management frameworks – whereby the frequency and intensity of quality audits become dependent on an assessment of risk level attached to their activities – for regulating and quality assuring universities and colleges. Risk tools and approaches have formed regulatory regimes across a range of sectors, and, in recent years, governments in the UK and Australia particularly have seen this as appropriate for higher education, too. Risk-based regulation, however, involves clear tensions, not least in higher education: for example, between a deregulatory urge by governments to let 'trusted' institutions take more responsibility for their actions and yet wanting to ensure that taxpayers and students receive affirmation that the courses taken reach expected standards. Such tensions spill over into the practices and routines of universities and colleges and constitute new sources of risk for them, not least for their reputations.

The risk university

Many businesses in the contemporary world operate with complex external environments and face numerous regulatory and risk challenges. Universities – as contemporary businesses – are little different. They, too, are becoming risk organisations. The 'risk university' appears more pressured by external risks than ever – legal, funding, ethical, security and social media and particularly by extending processes of external evaluation, such as rankings, quality assurance and professional accreditation. But internally, too, risks abound – from colleagues, professional groups, trade unions, managers and so on.

Many of these processes have the potential to have a huge impact on a university's reputation if anything goes wrong. There are various, and often competing, interests looking to claim organisational attention and resources. As higher education sectors, such as that in England, become more diverse and heterogeneous, it is not clear to what extent regulators and quality assurers are able to rely on the capacity of different institutions to take self-responsibility for internal standards and control.

Consequently, these growing external constraints (and potential risks) on universities and colleges – which nonetheless positively are aimed at improving university accountability, not least in the eyes of the public – have worried some governments. In UK governments, for example, there is concern that the emerging risk university potentially is the 'risk averse university'. Ministers fear a danger that institutions will become increasing reluctant to take any risks at all, even those undertaken carefully with managed entrepreneurialism in mind. Innovation and global competitiveness could suffer.

To counteract these negative consequences, the UK government has introduced the higher education sector in England to the notion and practices of risk-based external quality assurance. Roger Brown has criticised such an approach as containing 'fundamental problems' and predicts that 'the risk-based approach will continue until, and only until, the first "low-risk" provider is found to have major quality problems' (Brown, 2013, unpaginated). Does risk-based regulation have any redeeming features, however, or should it be discarded?

Risk-based regulation

The aim of risk-based regulation is that regulation should be proportionate to the problem (or perceived risks) in hand and, if at all possible, should reduce associated bureaucratic costs and stilted processes ('red tape') for both regulator and the regulated. It does so by focusing regulatory attention and resources predominantly on those 'riskier' parts of the sector that the agency's methodologies have helped to identify. 'High risk' entities, where the probability of a significant adverse event occurring is regarded as relatively high, are usually interpreted as being either relatively new or relatively unknown (to the regulatory system). But, in Australia, for example, a highly-formalised, strongly data-driven methodology has been employed by the Tertiary Education Quality and Standards Authority (TEQSA) to fully scope the system for risk and to classify institutions as ranging from high to low risk (TEQSA, 2015).

The contrast is with more traditional and standardised approaches to external quality assurance, where everyone is monitored broadly in the same manner, usually through periodic institutional visits by regulators. Such an approach – 'one size fits all' – is considered no longer appropriate for more diverse higher education sectors.

A key objective of risk-based regulation is deregulatory – to lift the bureaucratic burden on the vast majority of providers who have experienced successful reviews in the past. Decision-making should also be superior, as a more focused, evidential and transparent approach should enable a more targeted and open use of its resources. Moreover, the risk appetites of both regulator and regulated should become more visible and allow more defensible positions by the regulator to be adopted by emphasising that not all risks or their crystallisation can be avoided.

Some argue, too, that risk-based external quality assurance is not that new anyway. Anthony McClaran, Chief Executive of the UK Quality Assurance Agency, has suggested that the risk approach is much more evolutionary than critics might argue, with 'some clear antecedents' (McClaran, 2013, unpaginated). He points out that a strong deregulatory momentum had already been achieved in quality assurance for higher education in England over recent years, including the removal of subject review in 2001, and discipline trails in 2005, to the gradually lengthening of the cycle of review since then. Moreover, risk has been used as the basis for determining the basis of review in Wales since 2009–10.

These comments indicate a strong view among many regulators that they nearly all practice some form of risk-based approach, even if they have not adopted the risk-based model formally. Regulators, it is suggested, do not have the time or resources to monitor everyone to the same level or with similar intensity – they have to prioritise. Yet there are key differences between an informal practice and a formalised approach. The latter can lead to more centralised decision-making within the regulator (as all the risk dimensions and the regulatory impact are scoped and deliberated), and can lead to increasing demands for data from an already data-burdened sector (which has been led to believe, nonetheless, that such frustrations would be eased by risk-based frameworks).

Risk-based frameworks necessitate quality agencies and similar risk-based regulators to begin by identifying the risks that they are seeking to manage, not the rules that they have to enforce. We now examine some of the drawbacks to the approach.

Risk and uncertainty

Risk may not be the approach that best suits the indeterminacy of most social processes. Risk implies a level of knowledge about the future based on belief in calculability and predictability. Yet uncertainty – a relative lack of predictive knowledge – more accurately characterises most institutional futures in higher education and undermines strong views as to where risks may be emerging. Regulators, such as quality agencies, can never be sure where the next 'accident' will occur, even if they possess ever more purportedly rationalist techniques and masses of data.

There is an ontological uncertainty characterising such social processes that is reflected in epistemological uncertainty, too. It arises from the extreme difficulty of obtaining adequate knowledge to calculate and predict future adverse events (risks) (Naime and Audrey, 2013; de Vries *et al.*, 2011). Research has shown that even insurers and actuaries – committed to rational calculability and predictability for their business models – resort to hunches and guesses for a considerable part of their activity in seeking to estimate levels of risk (Ericson *et al.*, 2003). Higher education and social systems are not tight technical systems but beset by messiness and uncertainty about the future. Where risk is to be found is very difficult to measure.

To overcome some of these difficulties with risk-based external quality assurance, the QAA in England (understandably) has sought proxies to guide its approach in determining the intensity and regularity of its visits to institutions based around perceived risk. A key signifier is track record or the successful accomplishment by the organisation of at least two reviews by the Agency. But 'track records', or looking back, may not be the best guide to where risk lies in the future.

Much risk arises from human or personnel factors as from technical issues and as a result is not easily predicted. Moreover, in looking forward, we should not necessarily assume that large and well-established universities are less likely to suffer risk misfortune that newer, smaller entities. Large organisations do pose risk management and regulatory problems, as research in other sectors demonstrates. Di Mento (1986: 156) shows that size often correlates with levels of differentiation in a firm: the greater the differentiation, the greater the possibility of non-compliance. Consequently, the larger, more complicated and more transnational an organisation (like many leading research universities today), the greater its potential to generate risks internally and externally, perhaps on a global scale.

The notion of risk with its emphasis on predictability and calculability needs to be at least alleviated by an approach that has allowances for uncertainty. Rather than data collection, the focus should be regular contact and dialogue (often informal) between agency and institutions, and on preparing for 'accidents', not by trying to predict the future as such, but by inculcating institutional resilience in order to bounce back and learn from errors and misfortune. The stronger and shorter the relational distance between the regulator and the regulated, the greater is the chance for organisational learning and compliance.

Reputational risk

A focus on uncertainty and resilience appears particularly appropriate when institutions are concerned increasingly with reputational risk. In many ways, the risk university appears as driven by reputation and the potential threats to it as by any other form of risk. Or, at least, university leaders tend to sweep up the different dimensions of risk into a more encompassing notion of reputational risk, as all other risks have an added reputational risk potential. Yet, reputational risks are those where a university's internal risk control systems seem to have the least leverage. The ownership of reputations does not so much reside in the organisation but is the attribution of others.

Hutter notes that '[c]orporate reputations are social constructs based on a range of criteria such as legitimacy, credibility, trust, reliability and confidence' (Hutter, 2011: 140). We might observe, too, that reputations or 'brands' tend to attract to whole organisations rather than parts of it. As such, a university may feel particularly vulnerable to the actions of its local actors, although its continuing 'loosely-connected' aspects as an organisation may provide some protection for the overall brand if necessary. Yet, the more corporatised and tightly hierarchical an organisation becomes, the more chance of both an adverse event occurring locally and its contamination of the whole organisation.

Reputation risk in the risk university is so salient because, once diminished or lost, high standing can take a long time to recover, if at all. Moreover, organisational reputation can be leveraged over a range of products. For example, a strong research-based university may be able to recruit well in the undergraduate market based purely on its research reputation (or on those rankings determined by research) even though many such students never see the research stars, and the university may have relatively poor teaching and learning processes.

Uncertainty-based regulation

Deliberation, intuition and resilience

Effective quality assurance rests on the ability by regulators to construct periodic and often informal interactions between specified agency personnel with groups of institutions for which they have designated responsibility. Such agency personnel need the skills of trained intermediaries and counsellors, including seeking to manage the tensions between quality control and empowerment. They should be expected to offer as much in the way of education and guidance, mainly drawn from best practice cases in the sector, as on detecting possible risk factors. The processes they use should be deliberative and conversational (King, 2014).

The professional judgements of quality assurers should be based as much on experience and knowledge, built-up over years, that allow risk intuition, rules of thumb and intuition as on systems and data. As the psychologist Gerd Gigerenzer (2014: 31) has argued:

> The mind can discover simple solutions to complex problems. It is called a heuristic (rule of thumb) because it focuses on the one or few pieces of information that are important and ignores the rest.
>
> (Gigerenzer, 2014: 31)

That is, ignoring information (that is, not wading through masses of collected data from institutions) can lead to better quality assurance decisions. Gigerenzer's point is that most parts of our brain are unconscious, and we would be lost without the vast experience stored there. Calculated intelligence may work for known risks, but in the face of uncertainty, intuition and tacit judgement is essential.

Relatedly, as most risks cannot be predicted, they must be managed proactively when they crystallise. The appropriate risk management and regulatory approach should be based on instilling organisational resilience and building up the capacity of systems to respond quickly and effectively when an accident occurs. However, rather than suggesting that resilience refers to an organisation's ability to return to normal functioning without too much delay following an adverse event of some kind that has produced a disturbance, it is better if adversity is used more positively. That is, rather than seeing resilience as the key to restoring an unproblematic systemic equilibrium, it should be regarded as providing an opportunity for organisational learning. Resilience should characterise the ability by universities and colleges, for example, to welcome change through adaptation and devising new ways of ensuring that quality is continuously improved (Prior and Hagmann, 2014).

Standards and quality

It is unlikely that external quality assurance without an increased focus on standards will meet the expectations of many stakeholders in higher education, not least government, taxpayers, employers and students. Dill (2011) has remarked on the difference between standards and quality. Academic standards may be seen as the knowledge, skills and attitudes achieved by graduates as a result of their academic programme. Quality may be defined as the system of processes, rules and norms that maximises, in as effective and equitable manner as possible, the academic standards achieved by graduates.

Yet, as Roger Brown (2013) has observed, it is institutions that are responsible for their academic standards, and in England at least, the Quality Assurance Agency (QAA) focuses on quality in its role as 'expert adviser' to the Higher Education Funding Council for England (HEFCE). That is, the Further and Higher Education Act (1992) placed a duty on the funding councils to assess the quality of education in the institutions they funded. This duty did not extend to reviewing standards (and this remains the situation currently, although the Secretary of State has the power to transfer such a function to the funding councils but has chosen not to exercise it). Under contract (and contractual guidance), therefore, the QAA assesses quality in institutions on behalf of HEFCE. HEFCE has the power to seek alternative organisations and ways of delivering its quality assessment duty and has announced that it will seek the opportunity that the conclusion of its present contract with the QAA offers to review current arrangements.

Collective action

David D. Dill, in Chapter 19 in this volume, but also in Dill (2011), provides an approach to external quality assurance that fits better the processes of deliberation and resilience than that of highly-formalised risk-based regulation. The key for Dill is to recognise that effective quality processes, and thus enhanced academic standards, are best achieved at a local departmental level. It is collective staff – and student – actions and deliberations, aided by comparative evaluative data drawn from student surveys and their competitive reputational consequences for institutions (not least at departmental level) that produces real change and commitment behind it.

The role of external quality assurers is to monitor how universities and colleges go about this task. Dill notes that there is little evidence that any other factors than the core academic processes of curriculum design, teaching, and student assessment have as much influence on academic standards.

Such an approach may help to remedy a key problem of the conventional external quality assurance of universities and colleges, especially where this involves an audit or 'meta-assurance' of an institution's own processes, procedures and self-regulatory capacities – and whose own internal data and control systems get turned inside-out for the purposes of the regulator. The problem is the tendency to ritualism and ceremonialism in the eyes of those being regulated – who pull out all the stops in preparing for institutional review, breathe a sigh of relief when it is over, but learn not very much and change even less as a consequence.

That is, institutional review visits can become a periodic event that may meet the surface goals of the regulator but which achieves very little in assuring standards or even generating much in the way of quality enhancement. A focus on risk frameworks only reinforces such largely symbolic gesturing and does not achieve lasting commitment at the local level.

Ceremonialism

A difficulty with conventional external quality assurance of universities and colleges, therefore, is the tendency to ritualism and ceremonialism in the eyes of those being regulated. The institutional review visit can become a periodic event that may meet the ritualistic goals of both sides but may involve little in the way of learning, development and commitment to raising standards. Risk-based quality assurance runs the danger of reinforcing such largely symbolic gesturing unless it is accompanied by regular dialogue and deliberation between the agency and institution.

A critical aspect for Dill (2011) is to recognise that effective quality processes, and thus enhanced academic standards, are best achieved at local departmental level. It is collective staff – and student – actions and deliberations that produces real change and commitment behind it. The role of the external quality assurer is to monitor how universities and colleges go about this task.

In Chapter 19, Dill extends his thinking to consider issues of governance and its relevance to quality and standards. He suggests that reliance on either state regulation or market forces alone is not the way forward. Rather, citing Ostrom (1990), a third way of collective self-organisation and self-governance can work a lot better. The issue is how best can quality agencies encourage and monitor institutions to develop the collective action of staff at departmental level to become focused on quality enhancement and standards.

Conclusion

Uncertainty-based regulation emphasises quality enhancement and empowerment as much as quality control and assurance in the role to be played by external regulatory agencies. A focus on data gathering and predicting the future is replaced more by underlining the importance of resilience and deliberation. Local academic action is a key instrument in improving pedagogy, utilising the benefits of external surveys, ratings and benchmarks, not least as made available through regular and informal action between agencies and institutions. Better information and ideas from more extensive higher education research on standards and quality should assist such processes. In this way, external quality assurance is not simply about regulation but is multifunctional and has quality improvement as a major objective.

Eschewing an approach that relies on establishing a synoptic legibility at the centre (an all-seeing regulator), and which produces targets, plans, rewards and sanctions imposed from on high, is a key part of what uncertainty-based quality assurance seeks to avoid. This is not to downgrade completely the requirement for external quality assurance. The public has come to expect protection from poor performance, and governments are concerned that accountability for tax-payers' monies is generated by the regular quality monitoring of institutions. For new providers it would be realistic to expect a strong focus on quality control in the early years, with the focus becoming more one of enhancement with maturity and experience.

It is clear, however, that for quality assurance agencies to fulfill their central tasks of quality assessment and enhancement, they must avoid being drawn into taking on a set of responsibilities that divert them from their core focus and methodologies. In England, for example, the QAA has taken on responsibilities from the Home Office (equivalent to an Interior Ministry in many countries) to determine eligibility by institutions for recruiting non-EU students and related visa and immigration processes. This is discussed by Geoffrey Alderman in Chapter 11 of this book. It may be better if a more inspectorial methodology, employed by another agency, is used for such purposes. The (well-established and culturally understood) peer-review systems established for quality assessment is best reserved for the quality functions for which the QAA was originally established.

Consequently, it also becomes necessary to redevelop and encourage trust in higher education professionals, and to monitor it, if quality enhancement on a sustained and resilient basis is to occur. Obsessively monitoring the sector for risk is a false turning that we need to avoid, a point that Roger Brown has long emphasised.

Bibliography

Brown, R. (2013) Risk-Based Quality Assurance: The Risks. In A. McClaren (ed.) *New Arrangements for Quality Assurance in Higher Education*. Oxford: Higher Education Policy Institute (unpaginated)

De Vries, G., Verhoeven, I., and Boeckhout, M. (2011) Taming uncertainty. *Journal of Risk Research* 14 (4): 485–500

Dill, D. (2011) Governing Quality. In R. King, S. Marginson and R. Naidoo (eds) *Handbook on Globalization and Higher Education*. Cheltenham: Edward Elgar: 438–453

Di Mento, J.F. (1986) *Environmental Law and American Business: Dilemmas of Compliance.* New York: Plenum Press

Ericson, R., Doyle, A. and Barry, D. (2003) *Insurance as Governance.* Toronto: University of Toronto Press

Gigerenzer, G. (2014) *Risk Savvy: How to Make Good Decisions.* London: Allen Lane

Hutter, B. (2011) *Managing Food Safety and Hygiene,* Cheltenham: Edward Elgar

King, R. (2014) Regulating uncertainty: risk, resilience and improvement in higher education. *Journal of Leadership and Governance* 3: 77–88

McClaran, A. (2013) *New Arrangements for Quality Assurance in Higher Education.* London: Higher Education Policy Institute

Naime, A. and Andrey, J. (2013) Improving risk-based regulatory processes: identifying measures to pursue risk-informed regulation. *Journal of Risk Research* 17 (3): 281–298

Ostrom, E. (1990) *Governing the Commons: The Evolution of Institutions for Collective Action.* Cambridge, MA: Cambridge University Press

Prior, T. and Hagmann, J. (2014) Measuring resilience: methodological and political challenges of a trend security concept. *Journal of Risk Research* 17 (3): 281–298

Tertiary Education Quality and Standards Agency (TEQSA) (2015) Risk Assessment Framework. Available at: www.teqsa.gov.au

Chapter 11

How the Home Office became a regulator of higher education in England

Geoffrey Alderman

Introduction

Historically, the British Home Office – a government department roughly equivalent to an interior ministry – has played virtually no part in the regulation of higher education in the United Kingdom and has very little formal statutory authority for so doing. However, its powers in relation to immigration control have recently permitted it to undertake an unprecedented intervention in relation to such regulation. This chapter explains how this has come about, and what its implications might be. The story it tells highlights the impact that the marketisation of higher education – in this case through the mass entry of private providers – has made upon the regulation of the entire sector in England.

Background

In July 2013, the Higher Education Funding Council for England (HEFCE) published a guide to the regulatory framework in which higher education providers – both taxpayer-funded and privately funded – currently operate in England (HEFCE, 2013). Entitled *Operating Framework for Higher Education in England*, the document purported to explain:

> [H]ow higher education providers in England are held to account and regulated. It also shows how these arrangements are changing to meet the needs of students and society, and to provide value for money for taxpayers. It describes the organisations that handle different aspects of regulation and the framework for effective oversight of higher education.
>
> (HEFCE, 2013, paragraph 1)

The *Operating Framework* guide contained numerous errors and omissions. It failed to mention the role of the Independent Schools Inspectorate, which regulates some privately funded providers that offer both further and higher education programmes of study. It was silent on the role of 'Ofqual' – the Office of Qualifications and Examinations Regulation – which regulates non-university awarding bodies offering vocational qualifications at levels equivalent to programmes at Bachelor's, Master's and Doctoral levels. The *Framework* stated (paragraph 97) that non-taxpayer-funded higher education providers with degree-awarding powers 'must seek renewal every six years'; this statement is not strictly accurate, and does not apply, for example, to the University of Buckingham – a private institution that operates under regulations entirely similar to other English HEIs. It might also be worth noting that the guide speaks of the European Union – another error, since the law relating to international students also excludes those originating from Iceland, Norway and Liechtenstein, which are within the European Economic Area but outside the EU.

But the purpose of this chapter is neither to offer an analysis of this guide nor to expound upon these errors and omissions. It is, rather, to focus upon and explore one noteworthy feature of the guide, namely its admission that amongst the many bodies now involved in one facet or another of the regulation of higher education in England, is to be numbered the Home Office.

The role of the Home Office

We should note at the outset that between 2008 and 2010 the entire system of entry schemes for all manner of migrants into the UK was radically overhauled, and a regime of inspection was introduced for providers in the privately funded higher education sector. A points-based system was designed, supplemented by the grouping of would-be immigrants into tiers. International students were grouped into Tier 4. To obtain a Tier 4 visa, a student had (and has) to be sponsored by a receiving institution. As the *Operating Framework* explains, all higher education providers in England – indeed in the United Kingdom – are required to have a Tier 4 sponsor licence in order to recruit international students. Tier 4 refers specifically to students originating from outside the European Economic Area, who are in principle eligible for temporary admission to the UK. This licence is granted by the Home Office following inspection (in one form or another) by the Quality Assurance Agency for Higher Education (QAA), the organisation responsible for quality and threshold standards across the HE system in the UK.

Since taxpayer-funded providers must in any case undergo QAA inspection ('review') as a condition of the receipt of public funds, the Home Office had not historically insisted on further scrutiny. But in respect of privately funded providers, an exceptional inspection regime, entitled 'Review for Educational Oversight,' has been developed by the QAA specifically for Home Office purposes. Accordingly, the HEFCE *Framework* (Section 5) quite correctly lists the Home Office amongst the departments and agencies of government that are now empowered to 'impose regulatory requirements' on the higher education sector. As the *Framework* puts it:

> The Home Office's role in higher education pertains to those education providers which wish to recruit and enrol overseas students or staff. Education

providers must act as sponsors for migrant students or staff through the Home Office's points-based sponsorship system. As part of this, the UK Border Agency [now 'UK Visas and Immigration' – UKVI] set[s] regulatory requirements which education providers must meet and demonstrate compliance.

To enrol foreign students, education providers must hold Tier 4 sponsor status. Along with other requirements for this, education providers are subject to an educational oversight review, which is conducted by QAA on behalf of the Home Office.

(HEFCE, 2013:52)

Prior to 2008, the Home Office played no part in the regulation of higher education in England. Insofar as any government department or agency had any formal say in such regulation, this privilege was restricted to the Privy Council (in respect of the conferment of degree-awarding powers and university title), the Department for Education (in respect of the overarching administrative framework in which higher education operated in England and Wales) and HEFCE, which distributed under strict conditions public funds to higher education institutions entitled to receive them. That is not to say that the Home Office had no formal contact at all with higher education providers: as the department of state responsible for law and order, for example, and for occupational health and safety, it certainly had responsibilities and powers in relation to higher education providers – but none in relation to the manner in which they structured, delivered and monitored the higher education they offered.

In England, universities and other degree-granting bodies were (and remain) academically autonomous, responsible to themselves alone for the academic standards attaching to the awards they offered – either directly or through collaborative arrangements with partner institutions throughout the world. Under the provisions of the Further and Higher Education Act of 1992, HEFCE (Section 70) was charged with the responsibility of inspecting the quality of education in taxpayer-funded institutions of higher education, whilst the Higher Education Quality Council, wholly owned by the sector, undertook audits of the manner in which these institutions managed the quality of their particular learning environments. Five years later, these functions were – in broad terms – brought together under the aegis of a new and supposedly independent body, the QAA, which offered one inspection regime – latterly termed institutional review – that resulted in published reports, of which HEFCE and other government departments might or might not have taken cognisance.

The Home Office played no part in these arrangements and procedures. International students were granted visas to study in the UK based on what has to be admitted was a cursory and almost entirely paper-based evaluation of themselves and the institutions at which they had been admitted for study purposes. This regime had inevitably permitted many bogus institutions to exist and indeed thrive, at least for a time (Alderman, 2006).

Bringing private providers into the fold

As we have already noted, as a result of the 2008–2010 overhaul of the immigration regulatory framework it became necessary for Tier 4 students to be sponsored by a receiving institution. But no such institution in the private sector, and not in voluntary membership of the QAA, could so act unless it had been inspected and deemed of a satisfactory standard by one of five bodies specially designated by the UK Border Agency (UKBA), which was established in April 2008 as an executive agency of the Home Office; its work was reabsorbed within the Home Office in March 2013 under the name of UK Visas and Immigration (UKVI). The five designated bodies were the British Accreditation Council; the Accreditation Service for International Colleges; Accreditation UK; the Association of British Language Schools; and the Church of England Ministry Division.

There were no formal agreements with any of these five inspectoral bodies, nor did the Home Office presume to dictate to them how they were to go about their work. Institutions that wished to be designated for Tier 4 sponsorship purposes were expected to apply to the most appropriate of these bodies for the purposes of inspection. Inspection reports were made available to the Home Office. Meetings between the bodies and the Home Office (or, more correctly, at that time, the UKBA) did take place from time to time, and anecdotal evidence suggests that, from time to time, comments made by the UKBA were taken into account in revising particular processes of inspection (for example, unannounced 'site' visits).

In April 2012, this system was swept away. The Home Office, under its new political head, Conservative Member of Parliament Theresa May, claimed to have discovered widespread abuse of the system within the private, non-QAA-inspected sector. I have, elsewhere, addressed the question whether this claim was or was not true. I do not propose now to revisit this matter. For my present purpose it is sufficient for us to note that the system was swept away and the five private bodies formerly charged with the inspection of non-taxpayer-funded institutions for Tier 4 purposes were told that their services were no longer required. Instead, and insofar as such institutions were concerned that delivered wholly or mainly higher education programmes, inspection – now graced with the title of Educational Oversight – had to be carried out by the QAA, which thus agreed, of its own volition, to become part of the immigration control machinery of the United Kingdom. But in so doing the QAA also opened the door to the intrusion by the Home Office into the machinery by which the UK's higher education sector is now regulated.

Why did the QAA agree to become – in effect – an agent of the Home Office?

In legal terms, under English law, the QAA is a company limited by guarantee, and a charity, and is governed by a Board of (currently) seventeen members.

Some of these are nominated by bodies representing the UK higher education institutions (such as Universities UK) and by the regional higher education funding councils. A majority of members are nominally independent, as is the QAA itself, but it is clear from a perusal of its Board minutes and supporting papers (available at its website) that it invariably responds favourably to invitations from government departments to undertake additional activities. In 2011, it enthusiastically agreed to an approach from the Home Office to undertake Educational Oversight.

Two years earlier, following a lengthy parliamentary inquiry, the QAA had been found wanting in the manner in which it carried out its core duties. The then chair of the House of Commons' Committee on Universities had publicly accused the Agency of being 'toothless', in that it had complacently presided over a decline in the academic standards of the higher education sector as a whole (House of Commons, 2009, paragraphs 206–20). The Committee's report, published in the summer of 2009, amounted to a public relations disaster for the Agency. So the approach by the Home Office, to undertake Educational Oversight, came as a welcome opportunity to restore the QAA's public image. It could be presented as a massive vote of confidence in the QAA and its work. It would extend the authority of the QAA because any institution – however prestigious – 'failing' a QAA review would lose (or fail to gain) its Tier 4 sponsorship licence. And it would boost the QAA's income.

A paper entitled *QAA's role as an Educational Oversight body*, prepared for the QAA's Board (1 July 2011) put the matter thus:

> The EOP [Educational Oversight Project] is a highly significant development for QAA and UK HE. Not only will it represent the largest single programme of review activity since the termination of Subject Review, it will also extend QAA's safeguarding role into areas of HE provision not previously directly covered by our reviews. It will help to establish QAA as the single agency for the assurance of all types of HE provision and establish a common framework for the oversight of academic standards.
>
> (QAA, 2011, paragraph 4)

Astonishingly, in agreeing to accept the Home Office's invitation to launch this new income stream, no formal written agreement appears to have been entered into. However, fearful of the financial implications of any legal action launched against it by an aggrieved private provider of higher education, the QAA wisely asked for a sweeping financial indemnity (of up to £1 million per annum of taxpayers' money) from the Home Office; the Home Office – secretly – agreed to provide one (August 2011). The existence of this indemnity was kept secret. But in 2012, following an appeal to the Information Commissioner under the Freedom of Information Act, a copy of it was supplied to the author.

Educational Oversight – as practised by the QAA – is based broadly upon the QAA's existing higher education review methodology. As originally envisaged, and set out in the first (September 2011) edition of the *Review for Educational Oversight Handbook*, the methodology involved the submission by the institution undergoing review of a self-evaluation, followed by an inspection visit and the publication of a series of judgments focused on the management of academic standards, the quality of the learning environment and the management and reliability of public information. But in 2012, without any consultation, the QAA added a further level to the methodology, by mandating that between each full educational oversight review (once every 4 years) there would be an 'annual monitoring process' involving – at a certain extra cost – a 1-day (or, exceptionally, 2-day) re-inspection, which results in an addendum to the published educational oversight report (QAA, 2014).

Annual monitoring visits do not feature in institutional review as applied to full subscribing members of the QAA. Why, therefore, do they feature in educational oversight? The answer is that annual monitoring was forced upon the QAA by the Home Office. On 23 July 2012, the Home Office website announced as follows:

> Privately-funded colleges will be required to undergo a 4-year assessment cycle. All those who applied to a designated educational oversight body by the September 2011 deadline (or by 28 May 2012 for colleges in Scotland) will receive an initial full assessment by the end of 2012, beginning their 4-year cycle. These sponsors will next be required to undergo a full assessment in 2016 and every fourth year thereafter (unless there is a material change in circumstances – see below).
>
> In addition to full assessments every 4 years, educational oversight bodies will now introduce risk-based interim health checks. Health checks will be a light-touch, shortened version of a full assessment with the format devised by each of the individual oversight bodies. They are designed to ensure educational standards and quality are being maintained throughout the 4-year cycle, without imposing the burden of a full assessment. The fees for health checks will be set by the educational oversight bodies on a cost-recovery basis. The educational oversight bodies will determine the notice given for the health check visit, but they may be carried out without notice or at short notice. Each educational oversight body will make available a report of every health check on their website.
>
> (QAA, 2014)

One can argue, of course, about whether annual 'interim health checks' are in principle a good thing and whether, if they are, they should be extended to the entire higher education sector, to taxpayer-funded as well as privately funded higher education providers. But the significance of their insertion into the educational oversight methodology is that they were included at the behest of the

Home Office. This information was volunteered by Dr Adam Biscoe, the QAA's then Head of Educational Oversight, at a question-and-answer session of a conference on educational oversight held by the QAA in London on 19 February 2013; the author was present at this session, and there can be little doubt that their insertion was in turn part of the Home Office's war of attrition against private providers.

The Home Office has thus metamorphosed itself from guardian of the UK's external borders to that of quality and standards in the higher education sector.

Further implications

This is a remarkable transformation. But it has even more radical implications. Historically, the QAA has had no power to enforce any of its findings: it has merely inspected institutions and published its findings in respect of them, leaving it to other agencies to act upon those findings as they have wished. There has been no instance – for example – of HEFCE sanctioning a taxpayer-funded university following a seriously adverse QAA report. In this sense the QAA really was 'toothless,' as the House of Commons' Committee on Universities alleged. But it is toothless no longer, because the possibility of the suspension or indeed revocation of a Tier 4 sponsorship licence is uncomfortably real, even in relation to a taxpayer-funded institution, as (for example) London Metropolitan University infamously discovered in 2012. In that case, the revocation was apparently triggered by an investigation that the Home Office (through the UKBA) had itself launched. But in respect of privately funded higher education institutions, it is now entirely possible for the QAA to trigger a licence revocation, which would certainly follow publication by the QAA of a seriously adverse educational oversight inspection report. For many privately funded higher education institutions, heavily reliant on international students, such a report would amount to a sentence of death. It is a risk they dare not run.

Scarcely less significant is the impact of annual monitoring. This exercise takes as its agenda an 'action plan' that each privately funded institution will have agreed with the QAA following an educational oversight review and which is then published as part of the review report. Even a cursory glance at any of these plans (all of which are available at the QAA website) will confirm that they constitute a regulatory exercise, covering a host of matters ranging from the manner in which a 'virtual learning environment' is constructed to the precise content of a staff development programme and the manner in which institutional committee meetings are minuted. The fact that an institution will be visited annually to assess to what extent such agreed actions have been carried out comes perilously close to micro management. It is certainly far removed from the goal of an arm's length audit function that the QAA was established to meet.

At present, annual monitoring affects only privately funded institutions. But in announcing publication of its first annual review of educational oversight (August 2013) the QAA's chief executive warned that:

> From January 2014, we will start to review private colleges going through educational oversight review using the same method we use for universities and further education colleges, bringing them a step closer in quality assurance terms to a level playing field.
>
> (Grove, 2013)

This might of course mean that annual monitoring will be dropped from the educational oversight methodology. But, in view of the QAA's relationship with the Home Office, this seems exceedingly remote. Much less remote is the possibility that annual monitoring, in some form, will be extended to reviews of universities in England. In this connection we might note that the QAA already submits each Scottish university to an 'annual discussion'. So the possibility of English higher education institutions being subjected to some form of annual monitoring does not seem remote at all. If that happens, the Home Office should surely take some of the credit.

Postscript

In November 2014, the Home Office announced that it had agreed to reinstate the previously suspended Tier 4 sponsorship licence of Glyndwr University, a taxpayer-funded institution situated in north Wales, on condition that Glyndwr close its London campus – a remarkable further illustration of the use that the Home Office is making of its Tier 4 powers to interfere in the internal affairs of higher education institutions (Havergal, 2014).

Bibliography

Alderman, G. (2006) *Memorandum submitted to the Home Affairs Select Committee of the House of Commons*, 25 January 2006

Alderman, G. (2009) The right to award degrees must be vetted regularly. *The Times.* 4 August 2009: 22

Alderman, G. (2012) Educational Oversight? The Incursion of the UK Border Agency into the Quality Assurance of Higher education Programmes. *Oxford Centre for Higher Education Policy Studies, Occasional Paper* 43

Attwood, R. (2009) MPs call for 'toothless' watchdog to be put down. *Times Higher Education.* 12 March 2009

Grove, J. (2013) Plagiarism warning for private colleges. *Times Higher Education.* 12 August 2013

Havergal, C. (2014) Glyndwr told to leave London campus as visa licence reinstated. *Times Higher Education.* 24 November 2014

HEFCE (2013) *Operating Framework for Higher Education in England.* Available at: http://www.hefce.ac.uk/media/hefce/content/about/introduction/working inpartnership/rpg/operatingframework/operating_framework_for_HE_ 11072013_2.pdf [accessed 31 July 2013]

House of Commons (2009) Students and Universities. *Committee on Innovation, Universities, Science and Skills 1.* London: HMSO

QAA (2014) *Recognition Scheme for Educational Oversight: Annual Monitoring.* Quality Assurance Agency. Available at: http://www.qaa.ac.uk/en/Publications/ Documents/RSEO Annual monitoring 2015.docx

QAA Board of Directors (2011) *QAA's role as an Educational Oversight body.* Paper presented to QAA Board in July 2011

Chapter 12

Making a difference

The roles of markets and the roles of quality assurance regimes

John Brennan

Background

The classic model of the university and of academic life was one of autonomy and academic freedom. Over recent decades, both have been compromised by external interventions in the work of individual universities and academics. This chapter considers the impacts of some major interventions, and the different kinds of responses they receive from universities.

In their organisational model of the structure of higher education systems, Becher and Kogan distinguished between the four levels of the individual, the basic unit (department, faculty, research centre), the institution and the central authority along with the two elements of normative and operational modes operating at each level (Becher and Kogan, 1992). For a significant part of his career, Roger Brown occupied a position on the boundaries between the institutional and the central levels of authority and decision-making in higher education. Such a location provides an excellent overview of the entire higher education system, its diversity, its politics and the relationships between its parts, as is clear from so much of Brown's writing (e.g. Brown with Carasso, 2013). Quality assurance regimes occupy interesting territory, embracing both the normative and operational modes and, at least potentially, affecting the relationships between all four levels in the Becher and Kogan organisational model.

In this chapter, I shall reflect on some past developments in order to speculate on future directions of change and development in higher education. I shall do so with particular attention to quality, its assurance and its development, and to markets, especially in relation to the roles of students as the key users or consumers of higher education's 'products'. The reference to students as consumers reflects today's language of markets and neo-liberalism, but students have always been having a major influence on the shaping of higher education. Depending on time and context, students have been conceived variously as 'learners', 'junior members', 'clients', 'consumers', 'co-creators' and 'co-producers'. While they may still be junior members in certain traditional collegiate settings, students have increasingly become clients and consumers in today's increasingly marketised higher education. Brown makes the point forcibly in a recent article:

> The real crisis that higher education faces is that universities, their leaders and many of those associated with them are pursuing status and position for themselves, their subjects and their institutions at the expense of their core activities of educating students and conducting research and scholarship to the highest possible standards.
>
> (Brown, 2014: 4)

The point that Brown and others are emphasising is that reputation, whether of individuals or institutions, has come to replace education and research as the principal concern of the academic community. In commenting on the research function of higher education, Craig Calhoun observed that the goal of research was increasingly becoming one of 'adding a couple of lines to my CV' rather than generating knowledge for the public good (Calhoun, 2006: 31). Whether between institutions, between academics or between students, competition has tended to take over from collaboration as the key element of relationships. Thus, as the pursuit of status and reputation takes over from the generation and transmission of knowledge, the role and experience of students and the conceptions and measures of quality in higher education also change.

Whose quality?

In the decades prior to Roger Brown's arrival at the Higher Education Quality Council, judgements of quality in higher education rested mainly with the academics themselves. As examiners, internal and external, they made judgements about the quality and standards of students' work. As reviewers, they made judgements about whether new projects should be funded and new articles and books published. Other interest groups might not agree with the judgements of the academics, but it was with the academics that authority generally rested. No-one really bothered whether the students were satisfied and, on the whole, no-one asked.

When system-wide quality assurance arrived in the UK with the creation of the Council for National Academic Awards (CNAA) in the late 1960s, authority remained clearly vested in the academic profession. The CNAA was the degree-awarding and quality assurance body for the polytechnics and colleges up until the ending of the binary line between these institutions and the universities in 1992. Central to the CNAA was the operation of a system of subject committees and boards with memberships drawn from all parts of the higher education sector, universities as well as polytechnics and colleges. The boards and committees decided whether courses could be approved and degrees awarded. They could and frequently did impose conditions on the approvals. Approval itself was for a fixed time period, usually 5 years, after which a stringent review and approval renewal process would occur. The interests of the board and committee members were generally closely connected to their disciplinary backgrounds. They wanted to protect and enhance the position of their disciplines within higher education institutions, to ensure that teaching was good, curricula were appropriate, courses properly resourced. Of course, these were broadly shared values, but decisions about whether they were being achieved could sometimes be contested by other interest groups, with institutional managements being the main other key players.

The authorities vested in the CNAA committees and boards in respect of the polytechnics and colleges were located within the individual universities themselves in the university sector. In those less managerial days, there was perhaps not so much difference between management and academic perspectives and most university managers were also academics, taking on management roles for fixed periods and often in a part-time capacity. The values and interests on which judgements were made did not differ hugely between academic staff and institutional managements.

However, with the expansion of the system, and other social and technical developments worldwide, wider interests and different values came into play. The growing higher education system was costing the taxpayer more; and users of higher education – for example, students and employers – had more choices to make within an expanded and differentiated system. Questions of value for money and fitness for purpose were being asked by different groups (or 'stakeholders') reflecting different interests. Was public money being put to good use? Were students acquiring the knowledge and skills they would need when they entered the labour market? Which course to choose at which higher education institution? And which graduate to select when hiring new employees? Different answers were available to such questions from different interest groups. Academic perspectives needed to be combined with different user perspectives to provide answers to them. Academic judgements were becoming just one of many voices in discussions of quality in higher education.

In the UK, the central 'quality question' was becoming 'who is best?' or 'who is better than who?' rather than 'is it good enough?' or 'how can we make it better?' As Brown later pointed out, status and reputation were taking over from education as key concerns about higher education quality. With the arrival of league tables and rankings and global competition, the goal for many was to achieve a high position rather than necessarily improve quality. In the UK at least, quality was now defined largely in terms of the research functions of universities, using quite limited measures, and generally ignoring the educational function in many institutions. A further change concerned the question of 'quality of what?' Whereas the course and subject had been the standard unit of analysis for academic judgements of quality (whether by external examiners of the standards of student work, peer-reviewers of research proposals and publications or members of external review teams of courses), decisions to be made about funding, employment, relevance or value for money were being made by different interests and focused on different perspectives, more specifically on institutions and institutional types than on courses and subjects. Increasingly, academic judgements were being used to inform decisions but the decisions were taken by others – institutional managers, national funding and policy bodies, students as consumers – and not by the academics themselves.

Systems of quality assurance were developed from the 1990s onwards which attempted to combine these different interests and deliver information and judgements to a wide range of interested parties, within and beyond higher education. The methods of quality assurance drew on all four levels of Becher and Kogan's structural model of higher education systems – central authorities, institutions, basic units of faculties and departments and individuals – academics and, increasingly, students too. There were frequently tensions between the different levels, especially in the case of institutions vs. central authorities, and faculties or departments vs. institutions. Reports and judgements about quality were now in the public domain and recontextualised to generate rankings and league tables of institutions within an increasingly differentiated system. A further tension was created by the movement away from decision-making based on professional judgements (whether of academics, managers or central authorities) to decision-making through the operation of markets. Within the more marketised model of higher education decision-making, student voices were becoming ever more powerful.

From students to consumers

There is nothing new about students being at the 'centre' of the UK higher education system. Institutions, departments and academics have always needed students. In the UK, the qualities of incoming students (entry grades and school attended) and the qualities of outgoing students (the quality of their degree, or the jobs subsequently obtained) have always been important, internally and externally, to the operation and the reputation of individual institutions as well as to the higher education system as a whole. What has changed in recent years is the attempt by government to transform students into consumers and a granting of power and authority to them over what counts as good higher education. Student/consumer satisfaction has come to assume a significance greater than learning and academic achievement as a key measure of higher education outcomes and comparative performance of different institutions and courses (and individual teachers).

While these trends are not unique to the UK, they have been stronger here than in many other countries. This is partly because UK higher education is a strongly vertically stratified system, where reputational position counts for all, rather than the more horizontally stratified systems in many parts of continental Europe where difference does not always imply better or worse (Clark, 1983; Teichler, 2007). All of that said, the higher education systems in many other countries are beginning to catch up with the UK obsession with stratification.

However, the student voice does indeed have a significance to questions of quality and, with the expansion and differentiation of the higher education system, their voice may be sending different messages at different times and in different places. In a recent study of student experiences at thirteen universities (Brennan et al., 2010), students were asked about their learning experiences and what they had valued most about their time in higher education. While there were differences in emphasis between different students, subject areas and institutions, one message came out clearly. Employment relevance and interest in their subject of study were generally important to students. However, something else stood out above those considerations in appraising their higher education experiences. This was the effect that higher education had on their personal development. Most of the students felt they were different people by the time of their graduation from the people they had been at the time of their entry to higher education. They had new values, new friends and new aspirations.

There were also institutional differences in what was emphasised by students. For some, higher education was valued primarily as an enjoyable social experience far from home, often delivered in elite institutions. For others, especially those living at home and working part-time, higher education was primarily an educational experience, acquiring knowledge and qualifications that would hopefully be useful in later life. It is interesting to observe that in the former group, social emphasis tended to be emphasised more. In contrast, the educational or academic dimension was commonly emphasised in the latter group, often in institutions that put greater emphasis on teaching. The following quotations from students drawn from the above study illustrate these institutional contrasts (Brennan and Patel, 2011). The first is from a sociology student studying at a 'top 20' institution:

> No I'm not working, I'm just . . . you find yourself just going out a lot because there's nothing like just hanging around, talking in people's rooms and stuff, going to base and just filling time really. It's just surprising the amount of time you can waste. Just sit and talk because I think you have to make that decision when you came here, because like at the end of the day you're only doing sociology for like 6–10 hours a week, so you've got to have your best friends in hall I think because they're the people you're with the most and stuff.
>
> (Brennan and Patel, 2011: 319)

The second two quotations are from sociology students at a university ranked in the 70s:

> Using my mind academically, writing essays, discussing academic subjects. I have never done that before, and I find myself happy doing it. I am a more confident person as a result of it. I am happier. It has been a very positive experience for me. (Student 1)

You learn the skill of er . . . you know, not to take things on face value. It teaches you to look from every angle. You know, way of consider that point that you wouldn't have done before, consider that. Especially with my degree it's about community and people. It just teaches you to look at things – don't take things on face value. Why somebody lives their life that way. It just teaches you to look deeply and think a little bit more as to why things happen as they do. Um, that's a skill like a mediator really. And it's like the tolerance. I think that's a skill in itself. To learn to be tolerant. Things like that. (Student 2).

(Brennan and Patel, 2011: 319)

A recent study (Ashwin *et al.*, 2014; Abbas *et al.*, 2012) has also indicated an inverse relationship between institutional status and academic orientation of students. The general conclusion here is that different students want different things and different things are on offer at different places. The extent to which students are satisfied with what they have experienced at university is indeed an appropriate measure of *consumer* satisfaction but that does not necessarily mean that it is also a credible measure of the academic quality of that experience. Academic quality is but one part of that experience and, for many students, certainly not the most important part.

Demand for places, attendance at lectures, amount and quality of submitted work, ambition and destinations are among the many aspects of the student experience of higher education which have quality dimensions. But they represent different measures of quality and may also reflect experiences that the students brought into higher education as much as the experiences enjoyed while being there.

Additionally, the expansion of higher education has brought with it a weakening of boundaries – not just between academic disciplines and individual institutions, but also between the experiences gained within higher education and experiences gained in other contexts and life situations. In one of his last publications, Martin Trow summed up the changes with these words:

The broad movement from elite to open access systems of higher education is associated with, and in part defined by, the increasing permeability of boundaries of all kinds – between institutions and the surrounding societies, between departments and disciplines as both teaching and research become more interdisciplinary, between universities and private businesses and industry, and between formal education and the informal learning that goes on in a learning society that depends on the constant accretion of new knowledge.

(Trow, 2010: 605)

It follows, therefore, that students are consuming many different things in their experience of higher education and that some things will be valued more by some students than others, irrespective of their qualities. Different people enjoy different things. Consumer choice, therefore, is not primarily about identifying the best but about achieving a good match between what is wanted by the individual consumer and what is available from the provider. It is about identifying differences between providers and presenting them in such a way that they can assist consumers in making choices and decisions between an increasing range of goods and provisions. They are not guarantees of quality in an academic sense and indeed may divert attention away from academic quality.

The student voice in quality assurance

In the UK, the student voice speaks to quality assurance, and the published outputs of quality assurance speak to students. In speaking to quality assurance, data from the National Student Survey are routinely referred to in quality reviews. These data concern the satisfaction of students – in a consumerist context – but the data are then used by institutions in a marketing context and by national quality agencies in a regulatory context. Additionally, students speak to course reviewers in most review processes. The performance and learning outcomes of students are frequently taken as important evidence of quality and, when linked to access issues and social origins, of value added. Looking at the other side of the relationship, in influencing student decisions about where and what to study, data on the quality of particular courses and institutions is increasingly available to inform student decisions about where are what to study. The national quality body (QAA) in the form of the Key Information Set, the National Student Survey and *Which?* (a consumer magazine) higher education reports are all important. Thus, the student experience is indeed at the heart of the quality assurance process in higher education, but it is about more than satisfaction and the student is more than consumer.

While the forms in which the student voice is expressed and heard may have evolved over the years, the ways in which it has been used have to some extent become more limited, reflecting the increasingly vertical differentiation of higher education in the UK where rankings have replaced analysis and judgement in assessing quality. There is also a sense that the quantitative has replaced the qualitative in judgements about quality.

Yet differentiation can also be horizontal, where differences are recognised and valued and not immediately converted into hierarchical rankings. Many higher education systems worldwide are still organised on binary lines with different kinds of courses provided in different kinds of institutions. Arguably, differentiation of this sort is better able to meet the needs of increasingly diverse student populations than systems of differentiation where institutions claim to be doing the same things, only better. Horizontal differentiation is certainly present in UK higher education but much of it is hidden by the obsessions with status and hierarchy. Provided the right kinds of questions are asked of them, the student voice can provide invaluable evidence of differences between courses and institutions that can help choice and decision-making. In so doing, it moves the question from asking 'Is it any good?' to asking 'What is good (or bad) about it?'

There is a market in higher education. Quality assurance can inform it. But to do so its findings and judgements must be communicated in ways that will genuinely assist its intended audience in making the right decisions. It needs to inform the consumers about the range of products on offer in ways that will assist decision-making. Once more, academic judgements are needed, but they are there to inform rather than to make decisions. Within the market, decisions must be left to the consumer. The butcher can tell me about a particular cut of meat, but he can't tell me what I want for my dinner. Similarly, in the case of the academic and the student, the former can explain the features of the course on offer, but only the latter can decide what he or she wants to learn.

Conclusion

Roger Brown has written quite recently that 'the pursuit of status will be the death of the university as we know it' (Brown, 2014: 21), and he has also commented that institutional reviews as conducted by quality assurance bodies tend to be mainly an exercise in reputation management. However, it is still the case that reviews conducted in the UK by the Quality Assurance Agency are not directly concerned with producing ratings and rankings. Higher education institutions may approach them with a concern about avoiding reputational damage, but they can also use them to make their own critical judgements about their current activities and to inform decisions about how they can be improved in future. External judgements of quality achieved through processes of external peer-review can make major contributions to the workings of markets. Markets need quality assurance regimes and their outputs. But quality assurance regimes need also to take account of markets and the diverse values and demands that these represent. They need to provide information of a kind and in ways that will inform users. And users are not only students but the societies of which students are but a part.

Bibliography

Abbas, A., Ashwin, P., and McLean, M. (2012) University League Tables Not Valid. *Network: The Magazine of the British Sociological Association*

Ashwin, P., Abbas, A and McLean, M. (2014) How do students' accounts of sociology change over the course of their undergraduate degrees? *Higher Education* 67 (2): 219–234

Becher, T. and Kogan, M. (1992) *Process and Structure in Higher Education.* London: Routledge

Brennan, J., Jary, D., Osborne, M., Richardson, J., Edmunds, R., Houston, M. and Lebeau, Y. (2010) *Improving What Is Learned at University.* London: Routledge

Brennan, J. and Patel, K. (2011) Up Market or Down Market: Shopping for Higher Education in the UK. In P. Teixeira and D. Dill (eds) (2011) *Public Vices, Private Virtues: Assessing the Effects of Marketisation in Higher Education*. Rotterdam: Sense Publishers: 315–327

Brown, R. (2014) The real crisis in higher education. *Higher Education Review* 45 (3): 4–25

Brown, R. with Carasso, H. (2013) *Everything for Sale?: The Marketisation of Higher Education*. London: Routledge and the Society for Research into Higher Education

Calhoun, C. (2006) The university and the public good. *Thesis Eleven* 84: 7–43

Clark, B. R. (1983) *The Higher Education System: Academic Organization in Cross-National Perspective*. Berkeley: University of California Press

Teichler, U. (2007) *Higher Education Systems: Conceptual Frameworks, Comparative Perspectives, Empirical Findings*. Rotterdam: Sense Publishers

Trow, M. (2010) Reflections on the Transition from Elite to Mass to Universal Access. In M. Burridge (ed.) *Martin Trow: Twentieth-Century Higher Education*. San Francisco: University of California Press: 554–611

Part IV

Marketisation and higher education pedagogies

Chapter 13

Shifting perspectives on research and teaching relationships

A view from Australia

Angela Brew

Introduction

In the 1980s–1990s, considerable work was undertaken to understand and to develop the relationship between research and teaching. Numerous qualitative and quantitative studies examined models of the relationship (e.g. Ramsden and Moses, 1992), its nature (e.g. Feldman, 1987), perceptions of it (e.g. Neumann, 1992), linking factors (e.g. Brew and Boud, 1995) and how it was linked to ideas of knowledge (Brew, 1999). Indeed, there were so many studies (my personal database lists over 400) that it is only possible to mention a few. In addition, seeking to understand and develop the relationship at that time, numerous institutions and individuals worked on a practical level to integrate research and teaching. From the early 1990s, Roger Brown brought together a group of people interested in developing the relationship. They met regularly in London for a number of years to explore how to do this. These meetings developed into the Forum described by Vaneeta D'Andrea in Chapter 16, and also mentioned by Alan Jenkins and Mick Healey in Chapter 15. These meetings culminated in two major events in 2004 and 2007 (held at Marwell in Hampshire) that aimed to bring together all the people who were researching in this area.

I remember sitting in the main conference room at Marwell at the second of these conferences surrounded by all the scholars from across the world who had contributed significantly to the literature on teaching and research. By that time, I had moved to Australia and was leading a strategic project at a research-intensive university to develop research-enhanced learning and teaching. Surely, I thought, given the length of time that had elapsed, the amount of research that had been published and the number of institutional and national projects that had resulted, a greater understanding of the relationship between teaching and research should have been developed.

This chapter arises from questioning why there was such interest in the relationship at that time, and what it was about how universities were developing, that brought about a questioning of it. It appeared at the time that the relationship between research and teaching, as central to the academic project of the university, was under threat, and a crisis of confidence had been created. In this chapter, I discuss how within the shifting landscape of higher education, successive waves of scholarly work and practical strategies have sought to understand and to strengthen the relationship between teaching and research.

The chapter first reviews developments in understanding and strengthening the relationship during the latter part of the twentieth and the first decade of the twenty-first centuries when the emphasis was largely on changing teaching to include more research. It then briefly explores a shift of focus to the scholarship of teaching and learning, which again tended to focus on teaching. It then examines the shift to student research demonstrating how this has brought into focus the research community and redefined the role of students in contributing to research. Finally it explores the ways in which engaging students in research is challenged by, but can make use of, contemporary counter trends. I argue that in doing this, such work and scholarly endeavour has contributed to changing the nature of concerns and shifted ideas about who should be engaged in the scholarly project of the university.

A big wave of concern: strengthen the relationship

Many aspects of university functioning were traditionally dependent upon a so-called nexus between teaching and research. It is embedded in the traditional idea of the lecturer as a research and teaching academic and the idea that academics do not need training as teachers is predicated on it. Although we now know that these assumptions are false and that practice is indeed changing, in a pre-mass-higher-education system, they went unquestioned. In the closing decades of the twentieth century however, people were increasingly examining the importance of strengthening the relationship. This tended to be conceived in terms of changing teaching to include research. The late twentieth century saw an exponential growth in such studies. It is very noticeable that of the fifty-three studies included in Hattie and Marsh's (1996) meta-analysis, only four appeared before 1970, perhaps suggesting a growing concern with the relationship at a time when developments in higher education were exacerbating the divide. This continued into the first decade of the new century.

Mass higher education brought with it a huge tide of concern about how traditional relationships between students and their teachers could be sustained. Two other significant developments, I suggest, highlight distinctive features of research and teaching and serve to drive them apart. These are the professionalisation of teaching, and the politicisation of research.

The closer students are to lecturers, the more conversational can be the teaching. As soon as class sizes increase beyond the levels required for good conversations, a distance is created between teacher and student. Pedagogical structures are then required, e.g. the specification of learning outcomes and assessment criteria. The larger the class size, the more important are the organisational strategies to manage the learning process. Learning is no longer assured through the conversations the students have with their teachers, who are assumed also to be researchers. Mass higher education brought with it armies of casual teaching staff, many of whom are not engaged in research. The challenges of organisation, together with an increasing number of pedagogical requirements at an institutional, and indeed national level, and the changing character of knowledge and knowing, have pointed to a growing demand for the professionalisation of teaching and learning in higher education. This draws teaching away from disciplinary research.

Quality assurance processes at a national level designed to check and then enhance research output have transformed research into a political instrument for competition at institutional, national and global levels. This politicisation of university research draws it away from teaching as academics focus on short-term publication rather than longer term gestation of ideas within teaching and collegial conversations.

Thus, different facets of the changing nature of higher education served to exacerbate the divide between research and teaching. It was a time when many higher education institutions expressed in their missions the desire to strengthen this relationship, which was viewed as central to the idea of a university. Roger Brown in setting up the idea of advanced scholarship and attempting to infuse this throughout his institution was one of the early Vice-Chancellors to recognise the importance of having an institutional strategy to integrate research and teaching. A survey of institutional missions in Australia conducted in 2009 suggested that at an institutional level, strengthening the relationship between teaching and research was pervasive. But the tide of concern was short-lived. By 2011, new priorities had taken their place and attempts at an institutional level to integrate research and teaching appeared to have gone out of fashion (Brew and Cahir, 2014).

At the level of the individual academic, the changing nature of the academic role with, for example, increased casualisation and teaching-focused positions, also made the integration of research and teaching problematic. This shift is reflected in the academic literature where discussions of attempts to integrate research and teaching have tended to move away from a generic focus on how this can be done, to focus more specifically on the implications in specific disciplines (e.g. Burke and Rau, 2010).

Understanding more about the nature of the relationship between teaching and research, then, went hand-in-hand with a strong tide of change that was serving to divorce it. New strategies were needed; ones that did not go against the tide, but that would ride with the wave of concern and ultimately change the focus of attention. There were two publications that I believe were seminal in shifting the focus of attention and in changing the course of debates. The first of these was Boyer's (1990) report on investigations in 800 US universities, which concluded that there was a need to re-define faculty scholarship to include the scholarship of teaching. The second was Hattie and Marsh's (1996) meta-analysis that concluded there was no inevitable link between teaching and research and argued that it was important to actively develop one.

Shift of focus: scholarly teaching

Since the early 1990s when Boyer published *Priorities for the Professoriate*, the scholarship of teaching and learning has captured the imagination of institutions and individuals concerned with professionalising teaching and learning. As demands for greater teaching expertise have intensified, work designed to elucidate scholarly teaching has provided criteria for measuring the quality of teaching and practices to develop it. Critically important has been the capacity of the scholarship of teaching and learning to provide a helicopter vision of teaching where academics frame and systematically investigate questions in relation to teaching and learning. Hutchings and Shulman (1999: 13) call this 'going meta'. Through the scholarship of teaching and learning, academics may be led to research their own practice. They may draft a philosophy of teaching and develop a portfolio of evidence about their teaching. The scholarship of teaching and learning has been fed into courses for university teachers and led to its own scholarly outputs. There have been institutional strategies to develop it (e.g. Brew and Sachs, 2007), and promotions strategies to reward it. There is also some evidence that engaging in the scholarship of teaching and learning leads to improvements in teaching (Brew and Ginns, 2008). Indeed it has become a huge movement that has changed ideas about the nature of teaching and teaching development across the globe.

The scholarship of teaching and learning has been seen as one of the ways in which research and teaching can be integrated. Engaging in research on teaching brings research into the teaching realm. Further, engaging students in the scholarship of teaching and learning draws students into the scholarly teaching work of the university (Hutchings, 2002).

However, it must be recognised that the scholarship of teaching and learning tends to emanate from committed teachers and teaching leaders in institutions, not from the research community. Although there are examples of leaders and managers of research and of teaching working together to develop research on teaching, these are relatively rare. The scholarship of teaching and learning tends to leave the research community relatively unaffected. In the current political context of research mentioned above, heads of department faced with improving research outputs are more likely to encourage academics to focus on disciplinary rather than educational research. So while the scholarship of teaching and learning has the capacity to integrate research and teaching, there have been strong forces still keeping them apart.

Shift of focus: students

Notably absent in discussions of integrating teaching and research that took place around the end of the century was consideration of students' perspectives. Teaching and research were activities of academics and the way to strengthen them was viewed as a question of influencing academic practice. However, since the mid-1990s, interest in understanding students' experiences of research has flourished (see, for example, Jenkins *et al.,* 1998). This work included studies of students' perceptions of what research is, how it is related to disciplines (Robertson and Blackler, 2006), students' perceptions of learning research skills and the extent to which students feel they develop them. This work highlights the distance, and in some ways the alienation of students from the research enterprise of the university.

Subsequently, numerous and varied accounts of undergraduate research have appeared in a range of different disciplines (see for example, Chang, 2006; Cuthbert *et al.,* 2012; Elsen *et al.,* 2009). There are now a number of studies that suggest how to develop research skills (Willison and O'Regan, 2007); how to include more non-traditional students in research (Strayhorn, 2010); how to motivate students to engage in it, as well as numerous journals for students to publish their research.

Not only have such studies flourished in recent years, the shift of attention away from an emphasis on what academics do in integrating their research and teaching, onto what students do and how they experience the university and their place within, has been noticeably successful in bringing research and teaching more firmly together and has dramatically contributed to changing the focus of debates.

In 2008, I personally shifted my emphasis away from a sole focus on academics' practice, to focus on involving students in efforts to integrate research and teaching. For me in Australia, this involved not only bringing undergraduate students into a national conversation about research and teaching relationships, but challenging some taboos about the capacity of undergraduates to engage in research. In the US, many institutions had accepted the contributions that undergraduates could make to their research enterprise. National funding bodies, such as the National Science Foundation have been putting resources into undergraduate research for many years. In Australia, there was widespread skepticism about whether undergraduates were capable of research.

A national summit on the integration of teaching and research in 2009 brought together leaders of Australian higher education institutions as well as leading experts from around the world. From this, a communiqué was prepared that concluded:

> The synergistic link between an educated workforce and economic development is undeniable. Exposing undergraduates to the vital link between teaching and research is one of the cornerstones on which a competitive Australia will be nurtured. If we fail to embolden our students to be creative, the future of Australia in 2020 and beyond, when our natural resources inevitably decline, will be bleak. It is vital that we now connect undergraduate students with research clearly and explicitly, to enable Australia to be a genuinely innovative knowledge society.
>
> (Brew, 2010: 15)

I like to think that the summit was important in breaking the taboos. Certainly there has been a great deal of development of undergraduate research opportunities both within undergraduate curricula and also in special research programmes and internships since that time. Many Australian universities now have significant programmes of undergraduate research opportunities, the Office of Learning and Teaching (an Australian Government body) has funded a number of major projects designed to develop undergraduate research. Three national undergraduate research conferences have been held and a fourth is planned. The Australasian Council of Undergraduate Research (ACUR) has been established to ensure continuity of conferences into the future. The Council is led by a steering group consisting of high level representatives of thirty-two Australian universities, four New Zealand universities and fourteen other organisations worldwide. In 2014, thirty-four students from sixteen Australian and two overseas universities presented their research to members of the federal parliament and senators in Parliament House, Canberra to showcase the excellent research that undergraduates were doing.

These developments are beginning to recognise the important contribution that undergraduates can make to the academic project of the university. Through such developments undergraduates become more a part of the university. This is not just an academic exercise. Nor is it simply to enhance students' engagement as Kuh (2008) has suggested it does. As much research has shown (see, for example, Lopatto, 2009; Laursen et al., 2010), the skills that students gain in carrying out research are important in preparing them for professional life.

Riding with the new wave

Traditional ways of attempting to integrate research and teaching tended to focus on the teacher and how they could utilise their research in their teaching. Redefining the task has brought students onto centre stage. At its simplest level, engaging undergraduates in research and inquiry involves setting up special programmes for groups of students to work with researchers on short-term research projects or introducing research and inquiry projects into courses. More radically, it involves designing whole courses and programmes to involve students in research and inquiry throughout their degrees. It involves undergraduates in course design and planning and research on teaching and learning. It involves some students mentoring others in research. Importantly, it involves researchers becoming involved in undergraduate education and strengthens the educative role of research. In other words, the relationships between undergraduates and the university and between students and academics are transformed. Students become co-creators of the curriculum, and partners in designing and pursuing it. Students learn with each other and with relevant others, e.g. academics including researchers. Students are producers of knowledge (Neary, 2010), agents of change (Healey and Jenkins, 2009) and researchers of both the content of the curriculum and curriculum processes.

These developments signal a new wave of thinking about the relationship between teaching and research. But if some of the earlier ideals of a nexus are to be achieved, the relationship needs to be embedded within the very fabric of university structure and functioning in respect of policy, administration as well as research and teaching. Indeed, the USA *Council on Undergraduate Research* lists twelve main categories of university functioning that are affected if excellence in undergraduate research and inquiry implementation is to be achieved: campus mission and culture, administrative support, research infrastructure, faculty professional development opportunities, recognition, external funding, dissemination, student-centred issues, curriculum, summer research programmes, assessment activities and strategic planning (Hensel, 2012).

Institutional and departmental contexts, the teaching and learning and research policy contexts, the disciplinary context as well as the external societal context, all are affected and in turn affect the nature of knowledge and the role of discovery in the university and challenge who has the authority to make decisions regarding the generation of new knowledge. This is a radical agenda that challenges old assumptions and requires new ways of thinking and new skills to be developed. If research and teaching are to be fully integrated, then both curricula and pedagogy for student research obtain their impetus as much from research traditions as from learning and teaching. This means thinking about a curriculum that integrates critical elements of the research process (Brew, 2013). It also involves the research community in undergraduate education.

New ways of thinking about the relationship between teaching and research draw attention to the need for awareness of differences in the nature of knowledge and different views about how, and whether, knowledge is discovered or generated, for example, in different disciplines. Many research projects that students engage in may include knowledge that is new to the student but also new to the discipline. This means that the place of content in traditional curriculum design is displaced.

Importantly, this challenges traditional authority structures. It challenges the extent to which particular individuals and groups at differing levels of the institution have the authority to make decisions about specific aspects of curricula. When students carry out research, the researcher, the teacher, the students or the community or external organisation that is perhaps sponsoring the research may initiate the project and define the questions to be addressed.

I have found that once students have had an experience of engaging in research and have taken a lead in negotiating a research project, they can very readily take the initiative to develop undergraduate research further. For example, in my university, students who in 2013 participated in research on teaching and learning, in 2014 on their own initiative set up a student mentoring scheme for others new to research, mounted an undergraduate research poster conference and are producing a website of resources for students. These students are not waiting for research opportunities to arise. They are participating in building capacity and actively seeking support for new initiatives. Students really are becoming part of the academic project of the university.

Going against the tide

But at the same time, as Alan Jenkins and Mick Healey argue in Chapter 15, there are elements of higher education working against the tide. As before, when people were trying to integrate teaching and research, there were trends drawing them apart. Some of these have intensified. So, this new wave of activity similarly is buffeted by a strong tide of competing trends.

The politicisation of research with its emphasis on research outputs and specialisation of research strengths militates against undergraduates engaging in research. Powerful vested interests work to consolidate research in particular institutions or centres, making it increasingly difficult for teaching academics to engage in it. In some institutions, teaching-only positions have been established on the assumption that research is not needed for undergraduate education. Research agendas affect curriculum decisions. There is a complex interaction between curricular intentions and research intentions as academics navigate this terrain. This does not make undergraduate research impossible, but it challenges it and is, in turn, challenged by it.

Mass higher education continues to pose challenges for institutions and academics wishing to introduce widespread undergraduate research and inquiry opportunities. The existence of large classes is often used as an excuse for not involving undergraduates in research or confining such experiences to elite or advanced students. Coupled with concerns about the size of classes is a concern with student engagement. This should provide an impetus for undergraduate research-based learning since, along with a range of other activities that are entirely consistent with it, for example, learning communities, collaborative assignments, community-based learning, internships and capstone courses, undergraduate research is one of the pedagogical practices identified as contributing to high levels of student engagement (Kuh, 2008).

In a standards-based higher education, which is a key focus of attention at the present time, standards are specified not primarily for the knowledge that students are expected to acquire but for the disciplinary skills that they will develop. For example, in Australia, threshold learning outcomes for science as defined by the Australian Learning and Teaching Council discipline scholars (ALTC, 2011) include the following:

Critically analyse and solve scientific problems by:

3.1. Gathering, synthesising and critically evaluating information from a range of sources
3.2. Designing and planning an investigation

3.3. Selecting and applying practical and/or theoretical techniques or tools in order to conduct and investigation

3.4. Collecting, accurately recording, interpreting and drawing conclusions from scientific data

(ALTC, 2011:13)

Concern for standards then can point to the development of research and inquiry across the whole curriculum and suggests that merely engaging a few students in special elite programmes is not sufficient. Despite disciplinary expectations about standards to be met, many decisions about how to implement these requirements are left to individual academics. This results in different pedagogies existing side by side within traditional patterns of lectures, tutorials, laboratory sessions and assessment. Contextual factors such as the spaces available, the ways time is divided, the resources available, career expectations, promotion criteria, use of evaluation data, all will affect the decisions taken.

It is little wonder that there are calls for the professionalisation of teachers in higher education. The simple lecture is no longer adequate to meet such complex demands. Academics need to find their way through perplexing territory for the decisions they have to take have become extremely complex and there are, as we have seen, a number of initiatives that are pulling and pushing in opposite directions. This is where the scholarship of teaching and learning comes into its own.

As far as the implementation of research-based learning experiences is concerned, a number of models have been suggested and these are useful for thinking through the implications of curricular and pedagogical decisions (see for example, Brew, 2013; Healey and Jenkins, 2009). However, critical in this process is the involvement of students in decision-making and in contributing to creating the kind of higher education that will meet their needs. Also important, and made possible through these developments, is the involvement of researchers and research communities in the educational project of the university.

Conclusion

This chapter has explored the challenges in strengthening the relationship between teaching and research over the past 40 years or so. It has argued that what has been noticeably successful not only in bringing research and teaching together, but also in bringing researchers and teaching academics together in recent years, has been the shift of attention onto what students do and how they experience the university and their place within it. The chapter has highlighted recent work where research and teaching are being integrated through engaging undergraduate students in research, including pedagogical research, and where students are increasingly involving themselves in the academic work of the university.

In these developments we see an enactment of the role of research in teaching, and the role of teaching in research. We are looking at a higher education where the relationship between teaching and research is redesigned. Academic authority is problematised, different kinds of spaces (online and physically) are used, students become co-creators in their own education; teaching is informed by staff and student research; students and academics experience and conduct research, learn about research, develop skills of research and inquiry and contribute to the university's research effort together; and students and academics design courses based on research. Such a higher education transforms the relationship between teaching and research and sets a new agenda for universities as they educate students to contribute to the generation of knowledge in an uncertain world.

Bibliography

Australian Learning and Teaching Council (ALTC) (2011). *SCIENCE Learning and Teaching Academic Standards Statement, Academic Standards Project.* Sydney, NSW: Australian Learning and Teaching Council

Boyer, E. (1990) *Scholarship Reconsidered: Priorities for the Professoriate.* Princeton, NJ: Carnegie Foundation for the Advancement of Teaching, University of Princeton

Brew, A. (1999) Research and teaching changing relationships in a changing context. *Studies in Higher Education* 24 (3): 291–301

Brew, A. (2010) *Enhancing undergraduate engagement through research and enquiry.* Sydney, NSW: Office of Learning and Teaching, Australian Government. Available at: http://www.olt.gov.au/resource-enhancing-undergraduate-engagement-research-enquiry-macquarie-2010 [accessed 9 January 2015]

Brew, A. (2013) Understanding the scope of undergraduate research: a framework for curricular and pedagogical decision-making. *Higher Education* 66 (5): 603–618

Brew, A. and Boud, D. (1995) Teaching and research: establishing the vital link with learning. *Higher Education* 29: 261–273

Brew, A. and Cahir, J. (2014) Achieving sustainability in learning and teaching initiatives. *International Journal for Academic Development* 19 (4): 341–352

Brew, A. and Ginns, P. (2008) The relationship between engagement in the scholarship of teaching and learning and students' course experiences. *Assessment and Evaluation in Higher Education* 33: 535–545

Brew, A. and Sachs, J. (eds) (2007) *Transforming a University: The Scholarship of Teaching and Learning in Practice.* Sydney, NSW: Sydney University Press

Burke, L.A. and Rau, B. (2010) The research–teaching gap in management. *Academy of Management Learning and Education* 9 (1): 132–143

Chang, H. (2006) Turning an undergraduate class into a professional research community. *Teaching in Higher Education* 10 (2): 387–394

Cuthbert, D., Arunachalam, D. and Licina, D. (2012) 'It feels more important than other classes I have done': an authentic undergraduate research experience in sociology. *Studies in Higher Education* 37 (2): 139–142

Elsen, G.M.F., Visser-Wijnveen, G.J., van der Rijst, R.M. and van Driel, J.H. (2009) How to strengthen the connection between research and teaching in undergraduate university education. *Higher Education Quarterly* 63 (1): 64–85

Feldman, K.A. (1987) Research productivity and scholarly accomplishment of college teachers as related to their instructional effectiveness: a review and exploration. *Research in Higher Education* 26 (3): 227–298

Hattie, J. and Marsh, H.W. (1996) The relationship between research and teaching: a meta-analysis. *Review of Educational Research* 66 (4): 507–42

Healey, M. and Jenkins, A. (2009) *Developing Undergraduate Research and Inquiry.* York, UK: Higher Education Academy

Hensel, N. (2012) *Characteristics of Excellence in Undergraduate Research (COEUR).* Washington, DC: Council on Undergraduate Research

Hutchings, P. (ed.) (2002) *Ethics of Inquiry: Issues in the Scholarship of Teaching and Learning.* Menlo Park, CA: Carnegie Publications

Hutchings, P. and Shulman, L. (1999) The scholarship of teaching: new elaborations, new developments. *Change* 31 (5): 10–15

Jenkins, A., Blackman, T., Lindsay, R. and Paton-Saltzberg, R. (1998) Teaching and research: student perspectives and policy implications. *Studies in Higher Education* 23 (2): 127–141

Kuh, G.D. (2008) *High-Impact Educational Practices: What They Are, Who Has Access to Them, and Why They Matter.* Washington, DC: Association of American Colleges and Universities

Laursen, S., Hunter, A-B., Seymour, E., Thiry, H. and Melton, G. (eds) (2010) *Undergraduate Research in the Sciences: Engaging Students in Real Science.* New York: Jossey-Bass

Lopatto, D. (2009) *Science in Solution: The Impact of Undergraduate Research on Student Learning.* Tucson, AZ: Research Corporation for Science Advancement

Neary, M. (2010) Student as producer: pedagogy for the avant garde. *Learning Exchange* 1 (1): 1–17

Neumann, R. (1992) Perceptions of the teaching-research nexus: a framework for analysis. *Higher Education* 23 (2): 159–171

Ramsden, P. and Moses, I. (1992) Associations between research and teaching in Australian higher education. *Higher Education* 23 (3): 273–295

Robertson, J. and Blackler, G. (2006) Students' experiences of learning in a research environment. *Higher Education Research and Development* 25 (3): 215–229

Strayhorn, T.L. (2010) Undergraduate research participation and STEM graduate degree aspirations among students of color. *New Directions for Institutional Research Special Issue: Students of Color in STEM* (48): 85–93

Willison, J. and O'Regan, K. (2007) Commonly known, commonly not known, totally unknown: a framework for students becoming researchers. *Higher Education Research and Development* 26 (4): 393–409

Zamorski, B. (2002) Research-led teaching and learning in higher education a case. *Teaching in Higher Education* 7 (4): 411–427

Chapter 14

Developing criticality in learning and teaching through pedagogical action research

Lin Norton

Introduction

For over 10 years, Roger Brown has been alerting us to the implications of reform on the higher education sector. Much of his work relates to the effects of marketisation and its impact on quality and standards (see for example, Brown, 2005, 2006, 2011; Brown with Carasso, 2013). One of his observations is that the separation of research and teaching funding has had the unfortunate and possibly unintended consequence that teaching is viewed as less prestigious:

> Research benefits more than teaching from the post-1980s emphasis on the role of higher education in contributing to economic growth and acting as the motor and vehicle for innovation.
>
> (Brown, 2010: 6)

This inevitably affects the extent to which we take a critical view of pedagogy. In this chapter, I put forward the case that one approach to counteract this potential decline is to encourage more academics to carry out action research in learning and teaching, which I term pedagogical action research (Norton, 2009). I contend that researching pedagogies not only contributes to theoretical knowledge but also compels university teachers to reflect critically and systematically on practice. In so doing, I build on Brown's assertion that when considering the impact of universities, student education should be key.

The purpose of higher education

In one of his latest works, Brown reflects on the fall of the public service model of UK higher education, giving us a careful and scholarly analysis of the way that UK higher education has developed since the 1990s (Brown with Carasso, 2013). He has described some of the main features of this UK reform in a *Higher Education Policy Institute Occasional Report*:

- An overall reduction in the public resources going into higher education
- A shift to a voucher system for funding teaching, so that for most subjects the only income institutions receive is the student fee

- The nearly threefold increase in the level of the full-time undergraduate course fee
- Competition on fees, fee waivers and bursaries and scholarships between providers
- A substantial deregulation of funded places
- The lowering of the barriers to market entry for new providers (and the exit of some existing ones)
- A number of moves to strengthen the role of students as consumers, supported by greatly increased information about institutions and courses

(McClaran and Brown, 2013: 8)

This last feature, which positions the student as consumer, links with the public demand for accountability in terms of quality of provision and the maintaining of standards. Somewhat paradoxically it could be argued that the combined forces of marketisation and quality assurance of higher education are actually damaging pedagogy. Although this has possibly had the biggest effect in the UK, similar situations face many other countries such as the US (Geiger, 2011), Australia (McCaig, 2011) and parts of Europe (Dobbins, Knill and Vögtle, 2011). At the very heart of this concern is the question as to what we believe the purpose of higher education to be? Students and their parents expect the cost of a university degree to be recompensed in the form of improved chances in the labour market. This employability drive has led to an emphasis on designing curricula that focus on graduate skills where pedagogies such as work-based learning, problem-based learning and skills acquisition take priority over more liberal-inspired values such as knowledge, wisdom and criticality. Williams (2012) makes the point that it is not just paying tuition fees that have positioned the student as consumer, it is also a result of political and educational shifts. The fact that pedagogy has been for some years powerfully moving against the transmission of knowledge to student-centred, experiential learning has perhaps had the unforeseen effect of conceptualising education itself as more instrumental.

The whole purpose of university education is constantly shifting and at present, the indications are that universities are rapidly becoming training grounds for employment rather than seats of learning. In the US, for example, the trend in liberal arts colleges has for the last 200 years been on character development, but increasingly the trend is towards career development (Altbach *et al.*, 2011). John Henry Newman in the late 1850s referred to university education as 'training of the intellect' (Newman, 1852), but few of today's students enter university for the intellectual experience (National Union of Students Experience Report, 2008). As Brown indicates, the pressure on students to get what they perceive as value for the money they pay for their degrees is understandable and might induce university teachers into providing what students appear to want. In the UK, we have seen the effect of such demands in the student call for more and better feedback. This has been a driver that has had a recognised effect as shown in the increasing measures of satisfaction in the National Student Survey (NSS,

Higher Education Funding Council for England, 2005–2013). Giving students better feedback can be defended pedagogically, but problems arise when student demands are in conflict with what we mean by higher learning, for example students who want their work to be easier. Yorke and Longden (2008) in a survey of over 6,000 higher education students found that a third of them reported that academic work was harder than they thought it would be. Hoeft (2012) found that the most frequently given reason for not complying with reading assignments was that students said they were too busy. Students may believe that they are not getting value for money when required to learn in ways that are pedagogically sound but require hard work. When measures such as the NSS have such profound implications for university success in terms of league tables, pedagogical values are continually threatened and academics may find it hard to resist students' expectations.

Teaching and learning in today's universities

It is easy in today's HE system to get demoralised by the forces that are pushing academics this way and that. In writing about the changes in the UK, the US, Australia and New Zealand, Fitzgerald (2014: xvi) says 'the nature of the academy, and what it means to be an academic, and undertake academic work, has also changed'. Most academics come into higher education as a result of their passion for their subject, a thirst to create and advance knowledge through research and their wish to pass it on; most are genuinely concerned that the student experience should be good, and some identify teaching as the main purpose of their role. However, they work in places where there is a necessity for institutions to make sure they stay afloat financially. This inevitably means that prioritisation of workload occurs.

Professionals who work in the higher education sector could perhaps be forgiven if they felt overwhelmed and paralysed by forces beyond their control. Seligman (1972) called this phenomenon 'learned helplessness', by which he means that people no longer try to escape from what they perceive to be negative situations, because past experience has taught them that they are powerless to change such events. In other words, the temptation is to think that there is nothing that the individual academic can do. My argument is that this is far from the case, but we need to think in terms of 'wriggle room' for those academics who prioritise learning and teaching and the student experience.

The first step is to reflect on the microlevel of practice, and at the level of individual beliefs. To do this, more criticality needs to be introduced in the way teaching and assessment practice are considered. Student satisfaction with the quality of their courses remains high in the UK (NSS, 2014) but satisfaction is not the only important measure; actual experience should also be noted. In the recent Higher Education Academy-Higher Education Policy Institute (HEA-HEPI) student academic experience survey of 2014, which involved over 15,000 students from all year groups across the UK, one of the questions asked of students was whether they felt their academic experiences had been better or worse than expected; 27 per cent said better, 50 per cent said better in some ways and worse in others and 12 per cent said it had been worse. When asked why their experience had been worse, 36 per cent said that they had not put enough effort into their studies, although worryingly, 27 per cent said that the teaching quality was worse than they had expected (Soilemetzidis *et al.*, 2014). Teaching quality can be defined in many different ways but is generally considered to be a mix of craft, skills, experience and subject knowledge based on research. More controversially, teaching quality should be enhanced by pedagogical knowledge, pedagogical research and reflective practice.

Pedagogical research is essentially research on learning and teaching but it is a vague term and can be linked to other types of research such as action research, teacher research, Scholarship of Teaching and Learning (SoTL) research, practitioner/professional research. Much of it has been influenced by education and the social sciences, particularly psychology, as regards research methods and approaches, but the philosophy and sociology of education also have contributions to make. In addition, the effect of the disciplines has influenced pedagogy and thereby pedagogical research:

> Pedagogical research is at its best when it assesses current practice, justifies good practice, looks in detail at teaching and seeks to find out how students actually learn successfully.
>
> (Reid, 2006: 5)

Pedagogical research in its widest sense could be used as a defence against overt marketisation of higher education, where empirical evidence might show deleterious effects of the current policies being enacted. An example of this might be the negative effect of large classes (see Gibbs, 2010), but either enough research has not yet been done to influence policy, or it has been ignored. Teichler (2013) points out the relatively minimal influence that higher education researchers in Europe have on those who determine policy and who claim to be experts on higher education. Brown puts it rather more chillingly when he refers to the marketisation of universities as:

> A real-time experiment which is being implemented without any control or fall-back position despite widespread evidence from the UK and elsewhere that an economic government controlled system limits the effectiveness, efficiency and fairness of a higher education system.
>
> (Brown with Carasso, 2013: 179)

The stark issue that faces us is how to increase the impact of pedagogical research on policy-makers in higher education.

The scholarship of teaching and learning

Linked to pedagogical research, the Scholarship of Teaching and Learning (SoTL) has steadily been gaining influence since Boyer's (1990) concept of the Scholarship of Teaching, which was later developed by the Carnegie Foundation for the Advancement of Teaching. While originally embraced in the US, the SoTL movement (Hutchings *et al.*, 2011) has been influential in many other countries, most notably Canada, the UK and Australia. However, it has not been without its critics. One of the barriers to a more widespread acceptance of SoTL might lie in the vagueness of its definition. Healey (2003) did valuable work more than a decade ago on academics' understandings of SoTL. He found that 75 per cent of a sample of seventy-seven respondents agreed with a statement based on the work of Martin *et al.* (1999) that:

> The scholarship of teaching involves three essential and integrated elements: engagement with the scholarly contributions of others on teaching and learning; reflection on one's own teaching practice and the learning of students within the context of a particular discipline; and communication and dissemination of aspects of practice and theoretical ideas about teaching and learning in general and teaching and learning within the discipline.
>
> (Healey, 2003: 5)

The ongoing debate about SoTL and its relationship to pedagogical research remains unclear. Kreber (2013: 857) 'challenges narrow interpretations of SoTL as evidence-based practice' although Gurung and Schwartz (2009) argue very strongly for the benefits of pedagogical research. They claim that in the US more departments are counting pedagogical research publications in decisions about tenure and promotion, although they acknowledge this is not universal. In the UK, the situation does not appear to be very different; the Higher Education Academy and the GENIE Centre for Excellence in Teaching and Learning (GENIE, 2009) report that in their survey of 104 higher education institutions, promotion criteria based on teaching were inconsistent, not always applied and 'often absent'. Another difficulty with pedagogical research, particularly practitioner or action research, is that it can be seen as lacking in rigour, and amateurish if carried out by academics in their own teaching contexts; however, to suggest this is to misunderstand its approaches, purposes and goals:

> Pedagogical research is important for helping us to better understand good learning and teaching practice and look for ways to improve it. It has a rightful place in the higher education sector but its status as legitimate research needs to be raised
>
> (Norton, 2014: 12)

Action research

In considering whether there is value in encouraging more academics to carry out pedagogical research, my argument draws on issues relating to the research-teaching nexus (see Jenkins and Healey in this volume, Chapter 15), but my focus is on action research in the university context, specifically on our students' learning experience and performance and our teaching and assessment practice. I contend that this form of research not only contributes to theoretical knowledge in pedagogy but also encourages university teachers to reflect critically and systematically on what they do when they teach. In so doing, I build on Roger Brown's assertion that when considering the impact of universities, student education should be key. Clearly being a reflective university teacher is a desirable asset (Brockbank and McGill, 2007; Cowan, 2006; Sotto, 2007) but on its own, it is unlikely to make a substantial difference. Introspective reflection is a weak process if it simply serves to confirm our assumptions rather than to challenge them. Only when we seek to disseminate and open up our reflective practice to others (either through peer-observation, professional learning dialogues or in research through peer-review) can these sometimes barely conscious assumptions be interrogated. In this sense, the reflective practitioner model alone is unable to demonstrate pedagogical effectiveness; this has sometimes led in the past to 'show and tell' presentations of a learning and teaching innovation where often the only indicator of effectiveness has been some measure of student satisfaction.

Because of its focus on changing and improving practice (Tripp, 2005; Whitehead and McNiff, 2006), action research in education is a specific form of research that may outperform other types of pedagogical research in terms of potential benefits to learning and teaching. Action research in education has been influenced in the UK by Stenhouse who argued that 'curriculum research and development ought to belong to the teacher' and that 'teachers should study their own work' (Stenhouse, 1975: 142). This British tradition of educational action research, albeit with school teachers, was given further impetus by the work of Carr and Kemmis (1986), who critiqued educational research because of its failure to relate to practice. Their alternative was critical educational science that could impact on practice through what they called emancipatory action research. This approach was based on the concept of a critical social science, by Jurgen Habermas in the 1970s. Habermas (1971) was concerned with processes involved in developing knowledge and challenged empirical analytical enquiry.

The other main tradition of action research has been more political and engaged with social justice. In pedagogical action research, both traditions of action research should be brought together. By carrying out pedagogical action research, the investigators, who may be lecturers or any other professionals concerned with university education, have an avowed aim of improving practice and may also have a political agenda (Norton, 2009). In higher education such a political agenda is taken to mean breaking with conventional pedagogical practices that frequently go unchallenged. An example in the UK is the external examiner system, which is held up as the guarantor of comparability between universities and the safeguarding of standards. External examiners in the UK are generally appointed for their subject expertise rather than for any specific pedagogical expertise:

> The most effective way of becoming an external examiner is through networking with discipline colleagues at conferences and meetings or through links developed in research and teaching.
>
> (Higher Education Academy, 2012: 2)

Action research with a more political agenda would enable academics to challenge the status quo as in the example just given. It also encourages the researcher to look closely at differing discipline-specific pedagogies (see Kreber, 2005 for a detailed analysis of how academic disciplines have influenced teaching and learning). Shulman (2005) introduced the term signature pedagogies, and there has been an enthusiastic movement to engage in discipline- specific pedagogical research, but caution must be exercised to ensure that the benefits of interdisciplinarity are not lost. There is much that academics can learn from disciplines other than their own so establishing discipline-based silos would be a pity. In a similar vein, to eschew the benefits that generic pedagogical research can provide would be to diminish the potential influence that pedagogical research can have on improving students' educational experience (Norton, 2014).

Potential and limitations of action research

If academics are to stand up against those forces of marketisation and instrumentalism which affect the quality of learning and teaching, they can as individuals choose to either comply or resist. My argument has been that pedagogical action research helps us to resist because its goal is to actively seek to refresh and energise teaching. In this type of research, we are required to reflect more broadly on the purpose of higher education by locating ourselves, our identities and values in the discipline, in the department, in the institution and in the higher education sector overall, where change is inevitable and can at times feel overwhelming. In so doing, pedagogical action research promotes the primacy of good teaching, and uses empirically based research to influence or, at the very least, inform policy-makers.

Pedagogical action research, however, is not without its critics. Because it is a non-linear process, it has links with complexity theory (Phelps and Hase, 2002) and does not follow the scientific paradigm of tightly controlling variables to ascertain cause and effect. Biesta (2007) states that the call for causality is dominant in educational research and yet, given the complexity of the student-teacher discipline-learning material interaction, establishing cause and effect is highly problematic. It is difficult therefore for those who situate themselves in the scientific paradigm to accept the 'messy' complexity of action research in which research and changing practice go hand-in-hand and happen at the same time. Like all types of research, it is important that pedagogical action research adheres to the criteria of rigour and authenticity rather than to the positivist criterion of generalisability. The acid test is whether reasonably minded professionals in the same area would be persuaded that the findings have something important to contribute to their own practice and context.

Conclusion

In writing this chapter, I have been influenced by many of Brown's writings and presentations, in particular his analysis of the effects of higher education policy on the student experience, which is fundamentally connected to the processes and practices of learning and teaching. Given that higher education encourages criticality in knowledge creation and dissemination, I have argued that the same level of criticality should also be applied to our thinking about pedagogy. All too often, education, at all levels, is swayed by the latest trend – currently, for example, we are persuaded that constructivism in learning is key and assessment for learning is crucial. We need to question these concepts and principles through a scholarly approach by reading the appropriate pedagogical literature and by looking for empirical evidence. For academics who are interested in critiquing and reflecting on their own teaching and assessment practice, pedagogical action research can be a powerful process. Rather than learned helplessness in the face of government, institutional and subject demands, there is much that the individual academic can do in response to the warnings that Roger Brown has formulated.

Bibliography

Altbach, P. G., Gumport, P. J., and Berdahl, R. O. (eds) (2011) *American Higher Education in the Twenty-First Century: Social, Political and Economic Challenges.* Baltimore, MD: The Johns Hopkins University Press, 3rd edition

Biesta, G.J.J. (2007) Bridging the gap between educational research and educational practice: The need for critical distance. *Educational Research and Evaluation* 13 (3): 295–301

Boyer, E. L. (1990) *Scholarship Reconsidered: Priorities of the Professoriate.* Princeton, NJ: Carnegie Foundation for the Advancement of Teaching

Brockbank, A. and McGill, I. (2007) *Facilitating Reflective Learning in Higher Education.* Buckingham: The Society for Research into Higher Education and Open University Press

Brown, R. (2005) Education, education, education – but will government policies produce 'an excellent higher education system'? *Higher Education Review* 38 (1): 3–31

Brown, R. (2006) *Higher Education and the Market: Further Thoughts and Reflections.* Oxford Centre for Higher Education Policy Studies, Occasional Paper Number 24

Brown, R. (2010) Research informed teaching or inquiry based education? *PRIME Pedagogical Research in Maximising Education* 4 (1): 3–19

Brown, R. (ed.) (2011) *Higher Education and the Market.* London: Routledge

Brown, R. with Carasso, H. (2013) *Everything for Sale? The Marketisation of UK Higher Education.* London: Routledge and the Society for Research into Higher Education

Carr, W. and Kemmis, S. (1986) *Becoming Critical Education, Knowledge and Action Research.* London: RoutledgeFalmer

Cowan, J. (2006) *On Becoming an Innovative University Teacher: Reflection in Action.* Milton Keynes: Open University Press, 2nd edition

Dobbins, M., Knill, C. and Vögtle, E. M. (2011) An analytical framework for the cross-country comparison of higher education governance. *Higher Education* (62) 5: 665–683

Fitzgerald, T. (ed.) (2014) *Advancing Knowledge in Higher Education: Universities in Turbulent Times.* Hershey, PA: ICI Global

Geiger, M. (2011) Markets and the End of the Current Era in US Higher Education. In P. N. Teixeira and D. D. Dill (eds) *Public Vices, Private Virtues? Assessing the Effects of Marketization in Higher Education.* Rotterdam: Sense Publishers: 3–18

GENIE (2009) Higher Education Academy and the Genetics Education Networking for Innovation and Excellence (GENIE) CETL University of Leicester. *Reward and Recognition in Higher Education: Institutional Policies and Their Implementation.* York: Higher Education Academy

Gibbs, G. (2010) *Dimensions of Quality.* York: The Higher Education Academy

Gurung, R.A.R. and Schwartz, B. M. (2009) *Optimizing Teaching and Learning. Practising Pedagogical Research.* Chichester: Wiley-Blackwell

Habermas, J. (1971) *Knowledge and Human Interests* (trans. J. J. Shapiro). London: Heinemann

Healey, M. (2003) The Scholarship of Teaching: An Evolving Idea. York: The Higher Education Academy [online]

Higher Education Academy (2012) *A Handbook for External Examining.* York: Higher Education Academy

Higher Education Funding Council for England (HEFCE) (2014) *UK Review of the Provision of Information About Higher Education: National Student Survey Results and Trends Analysis 2005–2013.* HEFCE

Hoeft, M.E. (2012) Why university students don't read: what professors can do to increase compliance. *International Journal for the Scholarship of Teaching and Learning* 6 (2): Article 12

Hutchings, P., Huber, M. T. and Ciccone, A. (2011) *The Scholarship of Teaching and Learning Reconsidered: Institutional Integration and Impact.* San Francisco: Jossey-Bass

Kreber, C. (ed.) (2005) *The University and its Disciplines: Teaching and Learning Within and Beyond Disciplinary Boundaries.* London: Routledge

Kreber, C. (2013) Empowering the scholarship of teaching: an Arendtian and critical perspective. *Studies in Higher Education* 38 (6): 857–869

Martin, E., Benjamin, J., Prosser, M. and Trigwell, K. (1999) Scholarship of Teaching: A Study of the Approaches of Academic Staff. In C. Rust (ed.) *Improving Student Learning: Improving Student Learning Outcomes.* Oxford: Oxford Centre for Staff and Learning Development, Oxford Brookes University: 326–331

McCaig, C. (2011) Trajectories of higher education system differentiation: structural policy-making and the impact of tuition fees in England and Australia. *Journal of Education and Work* 24 (1–2): 7–25

McClaran, A. and Brown, R. (2013) *HEPI (Higher Education Policy Institute) Occasional Report (6): New arrangements for Quality Assurance in Higher Education.* [online] Available at: http://www.hepi.ac.uk/2013/05/02/new-arrangements-for-quality-assurance-in-higher education-2/ [accessed 4 January 2015]

McNiff, J. and Whitehead, J. (2006) *All You Need to Know About Action Research.* London: Sage

National Student Survey (2014) NSS results. [online] Available from http://www.hefce.ac.uk/lt/nss/results/2014/ [accessed 11 August 2015]

National Union of Students (2008) *NUS student experience report.* Available at: http://www.nus.org.uk/PageFiles/350/NUS_StudentExperienceReport.pdf [accessed 4 January 2015]

Newman, J. H. (1852) *The Idea of a University.* National Institute for Newman Studies (2007) *The Idea of a University (1852 and 1858/1873) Part I.* Available at: http://www.newmanreader.org/works/idea/discourse7.html [accessed 4 January 2015]

Norton, L. S. (2009) *Action Research in Teaching and Learning: A Practical Guide to Conducting Pedagogical Research in Universities.* London: Routledge

Norton, L. (2014) Legitimising pedagogical research in universities: raising the quality. *Journal of Academic Development and Education* 1 (1): 5–14

Phelps, R. and Hase, S. (2002) Complexity and action research: exploring the theoretical and methodological connection. *Educational Action Research* 10 (3): 507–524

Reid, N. (2006) *Getting Started in Pedagogical Research in the Physical Sciences. A Physical Science Practice Guide.* York: Higher Education Academy

Seligman, M.E. (1972) Learned helplessness. *Annual Review of Medicine* 23: 207–412

Shulman, L. (2005) Signature pedagogies in the professions. *Daedalus* 134 (3): 52–59

Soilemetzidis, I., Bennett, P., Buckley, A., Hillman, N. and Stoakes, G. (2014) *The HEPI–HEA Student Academic Experience Survey 2014.* York: Higher Education Academy

Sotto, E. (2007) *When Teaching Becomes Learning: A Theory and Practice of Teaching.* London: Continuum International Publishing Group (2nd ed.)

Stenhouse, L. (1975) *An Introduction to Curriculum Research and Development.* London: Heinemann

Teichler, U. (2013) Academically ambitious and relevant higher education research: the legacy of the Consortium of Higher Education Researchers. *European Journal of Higher Education* 3 (3): 242–254

Tripp, D. (2005) Action research: a methodological introduction. *Educacao e Pesquisa* [Education and Research] 31 (3): 443–466

Whitehead, J. and McNiff, J. (2006) *Action Research: Living Theory.* London: Sage

Williams, J. (2012) *Consuming Higher Education: Why Learning Can't Be Bought.* London: Bloomsbury Academic

Yorke, M. and Longden, B. (2008) *The First Year Experience of Higher Education in the UK.* York: Higher Education Academy

Chapter 15

Reshaping understandings, practices and policies to enhance the links between teaching and research

Alan Jenkins and Mick Healey

> *'Universities should treat learning as not yet wholly solved problems and hence always in research mode.'*
>
> (Humboldt, 1810 translated 1970, quoted in Elton, 2005: 110)

The changing international context of higher education

The marketisation of universities needs to be seen in the context of major changes in international higher education. The expansion of higher education has led to a questioning of the traditional Humboldtian conception of the university as an institution where teaching and research are interrelated. Other developments include the problem of meeting the costs of expansion, and in many national systems the concentration of research funding in a limited number of high level research-focused universities. Such developments question the long prevailing view that effective teaching needs to be underpinned by an institutional environment where most staff are involved in research.

For example, in 2000, Howard Newby, then President of Universities UK, and soon to be Chief Executive of the Higher Education Funding Council for England (HEFCE), spoke at an early meeting organised by Roger Brown of what would become the Research and Teaching Forum. The report of the meeting states:

> [. . .] the effect of massification [is] requiring *HE to move away from a position as part of the publicly funded service economy to make an important contribution to the 'productive economy'.* [. . .] Even the notion of the university is caught up in this change [. . .] in particular to the links between teaching and research. As such it will require *greater clarity about the benefits the link brings.* [. . .] In the context of the UK, Newby contended that [. . .] the expansion towards a mass system meant that *funds are no longer adequate to support the increased population of staff to be involved in both research and teaching*
>
> (Southampton Institute, 2000: 7; emphasis added)

We explore in this chapter the role played by what became known as the *Research and Teaching Forum* – which we use as an umbrella term that refers to the series of initiatives Roger Brown launched and led between 1998 and 2009. Here we focus on the impact of disciplinary research on teaching. We were both centrally involved in the Forum during that decade as Steering Group members and as participants in its events. A related discussion of the Forum (under the name of R & T Group) is given by D'Andrea in Chapter 16 in this volume.

Developing international understanding of links between teaching and research

In the early years of the Forum, whenever the issue of whether the research evidence validated the Humboldtian conception of the university as an institution where teaching and research are interrelated, the dominant discussion revolved around whether to be an effective university teacher one also needed to be an effective researcher. Particularly important was the research by Hattie and Marsh which concluded that 'the common belief that teaching and research were inextricably intertwined is an enduring myth. *At best teaching and research are very loosely coupled*' (1996: 529; emphasis added). This research was often cited to cast doubt on the benefit of disciplinary research to teaching. Indeed the 2003 UK white paper (Department for Education and Skills, 2003) used this research to justify the development of what came to be informally called 'teaching-only' or 'teaching-intensive universities'. However, Hattie and Marsh in a later paper for the Forum's Marwell conference, argue that:

> The greatest misinterpretation and misrepresentation of [our] overall finding is that it leads to the conclusion that research and teaching should be separated for funding purposes. . . . *The fundamental issue is what we wish the relation to be, and then we need to devise policies to enact this wish*
>
> (Hattie and Marsh, 2004: 1; emphasis added)

Other researchers (e.g. Jenkins, 2004; Jenkins *et al.*, 2007; Healey and Jenkins, 2009), many of whom presented at conferences organised by the Forum, moved the research and policy focus more to the student and staff experience of the relationships between teaching and research and how departmental, institutional and national cultures and policies shape these relations. For example, a study at the University of East Anglia in the UK, found that:

> While students value being close to research, and to the idea of a university as a research community in which they are included, there are many ways in which they feel excluded
>
> (Zamorski, 2000: 1)

In terms of reshaping institutional and national policies, a major research direction has been the analysis of how institutions conceive and shape the relations between teaching and research. These studies generally reveal that while many national systems and institutional policies espouse teaching and research as linked activities, in practice the policies conceive and deliver them as separate activities (Coate *et al.*, 2001). For those who value students learning in a research environment, there has recently been a wide range of studies showing the positive impact on students' learning of various forms of inquiry or research-based learning. For example, Justice *et al.* (2007) have shown that a first year inquiry course had a clear learning gain in terms of grades the students obtained on subsequent courses they took at McMaster University (Canada). Baxter-Magolda (2009) has suggested that adoption of these kinds of pedagogies speeds up the intellectual development of students towards what she calls 'self-authorship' and helping them to move from seeing knowledge as facts to seeing knowledge as contested and uncertain. This conception of university teaching is similar to Barnett's (2000) view that university teaching should seek to develop student understanding the 'supercomplexity' of knowledge.

Conceptual models and languages

One of the conclusions from the 2000 Conference was the ambition to 'develop the language concerning teaching and research in order to develop a higher order of common understanding' (Southampton Institute, 2000: 11). Griffiths (2004) provided a conceptual schema, which Healey (2005) then represented and further developed into a now widely-used model. He distinguished between research-led, research-oriented, research-based and research-tutored ways of engaging students with research and inquiry. Since then, other conceptual models have been developed (in particular Levy, 2011; Spronken-Smith and Walker, 2010; and Brew, 2013) which have supported practitioners and institutions in enhancing their curricula to link teaching and research more effectively.

Their importance lies, in part, in moving the focus of international discussions away from the research attributes of individual faculty to the student experience of the institutional research environment. These conceptual models also support course teams and institutions to develop a common language to enhance their practice. Thus, recent research in a Finnish research-intensive university revealed a 'plethora of conceptions of research-based teaching and [. . .] to enhance teaching quality [. . .] cooperation in the development of common conceptions is necessary' (Blomster *et al.*, 2014: 62).

Enhancing practice and policies

This growing body of research has supported the enhancement of international practice and policy through linking teaching and research in ways that are realistic in a context of mass higher education systems:

- It is possible, and we would argue essential, to hold on to the Humboldtian ideal; but the focus should now be on the undergraduate *student learning through their involvement in research and inquiry*

- Undergraduate students need to feel that they are central gainers from the university research environment, and for many students, perhaps particularly those in professional disciplines, they need to see how this understanding of knowledge 'supercomplexity' (Barnett, 2000) will help them in employment
- Realistically it is not possible, or perhaps even desirable, for all staff to be involved in publishing in high level research journals. What is important is that they are immersed in the scholarship of their discipline; and have a conception of teaching that focuses on developing students' understandings of knowledge complexity and students learning in research mode (Jenkins and Healey, in submission)
- Departments, institutions and national systems need to note the overwhelming research evidence that too often teaching and research strategies are not linked, and that a common pattern is for research to be separate from, and undermine the institutional focus on, teaching
- Realistically there will be significant differences between the forms of research learning possible in international research universities and in local community colleges (Jenkins and Healey, 2007; Healey *et al.*, 2014). But in all higher education institutions, effective policies and strategies can ensure that all students learn through and about research.

Such research-based understandings are now making clear impacts on practice and policies – particularly in the practice of course teams and disciplinary communities, as shown in the next section.

Reshaping course team, disciplinary and institutional practices

Over the last dozen or so years Healey and Jenkins (2014) have collected numerous practices about linking teaching and research from a wide range of disciplines, institutions and national systems, which are regularly updated. The experience of undertaking workshops and consultancies in many countries shows that faculty strongly welcome examples from their own or related disciplines, and look positively on developing student learning through research and inquiry as a central focus for improving university teaching.

However, examples of strategic practice at departmental and institutional level that address issues of progression and embedding across the curriculum are much rarer. One such is the engineering department at Taylor's University in Malaysia, which has re-organised their teaching and research strategies around key engineering challenges, as identified by the US National Academy of Engineering. Faculty research groups support student research-based learning structured through the 4-year curriculum (Al-Atabi *et al.*, 2013). An example of a strategic institutional intervention is Durham University in the UK, whose Senate (the governing body of the University) in 2011 required research-led education – understood 'as in its broadest sense encompassing all four types of research-led education' identified by Griffiths (2004) – to be embedded within the curriculum of all programmes of study in a 3-year implementation plan (Durham University, 2012).

These, and many other interventions, are strong positive developments. However, (with a few significant exceptions such as Taylor's University) these interventions are almost entirely through the 'teaching strategies' of the university. A general pattern is for the university research strategies to claim they support teaching, but they are often silent about mechanisms of implementation.

Seeking to shape national policies

University strategies and practices regarding teaching and research have long been shaped by national views of the roles of universities, and through higher education funding and governance. In the UK, national funding for teaching and research used to be allocated through block grants to institutions to shape and link the teaching and research roles of the university. This was moulded by a national perception of the interdependence of teaching and research (Committee on Higher Education, 1963).

But that was before the period of mass expansion of higher education, which shaped the separation of funding for teaching and research in the UK, and before research funding became highly competitive. This led to increasing fragmentation between what are often informally termed as 'research-intensive' and 'teaching-intensive' universities; and to the further fragmentation of faculty roles between teaching and research within universities. These developments are mirrored in many national systems.

In 1963, Clark Kerr's lectures at Harvard University developed the concept of a 'multiveristy' with a fracturing between high level research universities and the rest of higher education, and inside universities between faculty teaching and research roles (Kerr, 2001; Marginson, 2008). Such developments and the increased insistent focus on national and global rankings, which really only value high level and commercially driven research productivity, explain both the devaluing of teaching and its fractured relationship with research in most institutional strategies. Yet there have been important national strategies that seek to reshape the Humboldtian vision of effective links between the roles of teaching and research including:

- *In the US*, in the 1990s the National Science Foundation (NSF) reviewed all its grant procedures to ensure undergraduate and postgraduate students being included in funding research projects. The NSF has since developed a range of initiatives to develop undergraduate research throughout US higher education, including in community colleges (NSF, 2006)
- *In New Zealand*, in 2000–2001 the Academic Audit Unit reviewed all universities for their effectiveness in linking teaching and research
- *In England*, in 2006 HEFCE allocated £40 million through the Research-Informed Teaching Fund to institutions to develop research-informed

teaching environments, with funds allocated inversely proportional to an institution's research funding
- *In Scotland*, in 2006–08 Scotland's Quality Assurance Agency supported national disciplinary groups and institutions to enhance teaching and research links (Land, 2013). This project revealed much good practice and succeeding in disseminating that practice, and to an extent embedding it, in revised departmental and institutional policies
- *In Germany*, in 2006 the German Research Council affirmed that research-based learning is essential to every kind of scientific programme of studies. In 2010, the German central government and state authorities announced large scale funding to improve undergraduate teaching with many of the institutional projects – including that at Humboldt University Berlin – focused on varied forms of research-based learning (Deike *et al.*, 2014).

These selected examples demonstrate a range of strategies from funding to quality assurance that national systems can employ *if* they value the potential interconnections between teaching and research.

The Forum's impact on UK national policies

The Forum, led by Roger Brown's vision and his links with many national and international agencies, sought to shape UK national policies. His contacts and understanding of how UK policies are shaped enabled members of the group to meet with the then Minister of Education, Charles Clarke, in 2006. Liz Beaty, then Director of Learning and Teaching for HEFCE, stated at one of the Forum's events that this meeting was central to the establishment of the Research-Informed Teaching Fund (see above). Members of the Forum were also significant in leading on a range of disciplinary and institutional funded projects, as well as publications funded by the UK Higher Education Academy (HEA) that also enhanced practice and policy internationally.

However, there are still areas where, as yet, little progress has been made. Particularly problematic have been the attempts to shape UK *research* policies. The Forum reached out to include the perspective of researchers and policy-makers who had been involved in the US undergraduate research movement. This resulted in a conference in November 2006, organised by the HEA and the Research Councils UK Executive Group – and which included Rosemary Haggett, then a central leader at the US NSF (HEA, 2006). While Ian Diamond, then chief executive of the UK Research Councils, participated at the meeting, it was unfortunately not followed-up by any significant initiatives by UK research councils to support the agenda.

In the UK, as elsewhere internationally, research funding is now highly selective and focused on internationally recognised research, in part because in a market environment high level research is increasingly seen as important to economic growth. But even in this context, one can ask how this research benefits under-graduate students' learning (Gibbs, 2014). Otherwise, why focus research fund-ing on universities? Members of the Forum saw the decisions in 2006–2007 to reshape the Research Assessment Exercise (RAE) to focus on research dissemina-tion as an opportunity to intervene. Again, Roger Brown's knowledge and con-tacts resulted in a meeting, this time with David Sweeney, then the Director of Research for HEFCE and centrally responsible for designing the revised research funding framework. The submitted paper argued that the Research and Teaching Forum:

> [. . .] recognises that dissemination is a longstanding weakness of UK research. Given that a high proportion of UK research will continue to take place in universities, the group believes that the impact on student learning should be a major criterion in future assessments.
>
> (Research and Teaching Forum, 2006)

Although the atmosphere at the meeting was very supportive, the final deci-sion was to exclude the impact of research on teaching. This policy has continued through subsequent revisions of the UK RAE, as Brown stated in relation to the re-named Research Excellence Framework (REF):

> [. . .] the only kind of impact excluded from the forthcoming REF is the impact on student learning in the department and institution where the research takes place.
>
> What better evidence could we have of the way in which UK policies on research continue to be oblivious to its interaction with teaching, even though the potential benefits to student education are the only justification for conducting research in universities in the first place?
>
> (Brown, 2010)

It is arguable that with the increase in student fees in England to a maximum of £9,000 in 2012, pressures on value for money may force universities to make more explicit and productive links between education and research so as to justify the cross-subsidies, especially from overseas students' fees, to staff research. For example, Michael Arthur, President and Provost University College London in the UK, recently stated that:

> At University College London, our top strategic priority for the next 20 years is to close the divide between teaching and research. We want to integrate research into every stage of an undergraduate degree, moving from research-led to research-based teaching.
>
> (Arthur, 2014: 22)

Conclusion

In the introduction to this chapter we cited a report on a speech given by Howard Newby in 2000, at a meeting of what later became the Research and Teaching Forum. He is reported as stating that changes in the international higher education system are impacting on the 'notion of a university' and of the relationship between teaching and research he stated that 'it will require *greater clarity about the benefits the link brings* [. . .] *The continuance of some form of funding* [. . .] *might depend on how important this relationship is shown to be*' (Southampton Institute, 2000: 7, emphasis added). We argue, from the evidence presented in this chapter, that the work of the Forum (and related interventions internationally) has demonstrated both the potential benefits to students of joining teaching and research, and how that could be achieved in a mass higher education system.

More problematic in affirming the importance of linking teaching and research is Newby's reported view that: 'the effect of massification [is] requiring higher education to move away from a position as part of the publicly funded service economy to make an important contribution to the "productive economy"' (Southampton Institute, 2000: 7).

One needs to ask whether this threatens the concept of a university as a place where teaching and research are both present and connected. A focus on the university as directly contributing to the productive economy links education to the marketisation agenda. Internationally, research is increasingly economy-oriented, and supported by economy-focused funding briefs, with very little regard for any potential impact on students. Faculty find many students wanting to ensure that spending on their higher education will help their employment, but a focus on them learning through research, as illustrated in this chapter, may not seem an important option, still less a requirement. While marketisation may support selected students wanting to learn in a research environment – that may in fact be restricted to those with parents who can pay the high fees to enter those institutions, such as the private US liberal arts undergraduate institutions. The information provided to parents and students in this market environment effectively sells them measures of student satisfaction and institutional prestige – not the potential benefits of research-based learning.

We concur with Brown's (2013) view of the dangers of such a market environment and see the way forward in national system-wide interventions such as:

1   Making the link a legal or semi-legal requirement for institutions
2   Introducing the link as one of the key criteria for research funding
3   Auditing the link through quality assurance;
4   Promoting research/teaching linkages through targeted initiatives.

In this chapter, and in the publications cited, we now have good examples of international practice and policy that show how this can be achieved. But whether through a market system or a government-funded regulated system, there is perhaps a more fundamental way forward. That is to affirm the distinctive values of higher education in moving students towards the complexities of knowledge and developing university students' learning through and about research. Marginson has argued that we need to reach back before Humboldt to Newman, citing his view that the purpose of higher education is 'an acquired illumination, a habit, a personal possession, and an inward endowment' (Marginson, 2008: 2). Alternatively, we would go back to Humboldt and value higher education institutions where teaching and research are linked, and see that connection in students learning the complexities of knowledge (Barnett, 2000; Baxter Magolda, 2009). In the final analysis it is not about markets or governments; it is about *values*.

Bibliography

Al-Atabi, M., Shamel, M. and Lim, X. (2013) A blueprint for research-led teaching at engineering schools: a case study of Taylor's university. *Journal of Engineering Science and Technology. Special Issue on Engineering Education*: 38–45

Arthur, M. (2014) From research-led to research-based teaching. *Research Fortnight* 30 April. Available at: http://www.researchresearch.com/index.php?option=com_news&template=rr_2col&view=article&articleId=1343435 [accessed 16 September 2014]

Barnett, R. (2000) Supercomplexity and the curriculum. *Studies in Higher Education* 25 (3): 255–265

Baxter Magolda, M. B. (2009) Educating for Self-Authorship: Learning Partnerships to Achieve Complex Outcomes. In C. Kreber (ed.) *The University and its Disciplines: Teaching and Learning Within and Beyond Disciplinary Boundaries*. New York: Routledge: 143–156

Blomster J., Venn, S. and Virtanen, V. (2014) Towards developing a common conception of research–based teaching and learning in an academic community. *Higher Education Studies* 4 (4): 62–75

Brew, A. (2013) Understanding the scope of undergraduate research: a framework for curricular and pedagogical decision-making. *Higher Education* 66: 603–618

Brown, R. (2010) The only impact worth having. *Times Higher Education* 22 April 2010. Available at: http://www.timeshighereducation.co.uk/comment/letters/only-impact-worth-having/411339.article [accessed 16 September 2014]

Brown, R. with Carasso, H. (2013) *Everything for Sale? The Marketisation of UK Higher Education*. London: Routledge and the Society for Research into Higher Education

Coate, K., Barnett, R. and Williams, G. (2001) Relationships between teaching and research in higher education in England. *Higher Education Quarterly* 55 (2): 158–174

Deike, W., Gess, C. and Rue, J. (2014) Increasing students' research interests through research-based learning at Humboldt University. *CUR Quarterly* 35 (1): 27–33

Department for Education and Skills (2003) *The Future of Higher Education*. Norwich: The Stationary Office. Available at: http://www.educationengland.org.uk/documents/pdfs/2003-white-paper-higher-ed.pdf [accessed 16 September 2014]

Durham University (2012) *Learning and Teaching Handbook*. Section 4.5. Available at: https://www.dur.ac.uk/learningandteaching.handbook/4/4/5/ [accessed 16 September 2014]

Elton, L. (2005) Scholarship and the Research and Teaching Nexus. In R. Barnett (ed.) *Reshaping the University: New Relationships Between Research, Scholarship and Teaching*. Maidenhead: McGraw-Hill and Open University Press: 108–118

Gibbs, G. (2014) *53 Powerful Ideas All Teachers Should Know About: 17 Research Can Help Student Learning*. Available: http://www.seda.ac.uk/publications.html?p=5_6 [accessed 16 September 2014]

Griffiths, R. (2004) Knowledge production and the research-teaching nexus: the case of the built environment disciplines. *Studies in Higher Education* 29 (6): 709–726

Haggett, R. (2006) The US National Science Foundation: The undergraduate curriculum and undergraduate research. *Bringing research and teaching together HEA and the Research Councils UK Executive Group conference*, London, 24 November

Hattie, J. and Marsh, H. W. (1996) The relationship between research and teaching: a meta-analysis. *Review of Educational Research* 66 (4): 507–542

Hattie, J. and Marsh, H. W. (2004) One journey to unravel the relationship between research and teaching. *Research and Teaching: Closing the divide? An International Colloquium*. Winchester, March 18–19. Available at: https://cdn.auckland.ac.nz/assets/education/hattie/docs/relationship-between-research-and-teaching-%282004%29.pdf [accessed 16 September 2014]

HEA and the Research Councils UK Executive Group (2006) *Bringing Research and Teaching Together Conference* 24 November, London. Available at: http://scotland.heacademy.ac.uk/events/detail/2006/research_and_teaching_conference_2006 [accessed 16 September 2014]

Healey, M. (2005) Linking Research and Teaching Exploring Disciplinary Spaces and the Role of Inquiry-Based Learning. In R. Barnett (ed.) *Reshaping the University: New Relationships Between Research, Scholarship and Teaching*. Maidenhead: McGraw-Hill and Open University Press: 30–42

Healey, M. and Jenkins, A. (2009) *Developing Undergraduate Research and Inquiry*. York: Higher Education Academy

Healey, M. and Jenkins, A. (2014) *Linking Discipline-Based Research with Teaching to Benefit Student Learning Through Engaging Students in Research and Inquiry*. Howden: Healey HE Consultants

Healey, M., Jenkins, A. and Lea, J. (2014) *Developing Research-Based Curricula in College-Based Higher Education*. York: Higher Education Academy

Jenkins, A. (2004) *A Guide to the Research Evidence on Teaching-Research Relationships*. York: Higher Education Academy

Jenkins, A. and Healey, M. (2007) Critiquing Excellence: Undergraduate Research For All Students. In A. Skelton (ed.) *International Perspectives on Teaching Excellence in Higher Education*. London: Routledge: 117–132

Jenkins, A. and Healey, M. (in submission) Institutional and departmental strategies to support faculty to teach through student research and inquiry: International perspectives. *CUR Quarterly*

Jenkins, A., Healey, M. and Zetter, R. (2007) *Linking Teaching and Research in Departments and Disciplines*. York: Higher Education Academy

Justice, C., Rice, J., Warry, W. and Laurie, I. (2007) Taking inquiry makes a difference - a comparative analysis of student learning. *Journal of Excellence in College Teaching* 18 (1): 57–77

Kerr, C. (2001) *The Uses of the University*. Cambridge: Harvard University Press (first published 1963)

Land, R. (2013) Undergraduate research in Scotland: an enhancement-led approach. *CUR Quarterly* 33 (4): 35–40

Levy, P. (2011) Embedding inquiry and research into mainstream higher education: a UK perspective. *CUR Quarterly* 32 (1): 36–42

Marginson, S. (2008) *Clark Kerr and the Uses of the University*. Centre for the Study of Higher Education, University of Melbourne Seminar, 15 December. Available at: http://www.cshe.unimelb.edu.au/research/res_seminars/issues_ideas/2008/docs/ClarkKerr15Dec08.pdf [accessed 16 September 2014]

National Science Foundation (2006) *Strategic Plan: Investing in America's Future*. Arlington, VA: Virginia: National Science Foundation

Research and Teaching Forum (2006) *Response to Reform of Higher Education Research and Funding*. Submitted to David Sweeney, Director of Research for the Higher Education Funding Council for England

Southampton Institute (2000) The relationship between research and teaching in higher education: present realities, future possibilities. *Report of a seminar jointly organised by Southampton Institute and HEFCE*. Chilworth Manor, Southampton, 19–20 January

Spronken-Smith, R. A. and Walker, R. (2010) Can inquiry-based learning strengthen the links between teaching and disciplinary research? *Studies in Higher Education* 35 (6): 723–740

Zamorski, B. (2000) *Research-Led Teaching and Learning in Higher Education*. Norwich: Centre for Applied Research in Education: University of East Anglia

Engaging the international scholarly and policy community through active dialogue on the research-teaching nexus

Vaneeta D'Andrea

Introduction

The focus of this paper is on the research-teaching nexus as a higher education policy issue. Roger Brown's leadership in this area has been exceptionally visionary and has created some of the earliest dialogues between scholars concerned with exploring the relationship between research and teaching and higher education policy-makers; first in the United Kingdom (UK) and then extended to the international higher education community. In the mid-1990s Roger Brown initiated a meeting of a small group of UK scholars who were working on questions surrounding the concept of the research-teaching nexus. This group evolved into what became known as the Research and Teaching (R & T) Group. At the start of its work the R & T Group focused on the research and teaching nexus within the context of UK government higher education funding policies. Its primary purpose was to review and critique UK higher education funding policies and their impact on research and teaching, separately and together. The aim was to provide an evidence-based approach for higher education policies. The group grew from the original group of four or five to twenty in 2000, to twenty-nine in 2004 and eighty in 2007.

Brief personal history of the research-teaching divide

The concerns of members of the R & T Group surrounding the research-teaching nexus in the UK were primarily linked to the government's funding policies, which separately funded each of these areas of work in higher education. My awareness of the issue originated from my personal experience teaching in higher education in the US in the 1970s. It was further heightened at a professional lecture I attended in 1975 by the eminent academician in my field of sociology, E. K. Wilson. The lecture was entitled: *Double Standards in Sociology: Research and Teaching,* and it assessed the research-teaching divide noting that there was a serious double standard to rewarding work in these two areas, as it applied to sociology (Wilson, 1975). However, it was clear that the argument being made could be applied to any discipline in higher education in the US at that time. The issues surrounding the double standard were not about how each area of work was funded, as both disciplinary research work and the scholarship of teaching and learning (though we didn't call it that just yet) were fundable in the USA at that time. Private charitable funding for higher education was, and still is, much more available in the US. For example, at that time I was involved in the national American Sociological Association Projects on Teaching, funded both by the pharmaceutical company Eli Lilly, which focused much of its philanthropy on education, and by the National Science Foundation Fund for the Improvement of Post-secondary Education (FIPSE). This work was a discipline-based project in conjunction with the American Sociological Association (ASA), which aimed to raise the status of teaching in the discipline and to upgrade both the professional teaching skills of university educators as well as increasing the scholarship of teaching and learning in the field. A few of the outcomes, which have continued to the present, include: a consultancy group of sociologists who developed expertise in higher education teaching, known as the Departmental Resources Group, who are available at nominal cost to sociology departments and the journal *Teaching Sociology* which has since been made an official journal of the ASA.

So instead of focusing on issues of double standards around funding, the lecture focused more on the differential career rewards available for each area of work, or as Wilson noted, the two major roles played by the academic. The point was a powerful one especially to a junior academic. By implication if you chose to engage in work related to teaching and learning, whether a form of scholarship or not, then you knew you were taking a high-risk approach to advancement in your academic career. Wilson was naming the elephant in the room. Once in the UK, my understanding of the research and teaching divide broadened to include the unequal funding policies of the government. For me, this moved the research and teaching question, as Mills (1959) would have described it, from a personal trouble of status and achievement, to a public issue of differential funding of higher education activities.

History of the R & T Group activities

In the first few years that the R & T Group met, its discussions focused on what was known through research about the research-teaching nexus both in the UK and elsewhere; and what needed be done to make the two more equal partners in higher education institutions (HEIs). Over the years, its work focused primarily on responding to UK government consultations relevant to the R & T Group concerns and organising colloquia focused on engaging, an ever increasingly international group of research and teaching researchers with higher education policy-makers, in a dialogue on the key issues related to the research-teaching nexus.

Thus, in 2000, at the time of the Higher Education Funding Council's (HEFCE) Fundamental Review of Research and Funding, the R & T Group started its programmatic work in earnest. Amongst the many strands of the review is 'the relationship between teaching, research and other outputs of higher education institutions' (Brown, 2000a: 4). The R & T Group responded by organising a seminar entitled *The Relationship Between Research and Teaching in Higher Education* and by submitting a response to the Review: *HEFCE Review of Research: Response by the Research and Teaching Group* (R & T Group, 2000).

The main purpose of the seminar was:

[. . .] to consider how, why and in what circumstance teaching and research, both subject-based and pedagogical, should be linked in the context of the move towards a mass system of higher education.

(Brown, 2000a: 4)

The seminar was by invitation only and brought together UK policy-makers from HEFCE, various UK government departments and agencies with selected members of the 'research and teaching' research community. The idea behind this pairing was to create an evidence-based dialogue between the researchers and the policy-makers – a rare opportunity indeed. The format for the seminar centred on three key background papers circulated in advance and five papers tabled during the seminar which 'reviewed the research evidence about the relationship between research and teaching' (Brown, 2000a: 4). In addition to these eight papers, the seminar also considered HEFCE's Fundamental Review of Research and Funding consultation paper (see Appendix for full list of papers).

The conclusions of this first R & T Group sponsored seminar were outlined in a report of the event and included the following:

1 It was agreed that the importance of the relationship [between research and teaching] could hardly be overstated, given that it is one of the distinguishing features of higher education
2 The seminar confirmed the need for a clearer understanding of the nature of the relationship . . . [and] greater clarification of the definitions of the terms 'teaching', 'research', and 'scholarship' [. . .]
3 There was some support for the view that a key to the link was through a focus on the notion of 'learning', with the proposition that learners should be taught by those who are themselves actively engaged in learning through research and scholarship
4 The seminar had provided evidence to lead both to a clearer understanding of the importance of the issues to the future of HE (higher education) and the new set of funding and policy drivers for the future shape of the sector.

(Brown, 2000a: 4–5)

Because the dialogue between the researchers and the policy-makers was a first for most, many found the event interesting and challenging but little change was recorded by either the researchers or the policy-makers on the key issues. In fact, disappointingly, HEFCE's Review of Research (2000) notes that:

> Despite the evidence of a synergistic relationship between teaching and research, we make no recommendation about this: it would be wrong to allow teaching issues to influence the allocation of funds for research.
>
> (Brown, 2002: 29)

However, although the funding issue had not been affected by the discussions, there were more positive outcomes from two UK higher education organisations funded by the government but acting independently of it (these are known as quangos in the UK): both the Institute for Learning and Teaching (ILT) and the Quality Assurance Agency for Higher Education (QAA) took positions to support the link between research and teaching (Brown, 2002). Evidence for individual membership in the ILT would now require that academic staff could demonstrate this link between their research and teaching in their application. The QAA degree descriptors also added the expectation that graduates could demonstrate an understanding of the complexity of disciplinary knowledge and the ability to evaluate evidence and arguments among other things. (Brown, 2002). These two changes were, in my view, indicators of the shifting narrative in the UK around the teaching-research nexus that was started by the work of the R & T Group led by Roger Brown.

External events continued to provide a prompt for the work of the R & T Group. Following the publication of the UK government's white paper *The Future of Higher Education* and the *Review of Research Assessment* (the 'Roberts Report') in 2003, the R & T Group submitted two responses: (1) *Liaison with Wider Stakeholders – Response from the Research and Teaching Group* (September 10) and (2) *Review of Research Assessment: Response to Roberts Report* (September 26). It also began planning a second colloquium/seminar to be held the following year in 2004.

Interestingly, around this time, policy-makers started to publically consider issues surrounding the research-teaching nexus. I would not suggest a direct correlation with the work of the R & T Group; however, it cannot be denied that the changing narrative had been influenced by the work of this Group. For example, in 2003, the Department for Education and Skills (DfES) announced:

> We will set up a [Higher Education] Research Forum to enable the dialogue with the sector [on Research and Teaching] to continue. Sir Graeme Davies has accepted the invitation to lead this Group, which will act as a sounding board for the Ministerial Group implementing "Investing in Innovation", feeding in technical advice on the practical application of the proposals.

Beyond that the Forum will focus on two issues. The first concerns the relationship between teaching and research. A major issue for all those involved is how to distribute inevitably limited research funds in such a way as adequately to fund the sharply increased volume of research in departments rated 5 and 5*, to maintain research excellence and allow the best research to compete globally in the long term. At the same time we need to ensure that we continue to maintain a high level of teaching quality.

(T. Brown, 2003)

A student member of the R & T Group was invited to participate in this forum. The following year the forum made a proposal to the Education Department (DfES) for funding support to develop a research-informed environment in less research-intensive higher education institutions. Though not equal to the funds available for research by any means, it was an important move in the direction of acknowledging the link between research and teaching. The funding decision from DfES (December 2004) was:

> The Higher Education Research Forum was set up a year ago under the chairmanship of Sir Graeme Davies, to look into how we could more closely link teaching and research. One of its main proposals was that less research-intensive institutions should be supported in developing a research-informed teaching environment. We support the principle of this proposal and have therefore included in the attached teaching grant figures sums of £2.5/7.5/15 million over the next three financial years for this purpose.
>
> (HEFCE grant letter quoted in Jenkins and Healy, 2005)

The following year the Higher Education Academy (HEA) developed a research scheme to fund projects on research and teaching (Burton, 2005). Around this same time it was decided that administrative support for the R & T Group needed to be moved to the UK Higher Education Academy. Prior to this, the work of the group was undertaken by staff at the home universities of members of the founding group. It was thought that moving these activities to the HEA would give the group a more permanent home and an infrastructure to underpin its work. By late 2004, the transition of the R & T Group to a forum of the HEA was well underway. A message to all members of the R & T Group listserv outlined the new plans which the HEA wished to initiate. These included:

- To raise the profile of the Group and to develop new links, for example in relation to the discipline-specific work of subject centres
- Moving the Group's web pages into the new Academy web site
- Changing the name of the Group to acknowledge its relationship with the Higher Education Academy to 'The Higher Education Academy Research-Teaching Forum'

(R & T Group Listserv, 2004)

These plans were given the go-ahead by the group members as well as international participants on the listserv: 'Like the change of title – now sounds like what it actually does' (Hattie, 2005). In 2005 it officially became a 'Forum of the Higher Education Academy' and the first meeting under the auspices of the HEA was held on February 11, 2005. The R & T Group remained a forum of the HEA, with Roger Brown as Chair, until its work ended in 2007; the last meeting was held in June of that year (HEA, 2014).

R & T Group developments

Work on the first R & T Group Seminar was via a listserv started in 2000 and was a private listserv for members of the Seminar Planning Group. A combined listserv consisting of the original Planning Group and another which included others who had attended the first two seminar/colloquia had a total of fifty-nine UK and international subscribers by the time it was moved to the HEA in November 2004. This listserv had become a means of sharing communications quickly among those involved with the group and included both researchers and policy-makers. By 2004, a website was created for the purpose of offering delegates to the second seminar/colloquium the opportunity to begin discussing the papers in advance of the event itself. The third seminar/colloquium followed suit. Materials from both of these seminar websites were migrated to the HEA, however they are no longer accessible.

Each seminar/colloquium extended the reach of the dialogue and each succeeding event involved more international delegates from a wide range of countries and funding regimes. The purpose of extending the discussion in this way was to find evidence both from international research and higher education policies that would support a revised funding strategy for higher education in the UK. Unlike the 2000 conference where there was one international observer, 2004 saw an equal number of international presentations to those from the UK. In 2004, there were invited delegates representing research and teaching researchers and higher education policy-makers from Australia, Canada, Finland, Germany, Hungary, The Netherlands, New Zealand, Qatar and the US. By 2007, a 50/50 mix of the sixty invited delegates from the UK and from abroad was enshrined in the seminar organisation. The invitation to international delegates in 2007 included the following note: 'Partly as a celebration of the bicentenary of von Humboldt, and building on the success of the previous conference, we are now in the process of planning a second international conference'. Each seminar/colloquium increased the breadth and depth of the discussions. The number and range of papers considered via the seminar website prior to the seminars expanded. In 2004 and 2007, there were ten times the number considered in 2000 (see Table 16.1).

In between these events, and following the last one, the R & T Group continued to meet to share additional research outcomes on the research-teaching nexus and to respond, as a recognised group, to a variety of UK higher education

Table 16.1 Purpose and scope of R & T Group seminars

	R & T seminars: purpose statements	Number of papers considered	Outcomes	Title of seminar
2000	The main purpose of the seminar was to consider how, why and in what circumstance teaching and research, both subject-based and pedagogical, should be linked in the context of the move towards a mass system of higher education.	3	Publication of proceedings (Brown, 2000a)	The Relationship between Research and Teaching in Higher Education: Present Realities, Future Possibilities 20 & 21 January
2004	The overall purpose of the Colloquium will be to achieve a better understanding of the relationship, if any, between teaching and research in higher education, and to identify the policies that will enable that relationship to be enhanced particularly for the benefit of student learning but also for academic staff and the intellectual life of the university.	31	Groupwork summaries on issues related to: a) individual academics and b) institutional policies (D'Andrea, 2004a, b) Publication of summary report of conference and its outcomes (Brown, 2004b) Proposal to produce a book Seminar website	Research and Teaching: Closing the Gap 17–19 March
2007	Purpose • To consider what has been learned from policies that have been applied since the last International Colloquium and to evaluate what is now understood about the relationship between research and teaching on the basis of that. This will include a 'stock take' with an update on work that has been completed since then. • To consider what a future discussion of the research-teaching relationship might cover.	31	Seminar website	International Policies And Practices For Academic Enquiry – An International Colloquium 19–21 April

policy consultations. Towards the end of the first decade of the twenty-first century, the work of this group came to an end. Yet, as noted below, it has had a profound influence on higher education funding policy in the UK and the continuing debates on the research-teaching nexus worldwide.

Impact of Roger Brown's visionary approach to higher education policy

Reflecting on the work of the R & T Group, it is evident that from the start it was propelled by Roger Brown's vision and leadership. It is my view that there were three major contributions he made to the research-teaching nexus debate. These are:

1   Creating an important (if not the first) dialogue between the UK academic research community and policy-makers on funding issues related to teaching and research
2   Encouraging the engagement of UK policy-makers with international debates on both the issues of evidence in policy-making and its application to funding higher education
3   Developing a changed narrative on the research-teaching nexus that helped to shift the paradigm of inequality between the two areas of academic work, particularly in the UK.

Right from the start, the first seminar/colloquium held in 2000 was aimed at both researchers and policy-makers. This was Roger Brown's idea, and it was an important shift from each group previously only talking to and among themselves. More than a decade later, David Willetts, the then UK Minister of State for Universities and Science, emphasised the importance of this 'new' dialogue between researchers and policy-makers during the 2013 Annual Lecture of the 'Campaign for Social Science' at the Academy of Social Science.

The first R & T Group seminar had one international observer from the US. Although the focus was on the UK higher education policy review, it was felt that this process might benefit from international input. Roger Brown was in strong agreement that international input would add value to the discussions. He was instrumental in finding the resources to fund the participation of an international expert on the research-teaching nexus and continued to do so for all the other events.

Over the decade and a half that the R & T Group worked on promoting an evidence base for issues surrounding the research-teaching nexus, the narrative on higher education policy issues has changed, and the expectation that policies should be evidence-based can be seen in the language used in policy documents today. This focus is also seen more broadly in the literature on higher education that has been produced since these early R & T Group discussions began. For example, in a recent message circulated via the UK Higher Education Funding Council email newsletter, the following was noted: 'I am writing to ask for your help in HEFCE's gathering of evidence to inform future policy and funding for knowledge exchange, anticipating the need to support new government priorities and a Spending Review next year' (HEFCE, 2014).

Yes, these changes have come about from the work of members of the R & T Group individually and collectively, but most importantly from the leadership of Roger Brown whose knowledge of policy processes, ability to bring together people with conflicting points of view to engage in constructive dialogues and wide-range of colleagues from both government and higher education organisations [funded by the government but independent of it] and academe were key to achieving the outcomes of this work.

Roger Brown's capacity to bring together issues of quality assurance and enhancement, the marketisation of higher education and the link between research and teaching was, and remains, a unique contribution to higher education policy debates. Witness his many articles and books on these topics over the last decade. One example of his conceptualisation of these links is evident in his book *Quality Assurance in Higher Education: The UK Experience since 1992*. Referring to a professorial lecture he gave at the University of Surrey Roehampton in 2000, he notes that the increasing separation of teaching and research is one of the challenges for quality improvement in higher education. He further elaborates this conceptualisation by quoting from the lecture:

> One of the greatest problems with the present accountability regime is the almost entirely artificial separation between activities which go under such titles as 'teaching', 'research' and (sometimes) 'other revenue generating activities'. In reality, teaching and research (each of which in turn covers a multitude of activities) are merely aspects or dimensions of the work of academic entity – an institution, a research group, or a department – which embraces a much wider range of things than can ever be captured in such simple terms. Such separation is not only misleading but actually dangerous because it is the connections between these activities and the ways in which they are capable of reinforcing one another that distinguishes higher education from other forms of education.
>
> (Brown, 2004a: 164)

In his later work on the marketisation of higher education (Brown, 2011) he draws these three areas – quality improvement in higher education; the teaching/research nexus; and marketisation of higher education – into an integrated whole. For example, his list of the ten conditions of a healthy higher education system in this book includes the following three items:

- [. . .] There is a balance between the public and private purposes and benefits of higher education
- There is a productive and mutually beneficial relationship between the core activities of institutions: student education and academic research and scholarship

- The system is effectively regulated in the public interest so that it produces worthwhile outcomes for both internal and external stakeholders [. . .]

(Brown, 2011: 4–5)

In each and every instance he also includes a reference to the importance of research evidence-based policy and practice. Thus, as the title of this chapter suggests, Roger Brown has succeeded in engaging the international scholarly and policy community through active dialogue on the research-teaching nexus.

Bibliography

Brown, R. (2000a) The Relationship Between Research and Teaching in Higher Education: Present Realities, Future Possibilities. *Report of a seminar jointly organized by the Southampton Institute and the Higher Education Funding Council for England.* Chilworth Manor, Southampton: 19–20 January

Brown, R. (2000b) *Accountability in higher education: have we reached the end of the road? The case for a higher education audit commission.* Professorial Lecture. University of Surrey Roehampton: 24 October 2000

Brown, R. (2002) Research and teaching: repairing the damage. *Exchange* Autumn (3): 29–30

Brown, R. (2003) The Research Assessment and Funding: Proposals for the Future-The Institutional Response. London: Church House Conference Centre: June 2003

Brown, R. (2004a) *Quality Assurance in Higher Education: The UK Experience since 1992.* London: RoutledgeFalmer

Brown, R. (2004b) Research and Teaching: Closing the Divide? *Report of an International Colloquium.* Marwell Hotel, Winchester, UK: 17–19 March

Brown, R. (ed.) (2011) *Higher Education and the Market.* London: RoutledgeFalmer

Brown, T. (2003) Email To: TRGROUP-UK@JISCMAIL.AC.UK Subject: Re: *Some hope from Charles Clarke* ??? 15 December 2003

Burton, L. (2005) Email To: R and T Forum sent on behalf of Professor Roger Brown Subject: *Research And Teaching: What Else? Research Projects Scheme*, 5 January 2005

D'Andrea, V. (2004a) Group Discussion A: 'The relationship at the level of the individual staff member', *Research and Teaching: Closing the Divide? An International Colloquium.* Winchester: UK (18–19 March 2004)

D'Andrea, V. (2004b) Group Discussion B: 'The policy implications at the level of institution', *Research and Teaching: Closing the Divide? An International Colloquium.* Winchester: UK (18–19 March 2004)

Hattie, J. (2005) Email To: D'Andrea, Vaneeta v.dandrea@city.ac.uk Subject: Re: FW: *Message from the Higher Education Academy.* 13 January 2005

Higher Education Academy (2014) Personal communication. 12 November 2014

Higher Education Funding Council for England (2014) *HEFCE requests for evidence to inform policy and funding for knowledge exchange. HEFCE alerts to higher education institutions.* 11 November 2014

Jenkins, A. and Healey M. (2005) *Opportunities for HEIs to Support 'Research-Informed' Teaching* [Posting to R & T Listserv] 13 February 2005

Mills, C.W. (1959) *The Sociological Imagination.* Oxford: Oxford University Press

R & T Group (2000) *HEFCE Review of Research: Response by the Research and Teaching Group.* 11 July 2000

R & T Group (2003a) *Liaison with Wider Stakeholders: Response From the Research and Teaching Group.* 10 September 2003

R & T Group (2003b) *Review of Research Assessment: Response to Roberts Report.* 26 September 2003

R & T Group (2003c) Planning Memo. *International Conference on the Relationship between Teaching and Research.* 17 August. 2003

R & T Group (2004) Programme. *Research and Teaching: Closing the Divide? An International Colloquium*

Willetts, D. (2013) Academy of Social Science, Campaign for Social Science's Annual Lecture series, Inaugural Lecture, London, UK, 28 October 2013

Wilson, E. K. (1975) *Double standards in sociology: research and teaching.* Lecture at Emory University. Atlanta, GA, April 1975

Chapter 16 Appendix

List of papers considered at R & T seminar 2000

Papers prepared in advance

Alan Jenkins: *Summary/Review of The Research and Scholarly Evidence on Teaching/Research in Higher Education*
Mantz Yorke: *Pedagogical Research in UK Higher Education*
Lewis Elton: *Research and Teaching: Possible Future Contexts and Considerations*

Papers tabled at seminar

Alan Jenkins: *The Relationships Between Research and Teaching*
Roger Brown: *Funding and Policy Drivers*
Graham Gibbs: *Institutional and Disciplinary Diversity*
Lewis Elton: *Research and Teaching Possible Futures*
Roger Brown: *Alternative Policy and Funding Scenarios*
Source: Brown, R. (2000) *The Relationship between Research and Teaching in Higher Education: Present Realities, Future Possibilities. Report of a seminar jointly organized by the Southampton Institute and the Higher Education Funding Council for England.* Chilworth Manor, Southampton 19–20 January

Part V

Universities' futures

Chapter 17

A critical reflection on leadership in higher education

Robin Middlehurst

Introduction

In the past 3 decades, increasing emphasis has been placed on strong leadership of universities and colleges. More recently, at policy and practice levels, this has also encompassed 'performance management'. Such rhetoric is visible not only in the UK, but also in the US, Australia and continental Europe (Middlehurst and Teixeira, 2012). Promoters of strengthened leadership and management of higher education institutions (HEIs) argue that reforms of governance are needed to achieve the modernisation of universities and colleges (European Commission, 2011) in a context of competitive globalisation. Critics, however, have described these developments as creeping or even rampant 'managerialism' (Trow, 1994; Kolsaker, 2008) aligned to the political ideology of New Public Management (Exworthy and Halford, 1999; Olssen and Peters, 2005) and the economics of 'marketisation' and 'privatisation' of higher education (Bok, 2003; Brown, 2010) resulting in the erosion of collegiality and democratic decision-making. Perceptions and attitudes are frequently polarised between proponents and critics of changing higher education governance, leading to sterile debates that neither advance understanding nor practice.

This chapter is an attempt to challenge a bipolar picture through analysis of relevant literature combined with reflection on experience. The experiential focus begins with observations on the leadership of Roger Brown, who was Chief Executive of the Higher Education Quality Council (HEQC), the UK's former national quality agency and Vice-Chancellor and Chief Executive of Southampton Solent University, formerly Southampton Institute. I was a member of Professor Brown's senior management team in HEQC (1994–1997) and for 4 years afterwards (1999–2003), served as an independent member of the Governing Board of Southampton Institute. From 2003 onwards, scholarship and experience converged in numerous professional and collegial dialogues with Professor Brown.

In juxtaposition to these observations, analysis of relevant literature begins with empirical research on leadership and management in UK universities, conducted by the author and colleagues between 1988 and 1992 (Middlehurst, 1989;

Middlehurst *et al.*, 1992) and subsequent study and development of leadership, management and governance in higher education, in the UK and internationally, over the last 25 years. Both sources of evidence provide the structure and content for the chapter.

Initial lessons from leadership theory

Contingency theories of leadership (Hersey and Blanchard, 1977; Hersey, 1984; Fiedler, 1997) have consistently pointed to the significance of context in any analysis of leadership, where context is interpreted widely. At the macro level, it can apply to leadership in different sectors and organisations, different political, economic, social or technological environments and different cultural settings (national, regional or organisational). At a micro level, context can apply to levels of leadership within organisations, to different disciplines and professional fields, to formal and informal leadership settings and to individual experiences of leading teams with different tasks, time horizons, individual personalities and personal circumstances and relationships between team members and groups. The academic disciplines of psychology, sociology, politics, anthropology, history and organisational behaviour have each contributed to perspectives and perceptions of leadership, highlighting the variables that make the exercise of leadership contingent on context and circumstance.

Despite manifold demonstration of contingency, there remains a persistent thread of leadership theory that focuses upon individual traits, suggesting generalisable leadership characteristics that remain valid over time with direct links to individuals' leadership behaviours, styles and relationships to other people. Individuals may become leaders through appointment or election to leadership positions, or may rise to exercise leadership through their own initiative, forced by circumstance or inner drive or both. In the former case, leadership may be expected of individuals – but not practiced – or may be successfully exercised and highly valued. In the latter case, leadership may be delivered and widely acknowledged, or may not be deemed successful or judged positively. Once again, perspectives on individual leadership can be applied at a macro level, for example in terms of political, business or intellectual leadership (Gardner, 1997) or at a micro level through studies of departmental or team leadership in universities (Ramsden, 1998; Gibbs, 2009; Kekale, 1997; Kennie and Woodfield, 2008). Leadership research over the last century has led to multiple refinements of the original hypotheses underpinning twentieth-century schools of thought (Bensimon *et al.*, 1989; Kezar *et al.*, 2006); and new disciplinary perspectives have more recently added to the richness and complexity of analysis (Wheatley, 1999).

Initial lessons from experience

Relating theory to practice, I now refer to two UK-based illustrations. Context was undoubtedly important in both: in relation to Roger Brown's leadership of the Higher Education Quality Council (HEQC), and of the Southampton Institute (later to become Solent University). In the former, government expectations of higher education were changing as more public money was channelled into a much-expanded system and the issue of institutional accountability became pervasive in the UK and beyond (Stensaker, 2011). In parallel, a political decision to change the status of polytechnics to universities in 1992 triggered questions overseas about the consistency and reliability of quality and standards across varied types of UK universities (Brown, 2004). The newly established HEQC was at the centre of these issues, needing to address the political and policy questions while protecting institutional autonomy and acknowledging accountability requirements set out in legislation. As a delivery agency, HEQC also had a technical task to translate policy into tools and instruments that recognised institutional realities. Contestation, negotiation, power-plays and pragmatism were all part of the mix.

In HEQC, the Chief Executive Officer's (CEO) role involved 'system-level leadership' combined with organisational leadership of a small, dispersed organisation with sites in three parts of the UK. At Southampton Institute, institutional leadership was a larger role (encompassing thousands of individuals), with system-level policy providing a context for institutional leadership, rather than being the main arena for strategic leadership as in HEQC. While there were undoubted differences in key stakeholders, organisational functions and leadership purposes, there were also similarities. Southampton Institute needed to change in an evolving political and economic context and after previous governance problems, and the institution was also embarking on a developmental path towards university status that now had to be earned, not acquired through legislative change. Both leadership agendas involved significant change towards more or less well-defined goals, with numerous stakeholders to be convinced to participate in the journey and assist in reaching the destinations.

Clearly, a variety of lessons were learned during each period and setting. Only those with the most significance over time and relevance to the present analysis are recorded here; the experiences are personal, albeit informed by leadership theory, observation of leadership in practice and 25 years of engagement with leadership development. There also remains a need for more detailed empirical evidence on higher education leadership, management, governance and administration, particularly across countries and regions.

A continuum of governance, leadership, management and administration

Roger Brown brought his UK civil service training into the internal operations of the organisations he led. This was easier in the smaller (and start-up) organisation of HEQC than in a large HEI. All HEQC communications, from internal memoranda to Board of Directors' committee papers, external presentations and publications, were subject to strict disciplines. The aim was not only consistency of message, but also responsibility at all levels of the organisation for the quality of the output, intellectually and professionally. Close attention was paid to sound administration (prompt responses and feedback) and responsible management (effective chairing of meetings, regular appraisal of performance with associated recognition and reward structures). Governance requirements in terms of audit trails, budgetary and staff responsibilities and accountability to the Board of Directors were also emphasised, and through the Board, accountability to wider stakeholders. Leadership was exercised through multiple channels of communication with staff who were left in no doubt about the purpose and functions of the organisation, the challenges ahead and the results expected. Each team's role and function was clear and operational and cultural differences and disagreements between teams were managed in a spirit of creative tension rather than dysfunctional acrimony. The CEO personally recognised and challenged performance, set high standards and actively mentored individuals; over the 5 years of his tenure, some individuals were promoted while others left for better or different jobs.

Within the leadership literature, there has been a long-running debate about the separation or integration of the concepts of leadership and management (Zaleznik, 1977; Bennis, 1989; Kotter, 1990; Mintzberg, 2004). There is little mention of governance or administration in these studies. However, the first lesson drawn from the experiences above is that, in practice, alignment of systems and processes of governance, leadership, management and administration – at all levels – is key to organisational effectiveness. Indeed, reports of institutional failures (including that relating to Southampton Institute) often draw attention to broken linkages between governance and management. In the context of the Governing Body of Universities (the main corporate committee of each institution), the relationship between the Chair of the Board/Council and the Principal (President, Vice-Chancellor or Rector) of the institution, is an important bridge between governance and leadership, and the role that the collective Board plays in terms of constructive challenge to the executive is equally important.

While structures of governance differ across countries, the dynamics of these relationships are likely to be similar. In terms of management and administration, classical bureaucratic principles, Weber (1947) and Fayol (1949) suggest that sound practice should lead to organisational consistency and order. Kotter's work on change in organisations (Kotter, 1990) describes the appropriate interplay between leadership and management, arguing that these two domains are complementary systems of action where leadership is about producing the momentum for innovation and useful change while the outcomes of sound management are predictability, order and consistent results, keeping complex organisations 'on time and on budget' (Kotter, 1990: 4). Context and circumstance determine the appropriate balance between the two systems of action; Kotter (1990) suggests that more emphasis on leadership is needed at times of change and uncertainty than in more stable and predictable conditions.

Balancing the needs of task, team and individuals

A model that draws attention to the task of leadership and associated management functions is Adair's 'action-centred leadership'. The central tenet of the model revolves around the requirements of leadership, at individual or collective, strategic or operational levels to balance the often conflicting requirements associated with achieving a task, building a team and developing the individuals involved. Adair (1983) defined eight functions of leadership in relation to these three key areas of leadership responsibility, creating a check-list that could be followed by individuals, groups and organisations. This model has been widely applied across sectors and countries and was one of the first leadership models to formally enter UK higher education in the mid-1980s through leadership development at departmental and institutional levels (Middlehurst, 1993, 2007). In building his model of leadership, Adair drew on US studies of motivation (Maslow, 1954; McGregor, 1960). McGregor's work, in particular, highlighted the potential impact that managers' positive (Theory Y) or negative (Theory X) assumptions about employees' behaviours could have on working conditions and on individual and collective performance. In more recent and related work on 'leader-member exchange theory', Sahin (2012) suggests that application of the different sets of principles underpinning these positive or negative assumptions will differentially affect the quality of relationships between managers and their staff, again with differential impacts on performance.

Bringing theory and experience together, a number of lessons can be drawn out. First, the combined impact of systems and procedures with leadership assumptions and practices can affect working conditions, the quality of relationships and the desire and ability of individuals and groups to achieve organisational and professional goals. Impacts can be positive or negative. At its best, HEQC was characterised by a pervasive 'can-do' organisational culture that was stimulating for the variety of professionals contributing to organisational outcomes, enabling them to achieve high levels of performance, as judged both against external evaluations of the organisation's work and internal appraisals. Second, successful performance was linked to high levels of motivation and satisfaction, a virtuous circle that is recognised in other studies of leadership (Bass, 1985; Kouzes and Posner, 1987) as well as in high performing professional organisations (Maister, 1993, 2001). A third lesson is related to the balance between the level of challenge and the level of support applied by leaders and managers in relationships with their staff. The balance will necessarily differ in relation to individuals or teams in different circumstances (Hersey and Blanchard, 1977). Getting the balance right for individuals has significant developmental potential; this may also be the case at an organisational level as models of 'the learning organisation' assert (Garratt, 2001; Senge, 1990).

Stepping up and stepping out: opportunities and challenges

The principles and practices of quality assurance (QA) and quality enhancement (QE) formed a significant part of Roger Brown's working life, as leader and public professional in the UK seeking to influence policy and practice. An important dimension of both QA and QE involves critical appraisal, to ensure standards are achieved and quality improved. These principles can be applied to any function and area of activity in universities and colleges: teaching and learning, research, service to businesses and communities, as well as to governance, leadership, management and administration. They can also be applied to individuals and groups, including the kind of system-level leadership practised by Vice-Chancellor's Committees or Rectors' Conferences in interactions with government and politics. Two of the five practices of Kouzes and Posner's 'exemplary leadership' model (1987) apply here: 'modelling the way', whereby leaders establish principles about the way people should be treated and goals pursued; and 'challenging the process', where leadership involves searching for opportunities to change the status quo, through challenging, experimenting and taking risks. Such exemplary leadership practices do not just relate to those in positions of leadership; any individual can challenge the process and arguably, academics and professionals are required to do so in their disciplinary fields, through public engagement, and to stimulate innovation in institutions. While Kouzes and Posner's model highlights certain kinds of leadership behaviours, lying behind these is the important human characteristic of courage (moral courage, in particular). Courage is commonly cited in trait theories of leadership and in studies of heroic leadership (Adair, 1989), but is also key in management settings (Klann, 2007). It is quintessentially associated with leadership, but is required well beyond its realms.

In HEIs, courage is needed at many levels – in research, teaching and knowledge exchange – but also to challenge the way things are done in the organisation. For those in leadership positions, there is an expectation that bad behaviours or poor practice will be confronted at individual and group levels, and in representing the institution (and higher education more broadly) leaders are also expected to step up and 'speak truth to power', using intellectual argument and evidence. 'Stepping up and speaking out' may also be part of exercising full institutional autonomy, or at the level of individual academics, of exercising academic freedom. However, experience suggests that exercising courage of this kind does not occur as expected among some who occupy organisational leadership positions in higher education. This is evident in different circumstances, for example: avoiding the potential for face-to-face conflict (in dealing with poor performance); avoiding situations where strong critique and negative emotions are aroused (over controversial ideas or allocation of resources); avoiding taking difficult decisions with potential for personal reputational exposure; or taking the path of least resistance against the tide of practice in other institutions or the prevailing political consensus. While judgement will always be required to decide when 'stepping up and stepping out' is necessary, the ability to do so is a key aspect of leadership and can be supported by effective governance and management.

Deploying courage appropriately (at an individual and organisational level) is part of military training; given the psychological pressures on leadership in today's media-rich world, when to deploy moral courage surely needs to be part of general leadership preparation. Military history was part of Roger Brown's education, and the principles outlined by von Clausewitz (1976) or Machiavelli (2003) did not seem distant, often emerging rhetorically. Such studies appeared to influence organisational planning and tactics in the light of shifting political circumstances and policy contexts. This is because an important part of management and governance work involved anticipation of future challenges and opportunities through scenario thinking, option appraisal, preparation of plans, development of communication strategies, in addition to operational tactics to deal with the here-and-now, as circumstances evolved. Preparation and anticipation brought levels of individual and organisational confidence that challenges could be met successfully. While confidence is not the same as courage, it can take individuals and organisations a long way towards the ability to deploy resources appropriately in the light of changing conditions. Senge's (1990) ideas on organisational readiness for change resonate here. At the 'least-ready' levels of anticipation, organisations and their leaders react to circumstances as they arise (reactive leadership). With enhanced levels of anticipation, organisations are able to prepare and adapt to changing conditions (adaptive leadership). However, the most change-ready organisations are those that anticipate shifting circumstances – through systematic collection and analysis of data and intelligence as well as strong networking capabilities – and intervene to change the rules of the game to their advantage (generative leadership).

Renewing or re-inventing higher education leadership, governance, management and administration?

Reflecting on theory and experience leads to a number of conclusions. The first relates to quality and standards in higher education, examined through the lens of leadership, management, governance and administration. The practices that are signalled through systems and procedures, including electronic communication systems for administration, and through the behaviours of individuals or groups in leadership positions, are often mirrored in behaviour through all levels of the institution, although in larger, complex organisations this effect may occur in lower level academic units and professional departments. Overly controlling systems and poor relationships between managers and staff may breed negative attitudes and behaviours between staff and students with consequences for institutional performance and reputation. Conversely, the principles of 'challenge balanced with support,' if applied rigorously and fairly, are likely to have a positive effect on staff and student morale, motivation and performance. In parallel, a culture of strong academic governance that combines ethical principles and rigorous scrutiny supported by data and evidence with active and engaged citizenship can engender a sense of community as well as ensure that standards are achieved and quality enhanced. Ideally, higher education governance structures and systems should be modelled on shared governance (Shattock, 2006) that is designed to provide checks and balances in decision-making between different sets of interests and levels of power. These checks and balances need to be not only preserved, but re-framed in the light of technological developments, resource constraints and other systemic changes (Middlehurst, 2013).

A second conclusion is that there is no inevitable misalignment between leadership and management theories from outside higher education with leadership contexts and cultures within higher education, as researchers have indicated (Ramsden, 1998). Where 'managerialism' is perceived and experienced, it is more likely to be the result of poor management practice and inappropriate leadership behaviours (whether related to levels of understanding and competence or other factors). Recent research and analysis in higher education contexts has sought to reconcile theories of leadership and management introduced from other sectors with practices that are part of university cultures and history, illustrating what happens in terms of positive or negative outcomes when there is effective alignment and when there is not (Bolden *et al.*, 2012). Other contributions revisit cultural traditions of collegiality and collegial decision-making, aligning these with positive leadership and management practices (Bacon, 2014).

These studies are important and useful, however, a third conclusion is that still more radical thinking, practice and theory is needed. Hamel has argued powerfully that theories of management applied to many businesses are significantly outdated, reflecting industrial-age not information-age assumptions and approaches (Hamel, 2007). In a subsequent study, Hamel provides examples of organisations that are structured, managed and governed very differently, in ways that blend freedom, creativity, discipline and responsibility (Hamel, 2012). Where higher education systems are importing models from other sectors, they can be applying anachronistic principles and practices, including hierarchical command-and-control systems with layers of management that favour compliance and conformity over creativity and innovation. Institutions may also be discarding systems that not only retain strong allegiances in the cultures of HEIs, but could also be well-suited to changing operating conditions. For example, stronger systems of academic governance may be needed to balance strong corporate governance systems given potential conflicts between decisions that could deliver market and economic advantage at the expense of academic or educational gain.

As Hamel (2012) illustrates, advances in communication and information technologies create a requirement and opportunity to lead and govern differently. Open source knowledge systems mean that management information can be widely accessible. Convergent data systems and analytical capacity can facilitate improved performance metrics as well as sharper tools for continuous improvement. Social networking structures and collaborative technologies offer the potential for wide engagement for students and staff. All of these enable ideas to be generated from multiple sources (crowd-sourcing) and decision-taking powers to be distributed to communities (peers, students and members of diverse communities). Important principles include self-management, accountability to colleagues for agreements made, developing a culture of meritocracy based on helping others and demonstrating expertise and adding value. Armed with data, information and authority, management can be broadened. Just as 'flipping the classroom' has become a popular metaphor for changing the relationship from lecturer and expert to mentor and manager of students' learning, so it is possible to imagine 'flipping management and governance' from hierarchies of (extrinsic) controls to hierarchies of influence that build on intrinsic controls of motivation, commitment and professionalism. Concepts and theories of leadership also need to change, the test questions for senior managers and governors are "Are others willing to follow you?" and "Are you making the rest of the institution successful?" Leadership needs to be widely distributed in ways that bring out the strengths of individuals and teams. Ideas that are embedded in positional leadership and selection practices, particularly at the vice-chancellor or principal level where an individual is expected to be the heroic 'visionary-in-chief', must change. Instead, the task is to act as 'organisational and cultural architect', distributing power, mobilising ideas, mentoring talent and expanding the scope of autonomy. None of this is to suggest that conflict and disagreement will disappear or should be ignored. Rather, dissent and diversity of views should be recognised and welcomed as means of fostering creativity and innovation.

Hamel's (2007, 2012) two volumes provide a wealth of detail on the nature and potential of post-modern governance structures and approaches to leadership for transforming organisations. But perhaps most significantly, Hamel points to the need to 'mend the soul' of management by embedding an ethos of community and citizenship to ensure that management serves a higher purpose. There are echoes here of debates taking place internationally. In Malaysian higher education, for example, a discussion has been led by the Ministry's Leadership Academy (AKEPT) in 2014 entitled *Soul-Driven Leadership: Reviving the Soul of Higher Learning*. The central arguments are about the sterility of focusing on instrumental learning outcomes and knowledge as an economic commodity independent of deeper considerations about holistic education aimed at developing responsible global citizenship. Such concerns are not limited to higher education. In the World Economic Forum's *Outlook on the Global Agenda for 2014*, trend seven of ten challenges for world leaders concerns a lack of values in leadership. It is time for HEIs to think more deeply and critically about aligning their governance systems both with their rapidly changing environments and with fresh thinking about the core values and purposes of higher learning.

Bibliography

Adair, J. (1983) *Effective Leadership*. London: Pan
Adair, J. (1989) *Great Leaders*. Guildford: Talbot-Adair Press
Bacon, E. (2014) *Neo-collegiality: Restoring Academic Engagement in the Managerial University*. London: Leadership Foundation

Bass, B. M. (1985) *Leadership and Performance Beyond Expectations.* New York: Free Press

Bennis, W. (1989) *On Becoming a Leader.* London: Hutchison

Bensimon, E., Neumann, A., and Birnbaum, R. (1989) *Making Sense of Administrative Leadership: The 'L' Word in Higher Education.* Washington DC: ASHE-ERIC Higher Education Report 1

Bok, D. (2003) *Universities in the Marketplace: The Commercialization of Higher Education.* Princeton: Princeton University Press

Brown, R. (2004) *Quality Assurance in Higher Education: The UK Experience since 1992.* London: RoutledgeFalmer

Brown, R. (2010) *Higher Education and the Market.* New York: Routledge

Bolden, R., Gosling, J., O'Brien, A., Peters, K., Ryan, M. and Haslem, A. (2012) *Academic Leadership: Changing Conceptions, Identities and Experiences in Higher Education.* London: Leadership Foundation

von Clausewitz, C. (ed.) (trans. M. Howard and P. Paret) (1976) *On War.* Princeton: Princeton University Press

European Commission (2011) *Supporting Growth and Jobs: An Agenda for the Modernisation of Europe's higher Education Systems.* Brussels: COM 567 final. Available at: http://ec.europa.eu/education/library/policy/modernisation_en.pdf [accessed 28 October 2014]

Exworthy, M. and Halford, S. (eds) (1999) *Professionals and the New Managerialism in the Public Sector.* Buckingham: Open University Press

Fayol, H. (1949) *General Industrial Management.* London: Pitman

Fiedler, F. E. (1997) Situational Control and a Dynamic Theory of Leadership. In K. Grint (ed.) *Leadership: Classical, Contemporary and Critical approaches.* Oxford: Oxford University Press: 126–154

Gardner, G. (1997) *Leading Minds: An Anatomy of Leadership.* London: HarperCollins

Garratt, B. (2001) *The Learning Organization: Developing Democracy at Work.* London: HarperCollinsBusiness

Gibbs, G. (2009) *Departmental Leadership of Teaching in Research-Intensive Environments.* London: Leadership Foundation

Hamel, G. (2007) *The Future of Management.* Boston: Harvard Business School Press

Hamel, G. (2012) *What Matters Now: How to Win in A World of Relentless Change, Ferocious Competition and Unstoppable Innovation.* London: Jossey-Bass Wiley

Hersey, P. (1984) *The Situational Leader.* New York: Warner Books

Hersey, P. and Blanchard, K. H. (1977) *Management of Organizational Behaviour.* Englewood Cliffs, NJ: Prentice-Hall, 3rd edition

Kekale, J. (1997) *Leadership Cultures in Academic Departments.* University of Joensuu: Publications in Social Sciences 26

Kennie, T. and Woodfield, S. (2008) *The Composition, Challenges and Changes in the Top Team Structures of UK Higher Education Institutions.* London: Leadership Foundation

Kezar, A., Carducci, R. and Contreras-McGavin, M. (2006) Re-thinking the 'L' Word in Higher Education: The Revolution of Research on Leadership. *ASHE Higher Education Report.* Washington DC. 31:6

Klann, G. (2007) *Building Character: Strengthening the Heart of Good Leadership.* San Francisco: Jossey-Bass and the Center for Creative Leadership

Kolsaker, A. (2008) Academic professionalism in the era of managerialism: a study of English universities. *Studies in Higher Education* 33 (5): 513–525

Kotter, J. (1990) *A Force for Change: How Leadership Differs from Management*. New York: Free Press

Kouzes, J. M. and Posner, B. Z. (1987) *The Leadership Challenge*. San Francisco: Jossey-Bass

Machiavelli, N. (trans. G. Bull) (2003) *The Prince*. London: Penguin Classics

Maister, D. (1993) *Managing the Professional Service Firm*. London: Simon & Schuster

Maister, D. (2001) *True Professionalism*. New York: Touchstone

Maslow, A. H. (1954) *Motivation and Personality*, New York: Harper & Row

McGregor, D. (1960) *The Human Side of Enterprise*. New York: McGraw Hill

Middlehurst, R. (1989) Leadership development in universities: 1986–1988. *Final Report to the Department of Education and Science CORE* 16 (1): 1992, Fiche 3 BO1

Middlehurst, R. (1993) *Leading Academics*. Buckingham: Society for Research into Higher Education and Open University Press

Middlehurst, R. (2013) Changing internal governance: are leadership roles and management structures in United Kingdom universities fit for the future? *Higher Education Quarterly* 67: 3: 275–294

Middlehurst, R., Pope, M. and Wray, M. (1992) The changing roles of university managers and leaders: implications for preparation and development. *CORE*. 16 (1): Fiche 5 E 11

Middlehurst, R. (2007) A challenging journey: from leadership courses to leadership Foundation for higher education. *Managing for Innovation: New Directions for Higher Education* 137: 45–57

Middlehurst, R. and Teixeira, P. (2012) Governance within the EHEA: Dynamic Trends, Common Challenges and National Particularities. In A. Curaj, P. Scott, L. Vlasceanu and L. Wilson (eds) *European Higher Education at the Crossroads: Between the Bologna Process and National Reforms. Vol. 2. Governance, Financing, Mission Diversification and the Futures of Higher Education*. Dordrecht: Springer: 527–551

Mintzberg, H. (2004) Enough Leadership. Opinion. *Harvard Business Review* 22 November 2014

Olssen, M. and Peters, M. A. (2005) Neo-liberalism, higher education and the knowledge economy: from the free market to knowledge capitalism. *Journal of Education Policy* 20 (3): 313–45

Ramsden, P. (1998) *Learning to Lead in Higher Education*. London: Routledge

Sahin, F. (2012) The mediating effect of leader-member exchange on the relationship between Theory X and Y management styles and affective commitment: A multi-level analysis. *Journal of Management and Organization* 18 (2): 159–174

Senge, P. M. (1990) *The Fifth Discipline: The Art and Practice of the Learning Organization*. London: Century Business

Shattock, M. (2006) *Managing Good Governance in Higher Education*. Maidenhead: Open University Press and McGraw-Hill Education

Stensaker, B. and Harvey, L. (eds) (2011) *Accountability in Higher Education: Global Perspectives on Trust and Power*. London: Routledge

Trow, M. (1994) Managerialism and the academic profession: the case of England. *Higher Education Policy* 7: 11–18

Weber, M. (1947) *The Theory of Economic and Social Organization*. New York: Free Press

Wheatley, M. (1999) *Leadership and the New Science: Discovering Order in a Chaotic World*. San Francisco: Berrett-Koehler Press, 2nd edition

Zaleznik, A. (1977) Managers and leaders: are they different? *Harvard Business Review* 55: 67–78

Chapter 18

Reflections on evidence and higher education policy

Gareth Williams

Background

In this chapter celebrating Roger Brown's career, I reflect on the relationship between higher education policy and practice and research into it: in particular, in the area in which I devoted most of my effort during the past 3 decades, and in which Roger Brown has become a major contributor, the economic foundations of the changing mechanisms of higher education finance.

My first public pronouncement on this topic was in my 1986 inaugural lecture at the Institute of Education (Williams, 1986). This was before two important legislative texts affecting higher education, the 1988 and 1992 Education Acts, which transformed relations between higher education and government in the UK. However, in 1986 already, it was clear that times were changing. In concluding my lecture I remarked:

> We suppliers of education have to keep our heads and ensure that the new tunes are not merely the educational equivalent of the top twenty in the popular music charts, on everybody's lips for a few weeks but completely lost from view a year later. If we are being forced into a free market situation it is long term marketing strategies based on real value for money that we must insist on, not short term income maximisation or crisis induced cost minimisation. [. . .] [I]t was interesting to note that one of the reasons given by Andre Previn for his recent resignation from the Royal Philharmonic Orchestra was that commercialisation was forcing it to give under-rehearsed performances and to concentrate to an excessive extent on 'safe' tunes. The effects of new ways of paying the piper extend well beyond public education.
>
> (Williams, 1986)

The function of higher education in a global context

Having spent most of my working life doing research into higher education, I am often finding myself asking what impact higher education research has made to the radical changes of the past 5 decades. This *Festschrift* for Roger Brown provides an opportunity to share some of my thoughts. During the past 4 decades, Roger Brown has experienced higher education from the viewpoint of research student, policy-maker and policy implementer, senior institutional manager and researcher. He has been able to view this tumultuous half-century from many different angles, and this wealth of experience enriches his recent publications.

Higher education systems are networks of able, intelligent creative and critical thinking people so it is not surprising that they interpret what they do in many different ways. Sometimes the narrative is almost theological in nature, a disinterested pursuit and dissemination of truth(s); sometimes higher education is seen as an extension of the family, completing the task of preparing each generation for the society it is inheriting; sometimes the main task is considered to be the maintenance of viable social and political order; and sometimes to act as licensed critics of that order. More recently higher education has come to be seen as investment in human capital, the main source of scientific and technological change that enables humankind to make progress. But no matter what interpretation we choose to accept, there can be no doubt that higher education institutions of the twenty-first century are global businesses. They are global because their networks, and often individual universities, cover the whole world, in their student and staff recruitment, their graduate destinations and their research sponsors. Furthermore, their raw material – knowledge – like money, can be flashed across the globe in an instant. They are businesses because the wide spread of university autonomy, financial and legal as well as academic, has resulted in universities competing fiercely for recognition in the global marketplace. Though I must say, I do sometimes wonder, especially when I look at universities global rankings, whether this aspect of globalisation is in practice an aspect of Anglo-lingual neo-colonialism and may well look different to people with other linguistic backgrounds and cultural traditions.

Global higher education teaching and research could in principle be closely regulated nationally and internationally. All higher education systems, like all banking systems have an element of regulation, from the long established, though fraying, California master plan which has underpinned the development of higher education in that state since the early 1960s, to the traditionally closely regulated public systems of many countries in continental Europe and Eastern Asia. The worldwide interest in the Bologna-inspired qualification frameworks is one example of evolving worldwide coordination arrangements. At the same time, the emergence of mass higher education, and the inevitable diversification that accompanies it, have resulted in a shift towards national systems in which individual higher education institutions have a great deal of financial as well as academic freedom. Almost inevitably, universities compete for students and research grants and in the past 2 decades, most universities in most countries have been remarkably successful in doing so. They have also been encouraged by governments to offer other knowledge-based services and have often been successful in extending their interests to cover a very wide range of knowledge-related 'third mission' ('enterprise' or 'community-based') activities.

But business expansion is rarely boundless or continuous. Universities, throughout their long history in Europe have grown in fits and starts. While the long term trend has certainly been upwards, there have been many periods of no growth and some of decline. Although Clark Kerr's well-known comment that the university is one of the very few European institutions to have survived since medieval times (Kerr, 1963) has often been quoted, it is important to remember that many individual higher education institutions have ceased to exist and those that have survived are very different institutions from those of earlier centuries. The great majority of the world's universities were established in the twentieth century – or later. All are in a continual state of evolution, sometimes painful, as a result of economic, social or political pressures. In brief, markets are not a unique threat and twenty-first century universities are likely to have as che-quered a history as their predecessors.

Higher education grew massively in most countries throughout the twentieth century, though growth was uneven and at different rates in different countries: like the economy, it grew in fits and starts, sometimes extremely rapidly and sometimes stagnating for several years. Though the timing was not the same in all countries, in general rapid growth in the 1920s was followed by a decade of stagnation in the 1930s. Growth resumed after the Second World War and accelerated in the 1960s and early 1970s. Then there was a decade and a half of stagnation in the late 1970s and 1980s followed by rapid growth again in the 1990s and the early years of the present century. The Organisation for Economic Cooperation and Development figures show that many countries may now be experiencing a period of relative stagnation at least in first degree enrolments (OECD, 2013).

In 2013, Britain celebrated the fiftieth anniversary of the publication of the Robbins Report, a seminal text that set guidelines for UK higher education expansion for the following 20 years, and for the first time formally promoted the notion of wider range access to university education. Although there were many changes of detail, all subsequent governments accepted the basic principles. In 1963, higher education in the UK was, by any criterion, a minority and elitist activity. It was also a secret garden. Universities published little factual information about themselves and what was available was rarely comparable between them. Even Oxford and Cambridge could not be rigorously compared. The Robbins Committee was 'struck by the paucity of information on higher educa-tion in general' (Robbins, 1963: 3), a deficiency which, as is well known, the Committee started to put right.

The emergence of higher education as a research field

Half a century later it would not be an exaggeration to claim that the reverse is true. I recently counted nearly 100 periodicals and journals in the Institute of Education library that deal exclusively or predominantly with higher educa-tion. In addition, economics journals, psychology journals, sociology journals frequently include articles dealing with higher education. There are also special-ised journals for medical education and engineering education, among others. So much information is published about higher education that it is now impossible for any individual person to keep abreast of any but a small portion of it. It has become a major field of study, and most universities now have at least one aca-demic group specialising in and often teaching the subject of post-school educa-tion. But what kind of subject is it? Does it have any value if it does not have an impact on policy and practice?

One problem is that higher education itself is strongly ideological. Three con-cepts have fuelled debates about its scope and magnitude for centuries. It is often seen as a continuation of primary and secondary education whose prin-cipal purpose is to encourage the full flowering of the abilities of individual human beings. Another view is that its purpose is to prepare individuals, espe-cially potential leaders, for the maintenance of ethical and cultural ideas which are believed to have served society well in the past and should continue to do, what Robbins called 'the transmission of a common culture' (Robbins, 1963: paragraph 28). The third idea, which has increased in importance as mass higher education has replaced older ideas of selectivity based on perceived academic potential, is that its principal role is to provide as many people as possible with advanced skills that will enable individuals, and the communities to which they belong, to prosper.

Until the middle of the twentieth century, student numbers increased at vari-able rates but mostly very slowly. There had been some growth in the sec-ond half of the nineteenth century when new universities were established in many European countries to provide for the growing needs of industry, both to train the technologists needed by the new industrial sectors and to provide opportunities to the children of the newly rich to absorb the cultural capital of their social superiors. This owed nothing to higher education research which did not exist; although there were intense disagreements between contemporary English academic authorities such as, for example, John Henry Newman (1852) and Matthew Arnold (1869), on one side, and Herbert Spencer (1861) and Mark Pattison (1868), on the other, about whether university education was primarily about encouraging the full flowering of superior individuals or about prepar-ing people for (leading) roles in increasingly industrialised societies. At the same time, led mainly by the German example, it was becoming clear that universities, as associations of intellectually able people could make an important contribu-tion to economic, social and cultural progress through the knowledge that their scholarly studies revealed about the physical and social world.

However, it was not until the middle of the twentieth century that rigor-ous academic research began to be applied to higher education itself led, in the United Kingdom, by the Robbins Committee. There had, of course, been research before Robbins that was relevant to higher education (see for example Bernstein, 1960; Clark, 1960; Floud and Halsey, 1957; Schultz, 1960) which were certainly influential in policy-making over subsequent decades but which were not undertaken primarily in order to influence policy directly. In the twenty-first century most research into higher education has to justify itself in terms of likely impact before it can even obtain funding to get started.

Research on the impact of university studies: the input of economists

From the outset, higher education research split into two main paths. One was concerned with access, student numbers, graduate employment and finance; in short, higher education as a social and economic policy issue. The other was concerned with the processes of learning and teaching and the relationship of teaching and research; in short, the core operational activities of universities and colleges. Obviously there are links between the two strands: expansion of student numbers has implications for the effectiveness of different teaching styles; research and teaching need resources that must come from somewhere; and what graduates have learned is an important economic issue. But as even a cursory reading of the research literature shows, they remain to a large extent two separate areas of scholarly activity: one rooted in sociology, political theory and economics and the other ultimately, in some aspects of applied psychology.

Another complication is that a considerable part of the literature derives, at least in part, from the personal experiences of the authors and participant observation. David Dill (2014) has recently written about critiques of the shift of higher education being considered primarily as a public good to one in which it is seen as a marketable commodity:

> [. . .] [R]ecent writings on the public good in higher education by sociologists, political scientists, and educationists have been largely critical (Calhoun, 2006; Tierney, 2006; Marginson, 2007; Brown, 2010; Rhoten and Calhoun, 2011). This literature suggests the policy reforms of the last several decades, which have introduced greater privatisation and market competition into higher education systems (i.e., so-called 'neo-liberal reforms'), have also lessened the 'public goods' provided by higher education institutions and are compromising academic activity within universities. This literature, written primarily by those who work within higher education institutions, makes valuable contributions, but has several limitations. First, it is largely rhetorical and qualitative, rather than empirical. When this literature is empirical, it is often focused on the views of academics themselves rather than on indicators of the outputs or outcomes of universities. Furthermore, in critiquing the impacts of current policies, many of these studies do not cite or assess the economic research on the increasing private and public returns produced by higher education noted above. While the impacts upon those actively involved in the production of higher education should certainly be included in any calculation of the public good and/or the social benefits derived from

higher education, focusing primarily on the impacts upon producers may not provide a totally objective assessment of the public good.

(Dill, 2014: 142)

Dill, although not an economist himself, is obviously sympathetic to much of what has been written in the past few decades by members of that discipline. So can the changes of the past 30 years be attributed to the work of economists?

To begin to give a sensible answer to that question, it must first be recognised that the financial changes of the past few decades have not been confined to higher education. The collapse of Soviet central planning, the development of a market system in communist China and the privatisation of many previously publicly provided services in Britain and Western Europe embraced wide sectors of the economy and for the most part impinged relatively lightly on the fundaments of higher education. So if academic economists have influenced the changes in the finance of higher education, it is likely to have been part of a much bigger debate about the ways in which economies can most effectively operate. Ultimately, it has been an ideological debate about efficiency and equity of which higher education is a small, though important, part. So how have the general debates that led to a shift from the planned public sector controlling the commanding heights of economies towards private monopolistic completion impinged on higher education?

Economists have, since the 1950s been researching the earnings of people with different levels of skills and educational qualifications. It has been well known for decades that there is a very good correlation between average lifetime earnings and level of education achieved. What have never been so clear are the mechanisms by which this has come about. While higher education was primarily a rite of passage for those from socially advantaged groups and a few very able people from less favoured backgrounds, it was quite possible that much of these higher earnings were the result of social and cultural advantages and innate abilities. There is a huge literature on this and it is still not conclusive (e.g. Harmon, Walker and Westergard-Nielsen, 2002; Psacharopoulos and Patrinos, 2002).

However, what more and more studies are now showing is that high average earnings of graduates conceal widening dispersion of graduate earnings (Green and Zhu, 2010). The differences between the highest earning graduates and those at the bottom, like earnings in general, are widening. While average rates of return to higher education remain high, there are growing numbers of graduates for whom this is not the case. In the UK, the average starting salary for graduates who went into investment banking in 2013 was £45,000 and for law £38,000 while for those entering public sector jobs it was £23,000. Subject of study makes a huge difference. The starting salary for medical graduates averaged over £29,000 and economics nearly £26,000, while for drama, media studies and music it was around £17,000. The London School of Economics is top of the list with starting salaries averaging £29,000 (Graduates.co.uk, 2014; HESA, 2014).

Such figures have not yet been the subject of detailed statistical analysis (BIS, 2013). But they do suggest that the graduate labour market needs to be analysed by policy-makers in a much more rigorous way than has been the case hitherto. Recent studies (Thompson and Bekhradnia, 2014) that show the probable increasing burden on future public funds of the means-tested repayment loans scheme currently in operation in England are in effect also showing that the dispersion of graduate earnings is becoming much wider than was assumed when the government introduced its full cost fees policy in 2012.

Another set of indicators that needs exploration is whether there are limits to the expansion of higher education. OECD figures suggest that some sort of plateau seems to have been reached in some of the countries that led the way in higher education expansion. Growth in the US and Japan, and in several other countries, has slowed in recent years (OECD, 2013). What also seems to be happening is that increasing numbers of graduates are opting for some form of postgraduate study, either immediately after obtaining their first degree or at some point later in their lives. This has important implications for both sociological and economic interpretations of higher education. There is evidence that it is mainly students from more affluent backgrounds who are able to do postgraduate studies and there are some reasons to believe that many UK first degrees no longer provide the knowledge, skills and attitudes that are required by an advanced economy (see Bekhradnia, 2009).

Conclusion

Roger Brown began the work that is needed with his programme on 'graduateness' when he was chief executive of the Higher Education Quality Council (HEQC, 1997). This was taken up by the Quality Assurance Agency in its programme on subject benchmarking. But most of the subject benchmark statements are essentially harmless platitudes, rather than clear statements of what a graduate ought to know or how s/he should think. We have a much better understanding of higher education in both its macro and its micro aspects than was available to Robbins half a century ago. But much remains to be done. And on my key question, I am still undecided. Is higher education research a significant driver of policy and practice or does research simply follow the changing whims of policy-makers and managers seeking evidence to support their decisions and actions?

Bibliography

Arnold, M. (1869) *Culture and Anarchy*. Oxford: Oxford University Press (new edition, 2006)

Bekhradnia, B. (2009) *The Academic Experience of Students in English Universities.* Oxford: Higher Education Policy Institute

Bernstein, B. (1960) Language and social class. *British Journal of Sociology* 11 (3): 271–276

BIS (2013) *The Impact of University Degrees on the Lifecycle of Earnings: Some Further Analysis.* Research Paper 112. London: BIS

Brown, R. (2010) *Higher Education and the Market.* London: Routledge

Calhoun, C. (2006) The university and the public good. *Thesis Eleven* 84 (1): 7–43

Clark B. R. (1960) The cooling out function in higher education. *American Journal of Sociology* 65 (6): 569–576

Dill, D. D. (2014) Assuring the Public Good in Higher Education: Essential Framework Conditions and Academic Values. In O. Filippakou and G. Williams (eds) *Higher Education as a Public Good: Critical Perspectives on Theory, Policy and Practice.* New York: Peter Lang: 141–162

Floud, J. and Halsey, A. H. (1957) Intelligence tests, social class and selection for secondary schools. *British Journal of Sociology* 8 (1): 33–39

Graduates.co.uk (2014) *Graduate Starting Salaries in 2013/14.* Available at: http://www.graduates.co.uk/graduate-starting-salaries-in-2013-14/

Green, F. and Zhu, Y. (2010) Overqualification, job dissatisfaction, and increasing dispersion in the returns to graduate education. *Oxford Economic Papers* 62 (4): 740–763

Harmon, C., Walker, I. and Westergaard-Nielsen, N. (2002) *Education and Earnings in Europe: A Cross Country Analysis of the Returns to Education.* Cheltenham: Edward Elgar

HEQC (1997) *Assessment in Higher Education and the Role of 'Graduateness'.* London: Higher Education Quality Council

HESA (2014) *Destinations of Leavers from Higher Education.* Cheltenham: HESA. Available at: https://www.hesa.ac.uk/pubs/dlhe

Kerr, C. (1963) *The Uses of the University.* Cambridge, MA: Harvard University Press

Marginson, S. (2007) *Prospects of Higher Education: Globalization, Market Competition, Public Goods and the Future of the University.* Rotterdam: Sense Publishers

Newman J. H. (1852) *The Idea of a University.* Yale: Yale University Press (reprinted 1996)

OECD (2013) *Education at a Glance.* Paris: Organisation for Economic Cooperation and Development

Pattison, M. (1868) *Suggestions on Academical Organisation with Especial Reference to Oxford.* London: Edmonston and Douglas

Psacharopoulos, G. and Patrinos, H. A. (2002) Returns to Investment in Education: A Further Update. *World Bank Policy Research Working Paper 2881.* Washington DC: World Bank

Rhoten, D. and Calhoun, C. (2011) *Knowledge Matters: The Public Mission of the Research University.* New York: Columbia University Press

Robbins, L. (1963) *Higher Education: Report of the Committee appointed by the Prime Minister under the Chairmanship of Lord Robbins.* London: HMSO

Schultz, T. W. (1960) Capital formation by education. *Journal of Political Economy* 51 (1): 1–17

Spenser, H. (1861) Education: Intellectual, Moral and Physical. *Essays on Education and Kindred Subjects.* London: Everyman Library (reprinted 1911)

Thompson, J. and Bekhradnia, B. (2014) *The Cost of the Government's Reforms of the Financing of Higher Education: An Update.* Oxford: Higher Education Policy Institute

Tierney, W. G. (2006) *Governance and the Public Good.* Albany: State University of New York Press

Williams, G. L. (1986) *New Ways of Paying the Piper: An Inaugural Lecture.* London: Institute of Education

Chapter 19

Academic quality and academic responsibility

A critical reflection on collegial governance

David D. Dill

Introduction

A recent set of intensive case studies of leading universities (Paradeise and Thoenig, 2013), which included the public University of California, Berkeley, and the private Massachusetts Institute of Technology in the US, attempted to develop generalisations regarding the internal governance processes by which contemporary universities sustain or attain standards of excellence in instruction and research. The studies were usefully comparative, evaluating differences in major countries, as well attentive to disciplinary differences, which is a particularly important and influential variable in academic behavior in all countries. The authors concluded that academic quality was primarily a function of social interactions that occur within and between academic subunits as well as within the host university. As they note, these processes play a major role in building shared identities as well as developing valuable common knowledge in instruction and research among academic staff members. These social interactions also help generate and communicate communal norms and values through socialisation and internal regulation. Finally, and importantly, as they emphasise, these processes legitimate certain decision-making criteria within academic institutions and have an impact as well on the distribution of authority and power within the university.

In sum, the studies (Paradeise and Thoenig, 2013) suggested successful performance within the best universities was related to shared goals and values among faculty members and administrators, values shaped by the 'soft' institutions through which universities communicate the attitudes and norms about how governance decisions ought to be made. Similarly Roger Brown's analyses (Brown, 2004, 2011; Brown with Carasso, 2013) and my own professional experience with academic quality assurance policies suggests the heart of the matter is better comprehending and improving of the design of university collegial processes for assuring academic standards. As our distinguished colleague Burton Clark (2008) noted at the close of his career, to understand university change we need to be able to 'reason inductively from the experience of on-the-ground practitioners':

> Only secondarily do we glance at broad frameworks developed in the study of business and public administration – resource dependency, path

dependence, isomorphism, management by objectives, total quality management. These borrowed approaches never get to the point of *how decisions are
collectively fashioned in complex universities,* each loaded with unique features
in an extended portfolio of missions and programmes, general and specific,
that need rebalancing from year to year.

(Clark, 2008: 542, emphasis added)

The new public management

In contrast, as Roger Brown (Brown, 2004, 2011; Brown with Carasso, 2013)
and other scholars have stressed, regulatory frameworks informed by the theories of the New Public Management are influencing academic work worldwide,
and these frameworks emphasise performance measurement systems that reify
markets, empowering greater consumer and managerial control of universities.
Embedded in this New Public Management worldview, they argue, is an attack
on professionalism, challenging the collegial decision-making authority of faculties and departments within universities.

The impact on internal university governance of policies shaped by the New
Public Management arouses significant concern because a basic premise underlying the distinctive organisation of universities is the complexity and uncertainty of
university curricula, academic work and research require that core academic decisions be determined by the professional expertise of the institution's academic
staff. Indeed a strong case can be made, particularly in the research university
sector, that well-designed collegial processes are efficient for society because academic staff are more likely to provide truly independent judgments on critical
academic decisions than are administrators (McPherson and Schapiro, 1999).

Innovations in information technology

Poorly designed higher education policies can distort academic incentives as well
as the internal governance of universities in a manner detrimental to the public
interest. However, I believe a focus primarily on government policy provides an
incomplete picture of the challenges now confronting universities. In the contemporary world, significant changes in the core activities of academic instruction
and research are being brought about as well by exogenous factors such as the
continuing innovations in information technology and these advances are also
influencing the effectiveness of the existing institutional rules in use for assuring academic standards. For example, a recent UK Institute for Public Policy
Research report titled *An Avalanche Is Coming: Higher Education and the Revolution Ahead* states:

> With world-class content available anytime for free, the ability of faculty
> to be present anywhere, and the rise of online learning as an alternative to

in-person instruction, we need to reflect on the nature of teaching and learning in a higher education institution.

(Rizvi *et al.*, 2013: 43)

Similarly IT innovations are also influencing the technology of academic research and scholarship as well as scholarly publication (Dill, 2014; Ostrom and Hess, 2007), thereby challenging traditional collegial norms and processes of governance in this area as well.

With regard to the technology of instruction within the university sector, the economist, former President of Princeton and thoughtful analyst of US higher education, William Bowen (Bowen *et al.*, 2014) recently conducted a rigorous study comparing the productivity of traditional university instruction and a hybrid version of on-line instruction. Bowen is well known as the co-author in the 1960s of the 'cost disease' concept, in which wages in certain labour-intensive industries such as the performing arts and higher education necessarily must rise at a rate greater than their growth in productivity. However, Bowen currently argues that productivity growth in higher education instruction is now both technically feasible and necessary.

Bowen acknowledges the serious need for systematic evaluations of different approaches to on-line learning in different subject fields and in different academic settings. However, his analysis led him to call for openness to new means of instruction by institutions of higher education and he emphasised needed reforms in our models of academic governance:

> [. . .] if wise decisions are to be made in key areas, such as teaching methods, it is imperative that they be made by a mix of individuals from different parts of the institution – including faculty leaders but also others well-positioned to consider the full ramifications of the choices before them. There are real dangers in relying on the compartmentalized thinking that too often accompanies decentralized modes of organization to which we have become accustomed.

(Bowen, 2013: 64)

In contrast to this call for more collective action in university governance, the market logic (Berman, 2012) of some higher education policies as well as the new information technologies influencing academic work appear to be providing incentives for greater privatisation of academic conduct, understood as the pursuit of autonomy for individual teaching and research, for programme development and for institutional prestige. There is some evidence that the motivation for this academic pursuit is less to better serve the public and more to maximise private benefit (Macfarlane, 2012). Consequently a major challenge to the assurance of academic standards is the growing chasm between the common or collective good of the university and the self-interest of the individual faculty member.

In this new, more competitive and complex environment of higher education, achieving the integration necessary for strategic academic decision-making will require development of more effective mechanisms for coordinating academic work and for promulgating the shared beliefs essential to achieving university purpose. How is this process of collegial coordination and socialisation best conceptualised?

The collegial model

The increasing application of political and economic perspectives such as the principal-agent model to the design of higher education policy and academic governance has renewed interest in the traditional collegial model of internal university governance most prevalent in the US and UK (Shattock, 2014). Recent analysis in the UK (Tapper and Palfreyman, 2010) has attempted to clarify the academic collegial model, but in my view this attempt – following English university tradition – adopts the 'collegiate university' model of academic governance characteristic of Oxford and Cambridge, featuring autonomous residential colleges emphasising undergraduate education. As a result this particular 'federal' conception of academic collegiality is of limited assistance in the design of public policies and internal academic governance for universities in other countries, including the US, which are not organised according to this model of education. Nor is it useful in designing more effective academic governance in distance-learning and/or emerging internet-based universities.

A more valuable framework for evaluating academic collegial organisation is the 'commons' model for addressing issues of collective action in self-governing communities thoughtfully articulated by the Nobel laureate Elinor Ostrom (2005). In her Nobel Prize lecture Ostrom (2009) argued that neither market forces nor the rules of the state are the most effective institutional arrangements for governing, managing and providing complex public goods. Instead, she has attempted to identify universal design principles that permit individuals in self-governing organisations to effectively address collective action dilemmas.

A commons perspective is most applicable in circumstances where more effective cooperation and integration among independent individuals is critical to performance, clearly and increasingly the case in university instruction, research and service. It is also most appropriate when organisations are self-organising communities, when the organisation's members share common values, when the organisation possesses a nested structure with multiple levels of rule-making (e.g. the federal model of academic governance) and when the organisation itself is of a size to facilitate the active participation of its members. All of these characteristics apply to most institutions of higher education in the US as well as to universities around the world. In addition, the external governance of US colleges and universities has traditionally assigned the *collective* faculty or academic staff of an institution primary responsibility for the quality of academic degree offerings, the content of the curriculum, the evaluation of teaching and research,

214 Davis D. Dill

as well as for the rules and norms governing instruction, research and public service (Kaplan, 2004).

I would suggest that Ostrom's commons perspective provides useful principles for redesigning academic collegial governance for the new conditions of global competition as well as for the challenges posed by innovations in the technology of instruction and research. Indeed in one of her last publications Ostrom (Ostrom and Hess, 2007) applied the commons framework to universities and argued they are best understood as humanly constructed, self-organising, 'knowledge commons'.

Principles of commons design

Ostrom's first principle of commons design addresses the nature of external governance in higher education by confirming the professional autonomy and responsibility of commons members to govern their own institutions. This principle thereby strengthens the members' motivation and commitment to invest the necessary time and effort in collective actions required to address contemporary challenges to assuring effective performance. The on-going debate in many countries about quality accountability versus quality enhancement in higher education reflects a similar problem. With regard to internal governance, additional commons design principles would encourage collective actions by commons members: 1) to develop more valid and reliable information for improving professional performance; 2) to enhance their ability to learn new means of improving professional activities from one another; and 3) to focus on the development of more effective governance processes.

Let me illustrate Ostrom's first design principle with examples of national policies intended to confirm professional autonomy and responsibility among academic staff. A great deal of literature has been devoted to research assessment systems similar to the former Research Assessment Exercise (RAE) in the UK (now the Research Excellence Framework, REF), which conducted retrospective evaluations of university research through the third party of the Higher Education Funding Council for England (Dill and van Vught, 2010). In comparison, less recognition has been given to the university research assessment system developed in the Netherlands where the government, consistent with a commons perspective, confirmed at the outset academic autonomy and responsibility by permitting the evaluation system to be collectively designed and implemented by the universities themselves in concert with national research organisations.

In contrast to the UK RAE, the research assessments in the Netherlands do not focus on assessments of research publications and are not tied to university funding. Instead, every 6 years, each university conducts an external peer-review of its research programmes involving internationally respected researchers, which follows a Standard Evaluation Protocol (SEP) (Jongbloed, 2010). The SEPs focus on the academic quality, scientific productivity and long-term vitality of each research programme and utilise a variety of information sources including onsite interviews, university self-reports, as well as bibliometric evidence. These evaluations are made public.

A comparative study of research funding and performance in selected OECD countries (Himanen *et al.*, 2009) revealed overall higher education research and development (R & D) expenditures (HERD) in the UK more than doubled from 1990 to 2005. Over this period the UK experienced moderate growth in their share of OECD research publications, but no growth in the UK proportion of OECD research citations. More significantly during this period three RAEs were conducted in the UK, but the ratio of research publications to HERD actually declined. In comparison during this same time period, when the Netherlands SEPs were in effect, the Dutch HERD hardly grew. But Dutch universities showed a constant increase in both publication output and citation impact and also exhibited continued growth in the ratio of publications to HERD. In fact the Netherlands showed the greatest output for the least input of the compared countries, which included Australia, Finland and Norway. Furthermore in contrast to the RAE, the collegially designed formative research assessment process developed in the Netherlands has been more stable and appears to provide more nuanced and useful information to each university on means of improving its research activities. As such these assessments likely can continue to make over time an effective contribution to improving research performance.

Of course this is but one study and the measurement of the quality of academic research is a complex issue. But precisely because of this complexity, principal-agent theory (Weimer and Vining, 1996) would predict a number of complications in research assessments, which were in fact experienced by the UK RAE. These included the need to continually adjust the measurement of outputs in order to address a product as multifaceted as academic research as well as the high costs of monitoring a complex output like university research performance. Furthermore, one would also predict difficulties in controlling cross-subsidies in an organisation like a university, which possesses the multiple outputs of teaching, research and public service, an issue raised by the UK QAA. In fact in the highly competitive American higher education market, the economist Ronald Ehrenberg (2012) provides convincing evidence of the extent to which instructional expenditures are increasingly cross-subsidising research expenditures in US universities and negatively effecting undergraduate educational performance.

A second example of a national policy that first confirmed academic autonomy and responsibility is the design of academic quality assurance policies in some EU countries (Dill and Beerkens, 2010). Consistent with the New Public Management, policy-makers in a number of countries including the US believe if student consumers have sufficient information on the quality of colleges and universities, their choices will provide a powerful incentive for universities to continually improve academic programmes, thereby increasing academic accountability and the efficiency of higher education. However, as Roger Brown (2011) argues and as research on student choice in the US and other countries suggests

(Dill and Soo, 2005), many higher education applicants are naïve consumers whose enrolment decisions are influenced by a wide variety of educational, social and personal factors, including the immediate consumption benefits of higher education. In fact a recent national study providing evidence of limited learning in US higher education concluded that '(t)here is no reason to expect that students and parents as consumers will prioritise undergraduate learning as an outcome' (Arum and Roksa, 2011: 137).

In contrast to the New Public Management perspective, the Education Ministers who initiated the Bologna process for strengthening higher education in the European Union argued early on:

> [. . .] consistent with the principle of institutional autonomy, the primary responsibility for quality assurance in higher education lies with each institution itself and this provides the basis for real accountability of the academic system within the national quality framework.
> (Conference of Ministers Responsible for Higher Education, 2003)

One can certainly debate the extent to which the quality assurance policies of particular Bologna-participating countries truly reflect this view, but as a consequence a number of EU countries have focused their quality assurance policies less on empowering consumers and university administrators and more on professionally-oriented quality enhancement. That is, on rebuilding and strengthening the capacity of faculty members within each institution to collectively assure and improve student learning (Dill, 2000; Dill and Beerkens, 2010).

Academic quality enhancement and research doctoral education

This focus on quality enhancement helps illustrate Ostrom's principles for cultivating the ability of commons members to learn new means of improving professional activities from one another and for focusing institutional efforts on developing more effective governance processes. For example, the adoption of the EU Lisbon Strategy in 2000, which set a goal of strengthening the European Research Area, as well as the acknowledged market competition of US research universities, increased incentives for EU universities to reform their institutional processes governing research doctoral education (Byrne, Jørgensen and Loukkola, 2013). In response, EU universities are now moving away from the traditional 'master-apprentice' model of doctoral training, which awarded substantial autonomy to the individual supervising professor, and developing a university-wide culture of shared values and commitment to research-doctoral education featuring new structures 'with defined processes that enhance quality and aim at coordinating individual efforts' (Byrne, Jørgensen and Loukkola, 2013: 13).

These changes in EU university internal governance were not made in response to external policy directives or managerialist incursions, but rather illustrate the types of voluntary collegial adaptations necessary to assure and improve academic quality in the more competitive global environment. For example, over the last decade many EU universities have implemented for the first time doctoral schools, often a university-wide unit similar to a US graduate school. In the US, a graduate school is a collegial governance structure engaging the collective academic staff of an institution in developing and implementing policies designed to assure the academic standards of each of a university's research doctoral programmes. Similarly in a number of EU universities, the collective faculty has been significantly involved in creating new university-wide rules and guidelines for doctoral supervision. These new rules include the adoption of doctoral committees to augment the expertise of the traditional thesis supervisor, the creation of university-level admissions committees for research doctoral education, as well as the creation of institutional spaces for the exchange of experiences and good practices among thesis supervisors via informal peer-learning groups and training opportunities. These largely voluntary efforts have, as noted in the PrestEnce studies (Paradeise and Thoenig, 2013), adjusted the distribution of academic authority within EU universities, shifting from the traditional governance system that granted significant personal authority to individual professors to a more balanced system featuring collegial or collective academic authority over research doctoral instruction and programmes (Clark, 1987).

Policy-makers and the public may understandably question whether university processes promoting, as I have just suggested, increased faculty discussion will contribute significantly to improving academic standards in instruction and research. But as Ostrom and Walker (1997) emphasise, face-to-face communication in social dilemmas is the most effective means of producing substantial increases in needed cooperation and coordination over time. These types of processes help stimulate the social ties necessary for the more effective observation, communication and enforcement of academic standards (Dill and Beerkens, 2010).

Academic quality enhancement at the programme level

A commons perspective is also reflected in a number of other EU academic quality assurance policies. Countries such as Denmark and Germany have required state-sponsored external peer-reviews of all or most subject fields in the university sector, but in contrast to the heavily criticised subject reviews conducted in England by the HEFCE, these reviews were more effectively focused on the enhancement of academic quality. As a consequence, a frequently reported positive impact of these subject assessments and accreditations is the incentive they provide for more frequent collegial discussions and actions at the programme level to improve teaching as well as the cohesion of academic programmes, i.e. the structure of academic curricula (Dill and Beerkens, 2010). The beneficial nature of these programmatic collegial actions is supported by research in the

US (Pascarella and Terenzini, 2005) indicating students' learning of academic content and their cognitive development are most significantly associated with the pattern and sequence of the courses or modules in which they enrol, by programme requirements that integrate learning from separate courses or modules, and by the frequency of communication and interaction among faculty members in the subject field.

Consistent with a third principle of Ostrom's commons perspective, the programme reviews that appear to have elicited the greatest respect and engagement of academic staff were those designed to encourage the provision of more valid and reliable information for collegial decisions regarding the assurance and improvement of academic standards. For example, the learning-oriented subject accreditation process developed by Teacher Education Accrediting Commission in the US (El-Khawas, 2010), the subject assessments developed in Denmark (Stensaker, 2010) and the accreditation process of the General Medical Council in the UK (Harvey, 2010) have in common a rigorous evaluation methodology conforming to social scientific standards of evidence (Dill and Beerkens, 2010). Accordingly these subject assessments and accreditations place much weight on assessing the efficacy of each institution's self-organised monitoring of educational outcomes. Peer-reviewers are trained, supported during the review process by professional staff, and employ systematic, standardised procedures and protocols. These external reviews all strongly emphasise development within universities of a culture of evidence (Shavelson, 2010) for assuring and improving academic standards.

However, these subject-level, external peer-reviews in the EU are costly to sustain for an entire system, their benefits tend to decline over time and therefore appear unsustainable. More critically, because they focus on the subject level, these external assessments and accreditations continue a tradition of centralised state control of academic programmes. Therefore, from a collegial perspective, these external subject reviews fail to reinforce internal university accountability. They do not provide real incentives for collegial actions by the university's collective academic staff (as previously noted in EU research doctoral education) to develop more effective institutional processes for planning academic programmes, implementing and evaluating them, as well as correcting and improving them based upon evidence of effective performance. This structural weakness in external subject assessments or accreditations is reflected in national policy shifts among several EU countries toward an institution or process-oriented focus for external quality assurance more similar to quality audit in the UK (Kehm, 2010; Stensaker, 2010).

In this regard, Ostrom's principle of collectively developing more valid and reliable information for improving professional performance might be pursued at the university level by a rebalancing of academic authority similar to the case of EU research doctoral education; for example, as at Cambridge and Oxford where the university academic staff collectively assume responsibility for setting and marking the exams of students in the constituent colleges seeking a degree. Or by the collective university academic staff designing and implementing rigorous evidence-based processes for assuring the effectiveness of teaching, learning and assessment in each university degree programme.

Conclusion

The PrestEnce studies' (Paradeise and Thoenig, 2013) emphasis on norms, values and forms of communication as a means of achieving necessary coordination and integration in universities reminds me of an earlier study by the sociologist Jerald Hage, *Communication and Organizational Control* (1974), which I consider a neglected classic of the organisation theory literature. Based upon extensive field studies of medical organisations in the US, Hage concluded that traditional hierarchical methods of coordination and control are ineffective in professional settings because of the complexity of professional tasks and the need for individual autonomy. Consequently, Hage argued that necessary coordination must be achieved through a process of socialisation that features high levels of communication and feedback about professional tasks. This communication is not vertical as with administrators, not primarily written as in reports and procedural documents, not episodic and does not focus on the detection or transmittal of sanctions. Rather, the communication is horizontal, with respected peers, largely verbal and face-to-face, continuous and focuses on the exchange of information about means of improving core professional tasks.

Similarly in an analysis of higher education and the public good Craig Calhoun, now Director of the London School of Economics, concluded:

> [. . .] (T)he productivity of academe depends upon the extent to which it is internally organized as a public sphere – with a set of nested and sometimes overlapping public discussions providing for the continual critique and correction of new arguments and tentatively stabilized truths [. . .]
>
> The answer must lie in the organization of academic institutions and academic work in fields which provide plausible boundaries to these critical debates, but boundaries which never allow for more than partial autonomy. There must also be boundary-crossing: physicists must sometimes question chemists, sociologists must sometimes question economists.
>
> (Calhoun, 2006: 35)

In short, Calhoun believes the public good is best served by academic institutions responding to their new, more competitive, environment by reorganising their collegial governance processes. In light of the thoughtful writing of Roger Brown (Brown, 2004, 2011; Brown with Carasso, 2013) and like-minded colleagues, I believe we still have much to learn from systematic research on the necessary collegial conditions for assuring and improving academic quality.

Bibliography

Arum, R. and Roksa, J. (2011) *Academically Adrift: Limited Learning on College Campuses*. Chicago: University of Chicago Press

Berman, E.P. (2012) Explaining the move toward the market in US academic science: how institutional logics can change without institutional entrepreneurs. *Theory and Society* 41: 261–299

Bowen, W.G. (2013) *Higher Education in the Digital Age*. Princeton, NJ: Princeton University Press

Bowen, W.G., Chingos, M.M., Lack, K.A., and Nygren, T.I. (2014) Interactive Learning Online at Public Universities: Evidence from a Six-Campus Randomized Trial. *Journal of Policy Analysis and Management* 33 (1): 94–111

Brown, R. (2004) *Quality Assurance in Higher Education: The UK Experience since 1992*. New York: Routledge

Brown, R. (2011) *Higher Education and the Market*. New York and London: Routledge

Brown, R. with Carasso, H. (2013) *Everything for Sale? The Marketisation of UK Higher Education*. London: Routledge and the Society for Research into Higher Education

Byrne, J., Jørgensen, T., and Loukkola, T. (2013) *Quality Assurance in Doctoral Education: Results of the ARDE Project*. Brussels, Belgium: European University Association

Calhoun, C. (2006) The University and the Public Good. *Thesis Eleven* 84 (1): 7–43

Clark, B.R. (1987) *The Academic Life: Small Worlds, Different Worlds*. Princeton, NJ: The Carnegie Foundation for the Advancement of Teaching

Clark, B.R. (2008) *On Higher Education: Selected Writings, 1956–2006*. Baltimore: Johns Hopkins University Press

Conference of Ministers Responsible for Higher Education (2003) *Realising the European Higher Education Area*. Berlin, Germany, 19 September 2003

Dill, D.D. (2000) Capacity building through academic audits: improving 'quality work' in the UK, New Zealand, Sweden, and Hong Kong. *Journal of Comparative Policy Analysis: Research and Practice* 2 (2): 211–234

Dill, D.D. (2014) Public Policy Design and University Reform: Insights into Academic Change. In C. Musselin and P.N. Teixeira (eds) (2014) *Reforming Higher Education: Public Policy Design and Implementation*. Dordrecht: Springer: 21–37

Dill, D.D. and Beerkens, M. (2010) *Public Policy for Academic Quality: Analyses of Innovative Policy Instruments*. Dordrecht, The Netherlands: Springer

Dill, D.D. and Soo, M. (2005) Academic quality, league tables, and public policy: a cross-national analysis of university ranking systems. *Higher Education* 49 (4): 495–533

Dill, D.D. and van Vught, F.A. (2010) *National Innovation and the Academic Research Enterprise: Public Policy in Global Perspective*. Baltimore: The Johns Hopkins University Press

Ehrenberg, R.G. (2012). American higher education in transition. *Journal of Economic Perspectives* 26 (1): 193–216

El-Khawas, E. (2010) The Teacher Education Accreditation Council (TEAC) in the US. In D. D. Dill and M. Beerkens (eds) *Public Policy for Academic Quality: Analyses of Innovative Policy Instruments*. Dordrecht: Springer: 39–58

Hage, J. (1974) *Communication and Organizational Control: Cybernetics in Health and Welfare Settings*. New York: John Wiley

Harvey, L. (2010) The Accreditation and Quality Processes of the General Medical Council in the UK. In D. D. Dill and M. Beerkens (eds) *Public Policy for Academic Quality: Analyses of Innovative Policy Instruments*. Dordrecht: Springer: 259–290

Himanen, L., Auranen, O., Puuska, H.-M., and Nieminen, M. (2009) Influence of research funding and science policy on university research performance: a comparison of five countries. *Science and Public Policy* 36 (6): 419–430

Jongbloed, B. (2010) The Netherlands. In D. D. Dill and F. A. van Vught (eds) *National Innovation and the Academic Research Enterprise: Public Policy in Global Perspective*. Baltimore: The Johns Hopkins University Press: 286–336

Kaplan, G. E. (2004) How Academic Ships Actually Navigate: A Report from the 2001 Survey on Higher Education Governance. In R. G. Ehrenberg (ed.) *Governing Academia*. Ithaca, NY: Cornell University Press: 165–208

Kehm, B. M. (2010) The German System of Accreditation. In D. D. Dill and M. Beerkens (eds) *Public Policy for Academic Quality: Analyses of Innovative Policy Instruments*. Dordrecht: Springer: 235–258

Macfarlane, B. (2012) *Intellectual Leadership in Higher Education: Renewing the Role of the University Professor*. New York: Routledge

McPherson, M. S. and Schapiro, M. O. (1999) Tenure issues in higher education. *The Journal of Economic Perspectives* 13: 85–98

Ostrom, E. (2005) *Understanding Institutional Diversity*. Princeton, NJ: Princeton University Press

Ostrom, E. (2009) Prize Lecture: Beyond Markets and States: Polycentric Governance of Complex Economic Systems. Nobel Media AB 2014. Available at: http://www.nobelprize.org/nobel_prizes/economic-sciences/laureates/2009/ostrom-lecture.html [accessed 17 August 2014]

Ostrom, E. and Hess, C. (2007) A Framework for Analyzing the Knowledge Commons. In C. Hess and E. Ostrom, (eds) *Understanding Knowledge as a Commons: From Theory to Practice*. Cambridge, MA: MIT Press: 41–81

Ostrom, E. and Walker, J. (1997) Neither Markets nor States: Linking Transformation Processes in Collective Action Arenas. In D. C. Mueller (ed.) *Perspectives on Public Choice: A Handbook*. Cambridge: Cambridge University Press: 35–72

Paradeise, C. and Thoenig, J-C. (2013) Academic institutions in search of quality: local orders and global standards. *Organization Studies* 34 (2): 189–218

Pascarella, E. T. and Terenzini, P. T. (2005) *How College Affects Students, Vol. 2. A Third Decade of Research*. San Francisco, CA: Jossey-Bass

Rizvi, S., Donnelly, K., and Barber, M. (2013) *An Avalanche Is Coming: Higher Education and the Revolution Ahead*. London: Institute for Public Policy Research

Shattock, M. (2014) *International Trends in University Governance: Autonomy, Self-Government and the Distribution of Authority*. London: Routledge

Stensaker, B. (2010) Subject Assessments for Academic Quality in Denmark. In D. D. Dill and M. Beerkens (eds) *Public Policy for Academic Quality: Analyses of Innovative Policy Instruments*. Dordrecht: Springer: 189–208

Shavelson, R. J. (2010) *Measuring College Learning Responsibly: Accountability in a New Era*. Stanford, CA: Stanford University Press

Tapper, T. and Palfreyman, D. (2010) *The Collegial Tradition in the Age of Mass Higher Education*. Dordrecht: Springer

Weimer, D. L. and Vining, A. R. (1996) Economics. In D. F. Kettl and H. B. Milward (eds) *The State of Public Management*. Baltimore: Johns Hopkins University Press: 92–117

Chapter 20

Policy, what policy?

Considering the university in the twenty-first century

Ronald Barnett

Introduction

Across the world, a more or less common policy framework has emerged for universities built around research (especially in STEM disciplines), the global knowledge economy, access, excellence and societal impact. Institutional leaders, policy-makers and administrators (and higher education specialists) can easily talk to each other since they are working worldwide within a common framework. But is it right to call this a policy framework? Is it not rather a set of taken-for-granted axioms and assumptions? I want to offer some critical reflections on this situation. *En route*, I shall essay some thoughts as to what it is to understand the university in the twenty-first century. My thesis will be that the very idea of policy in relation to the university is fraught with difficulty and is best re-imagined.

Global consensus

From Beijing to Washington, from London to Santiago, from Pretoria to Ottawa and from Stockholm to Canberra, there has developed something of a global consensus as to a framework within which higher education policy should be developed. The elements of this policy framework include – give or take – the following:

1 A horizon of a global knowledge economy
2 An emphasis on research, coupled with a growing wish to see it have impact on the wider world
3 Encouragement for internationalisation and/or transnational activities
4 A wish to advance the quality of teaching (as judged by national audit agencies, themselves often working within systems of cross-national coordination)
5 Learning having explicit outcomes, characteristically in the form of employability skills
6 Capitalising on new technologies
7 Academic staff being seen as (human) resources to be managed

8   A definite use of the private sector (in most but not all systems), this against the background of the state both withdrawing from the funding of 'public' services and finding the funding of higher education especially burdensome

9   A sense that higher education yields significant personal benefits and a lifetime earnings supplement, so giving rise to reservations as to the public funding of higher education (again, not in all regimes) and to a tilting of the financing of higher education towards students (so rendering students as customers)

10   A determination to widen access to higher education, especially from socioeconomic classes hitherto weakly represented in such systems.

As stated, this ten-fold framework is more or less to be found across the world. Its ubiquity allows institutional leaders, higher education ministers and politicians, senior officials of transnational bodies, national planners and think-tank members (not to mention higher education scholars) to engage seamlessly with each other. This framework has come to constitute a *lingua franca* of meetings and interactions within higher education policy circles, both nationally and internationally. It also has come to allow universities to form particular network groups across the world and to establish international collaborative arrangements, both in research and in curriculum provision. What has emerged here is nothing short of a global 'discursive regime'.

That this discursive regime is *global* can be explained only as the outcome of a set of influences at work that are themselves global. They include the emergence of 'the entrepreneurial university' as a universal trope; the advance of global knowledge and learning economies; the marketisation of higher education (and higher education becoming a part of the neo-liberal colonisation of public services); increasing financial pressures on governments leading to a parsimonious approach to higher education funding and an encouragement of the private sector (to take over some of the burdens of state funding); evolving relationships between the private and public sectors of higher education; the emergence of hybrid institutions that are at once both private and public; and a digital revolution that seems to offer answers to policy dilemmas. The large number of underpinning forces that are more or less global in character help to explain the near ubiquity of the ten-fold policy framework just listed. There is a common language at work because there exists this set of huge and powerful forces at work, bearing down on higher education.

What lies before us here, surely, is nothing less than a set of global 'generative mechanisms', to draw on a concept from Roy Bhaskar's philosophy of Critical Realism (Bhaskar, 2008). The developing presence of a global knowledge and learning economy, given added impetus by the digital revolution, a private sector of media organisations looking to insert itself into higher learning and knowledge transfer, and a readiness to expose higher education and universities to market mechanisms have come to constitute a concatenation of forces that are having impact upon the internal life of universities in much of their functioning.

Teaching, research and third stream (wider engagement) activities are affected by the global movements and forces just identified. The contemporary university, therefore, to a significant extent, is being shaped by global structures; a set of structures that we might term 'global digital capitalism'.

Options, yes – but of what kind?

If anything of the picture just sketched carries water, certain implications flow. One is that the very idea of the university is in difficulty. For the literature on the idea of the university – stretching back at least to Kant (1992) – implies that there is point to thinking about the very idea of the university, that the university could be this or that, and that there are options before the university as to its being in the world. Our reflections so far, however, could be taken to intimate that – now, at least – such a way of construing the university is at best fanciful and at worst misguided. If the university is largely given, if it is bound and positioned by massive global forces, if it possesses a deep ontology in the ways suggested, then the very idea of the idea of the university – the idea that it makes sense to contemplate the university as if it has options in front of it – begins to dissolve. And some have suggested just this, variously that the idea of the idea of the university is problematic (Rothblatt, 1997: 38–48) and even that the university has been hollowed out (Scott, 2000: 205).

Ideas of the university have, after all, been expressive of certain ideals of the university – around untrammelled inquiry and truth-seeking, unfettered critical dialogue, unconditioned knowledge, independent reasoning, academic freedom and a flourishing of human being. But such ideals are now mere mirages if the global forces are so all-embracing that the university not only has little room for manoeuvre, but also is being oriented in quite other directions – of instrumentalism, inequitable market forces, reason dominated by use-values and students-as-customers.

Another implication of the rise of global forces acting on and positioning the university – and which must take our more considered attention here – is its impact on the idea of policy. For if thinking about the idea of the university opens up the possibility of there being alternative *ideas* of the university, thinking about policy opens up – or should open up – the possibility of there being alternative *practical* options before the university.

Here, we set against each other the university as idea and the university as institution. The concept of policy makes sense where there are significant options open to the university. And it may seem, *prima facie*, as if there are significant options open to the university. After all, do we not see the university developing in the direction of the entrepreneurial university, or the corporate university, or the digital university; and do we not also see debate and urgings as to the prospects for the emergence of the engaged university, the civic university, the public university and the university of wisdom? There appear to be all manner of options open to the university. Indeed, it is surely the case that – in the 900-year history of the western university – there has never been such a surfeit of ideas and options available to the university.

At one level, this sense of multiple options being available to the university is valid. There are options open to the university: the university is not bound in and still less determined entirely by structures beyond its control, but has measures of agency of its own. We may even consider the university to be a corporate agent (List and Pettit, 2011). The long-standing structure-agency debate within social theory bears in here upon the university qua institution. The university has more autonomy to choose the direction(s) of travel available to it than is often portrayed. At another level, however (and at a level of immediate concern to us here), to play up this optionality is misguided.

There is a danger here, in holding on to the optionality available to the university, of confusing the university as institution and the university as idea. The university has optionality to it as an *idea*: many ideas of the university are now being contemplated in a way such as never before. However, as an *institution*, as a matter of fact, across the world, the university is constrained within a tight envelope of institutional forms. However, to say it is constrained is not to say it is utterly determined. To the contrary, there are considerable spaces available to the university, and imaginative possibilities are being pursued by some universities. But the dominant patterning of universities is largely confined within a set of boundaries, the boundaries marked out by the near-global consensus that we identified earlier.

Policy vacuum

Qua institution, then, the university moves within a global set of horizons, a set of horizons marked out by a taken-for-granted set of axioms as to what it is to be a university in the twenty-first century. It is this taken-for-grantedness character of these understandings that enable communication about higher education to be relatively unproblematic across national borders. Yes, there are aspects of the micro character of university systems that need to be clarified on occasions – the nature of the pedagogical relationship, what it is to be a 'professor', the extent to which there is a separation of academic identities – as between teaching and research – and the degree to which 'third mission' or public engagement activities are being developed *but*, for the most part, communication across higher education systems can take place without fundamental difficulty. The main planks of what it is to be a university in the contemporary world are, as stated, several and more or less uniformly understood. The ten axioms earlier identified constitute tacit, and so *largely unquestioned*, understandings that are held internationally. What it is to be a university moves on an 'assumptive' plane (Sabri, in press) across the world.

If this is so, a major problem emerges here so far as the concept of 'policy' is concerned. If there is a large consensus – not uniform, certainly, but still extensive in its scope and global in its reach – as to what constitutes a university in the twenty-first century, policy formation is taking place within a tight set of parameters (and, as stated, as largely unquestioned parameters at that). The formation of a policy framework in any one jurisdiction is going to take the form of a tinkering within the global university framework. As intimated, there will remain much variation, especially at the micro levels (of individual academics, programmes of study and discrete cohorts of students) and even at the meso levels (of teaching approaches, academic identities and research strategies within disciplines and universities). At the macro level, however, of university systems, and of the broad character as to the relationships between universities and the economy and the wider society and their valuing, there is much agreement and so much uniformity.

Accordingly, policy formation in higher education becomes largely a tinkering with the relationships between the various (ten) elements in the global framework. A little more state funding here, a little more expansion of the private sector there, a greater emphasis on the student-as-customer and self-payer here, a larger encouragement for the digital revolution there: these are but adjustments within a taken-for-granted framework of understandings. That quite different kinds of university might be sponsored or encouraged is not characteristically on the cards. The university of the twenty-first century is at once global, entrepreneurial and digital, and playing its part in the formation of cognitive capitalism (Boutang, 2011). *That* overarching framework is taken-for-granted. Policy formation, accordingly, is hemmed in and narrowly bounded.

We are, in this situation, permitted to ask as to whether we are ever seriously in the presence of a policy framework, when any such framework begins from and works within a taken-for-granted horizon of axioms of the university (that it should advance the economy of the nation-state, that it should develop its own resources so as to manage itself in a global knowledge economy, that it should generate income for itself, that it should orient the development of students towards their employability and that it should recognise its students as being customers of its services). If such a set of axioms sets up horizons within which a national framework takes its bearings, we are entitled to doubt that we are in the presence of a policy framework. Rather, the possibility emerges that we are in the presence of a policy *vacuum*.

Tacit backing for such a possibility is to be found in the authoritative overview of the modern history of *Making Policy in British Higher Education, 1945–2011* by Michael Shattock (2012). In essence, Shattock argues that UK higher education policy over the post-war period has never been especially ideological, but has been largely steered by the UK Treasury, albeit influenced over time by haphazard gentle politicking by policy networks. In other words, there has been a political consensus that higher education policy should be largely determined by financial concerns; and this would include judgements about financial rates of return both to individuals and to the state. But this is to say, in effect, that there has been a policy vacuum in the UK with regard to higher education, in the terms being set out here. Little serious consideration has been given to the matter as to what is to count as 'higher education' or 'university'. So-called higher education policy has actually been held and steered within a tight set of financial parameters.

The possibility of possibilities

The question arises, then: how is this policy vacuum to be understood? Is it an inevitable feature of the position of universities or might matters be different? To put the matter sharply, if somewhat crudely, and placing it in the context of the structure-agency debate in social theory: is the university largely hedged in and determined by global structures acting upon it or does it have some room for manoeuvre, some agency, of its own? Is it possible that the university has possibilities before it? Does it possess the possibility of its own possibilities?

At one level, these questions are empirical; and it would be possible – and sensible – to point to examples of universities expressing their own agency and declining to be bound by the ideology of the entrepreneurial university. Two forms of such disinclination are apparent. On the one hand, there are university systems, especially in continental Europe (notably Germany), in which universities are perceived as fulfilling public goods and where the marketisation of universities has only a weak hold. This is a weak form of opt-out. On the other hand, instances of stronger forms of opt-out may be observed. For example, some universities are wanting to see themselves as incarnations – in their own locality, in their own ways – of 'the civic university' or, say, 'a university of wisdom' or 'the engaged university'. Such universities are understanding that they are corporate agents with their own agency – and thereby too their own responsibilities. They are also wanting to advance that agency as expressive of a set of values that they have chosen for themselves, values that stand out against the instrumentalism and economic reason marked by the dominant university conception of our age, that of the entrepreneurial university.

Such empirical lines of enquiry are crucial in identifying the range of concepts of the university that are actually to be seen as being instantiated across the world. But this practical empiricism, while valuable, cannot be the last word in opening up a horizon of possibilities. There is another tack available to us. This is that of dwelling on the idea of the university itself. For the idea of the idea gives rise to possibilities for the university.

Such a task is not to dwell in the ruins of past ideas of the university (Readings, 1997) but to bring forth new ideas that might do justice to the university in its present (twenty-first century) age. And nor is it to lose sight of the university as an institution, beset by the forces that we identified earlier (for a certain realism has to be part of this stance). But it is to enter a set of 'thinking spaces' in 'new time-space arrangements', 'spaces of inspiration incorporating many possible worlds' (Thrift, 2008: 42).

Here, the mind frees itself from the empirical world and commits itself not so much to a being a 'space of reason' (Bakhurst, 2011) but to a space of *imagining*. There is a curious dual relationship here between the university as imaginative idea and the university as institution. This imagining tenuously retains the sutures that connect it to the university as institution; but it also reflects the fluid and dynamic character of the university. For all its complexity and interwovenness, the metaphor of rhizome bequeathed to us by Deleuze and Guattari (2007) is surely far too static and rigid. Now, to do justice to the university in its contemporary manifestation, we need a much more lively and far-reaching metaphor. Has the university not become a *squid*? This university reaches far abroad and moves swiftly, even across the world, its tentacles now able to squeeze into the smallest apertures. It has a hard shell and moves effortlessly in a liquid space.

Possibilities open for this university. Just which spaces is it to inhabit? What is its reach to be? With which other entities does it feel most comfortable? Which will give it some kind of succour? The contemporary language of collaboration – even, say, 'the collaborative university' (Walsh and Kahn, 2010) – is surely again too static. A richer language of engagement, marriage, partnering, tension, joint creativity, forgiveness, care, concern and even antagonisms is necessary here.

The antagonistic university

Antagonism in the university is not to be denied, repudiated or neglected. It is part of the university, both as institution and as idea. As institution, we see antagonism in the university daily, in denials of academic freedom, in internal conflicts between the faculties (Kant lives on!), in tensions if not downright battles between the managers and the academics, and in ideological strife (not least between student societies). But, again, alongside the empirical story, there opens here a glimpse of the antagonistic university as an *idea*.

How might *this* antagonism be understood? The standard reading is that it is an external antagonism, that of the university besieged by external forces against which it is largely weak and is being overrun. If only the university was stronger in some way, then it would (re)gain some autonomy for itself. As it is, variously the state, the corporate sector or, more nebulously, the global economy and 'neo-liberalism' are conspiring to rob the university of its internal integrity. This story has validity but it is not the full story. Less noticed is that the university is now an institution characterised by internal schisms, in which the university is battling against itself. Disputes among the disciplines, between the managers and the academics, over ideological stances (for example, towards the market, Israel, student fees, investments in the corporate sector or in receiving gifts from certain donors) are but symptoms of fundamental differences in value stances on campus.

These internal conflicts bequeath a particular feature about – to put it rather grandly – the ontology of the university. If the former conflicts, the external conflicts, were to be resolved, the university as such would still exist. However, the latter set of conflicts – those reflective of inner antagonisms – are indicative of the contemporary character of the university's ontology. For internal antagonism has become an essential part of what it is to be a university in the twenty-first century. No internal battle, no university! An institution that is entirely at peace with itself cannot any longer constitute a university.

Proliferating – and competing – universalities

A way of interpreting these conflicts, especially the internal conflicts, is as conflicts between universals. Until recently, universities stood in a limited space of universals, marked out by terms such as knowledge, truth, reason, academic freedom and critical dialogue. That conceptual landscape has largely disappeared, being overlain by universals such as markets, globalisation, employability and economic return. This disappearance of the universal landscape of universities has been aided by post-modernism, which declared an 'incredulity towards grand narratives' (Lyotard, 1984: xxiv). But universals are a long time a-dying. To the contrary, the universals with which universities are associated are now *proliferating*. Access, sustainability, learning, life chances, social value, personal benefit, wellbeing, public good and civic engagement are characteristic of the large ideas through which the university is now not only understood but judged. And their forming and congregating are indicative of the way in which universals of the university are growing.

Inevitably, this proliferation of the universals of the university is accompanied by conflicts among them. Economic reason vies with social benefit, equity squares off against excellence, tension erupts between truth and impact, public benefit runs against personal benefit, 'civic engagement' conflicts with 'academic community' and understanding struggles against performance. A problem, in turn, for the contemporary university thereby becomes that of living not only with discrete antagonisms that beset it but also with antagonism *per se*. After all, the universal landscape is promising to witness continual growth in the range and number of universals in and of the university. 'Wellbeing', 'wisdom', 'ecology', 'care', the idea of the 'public', 'identity' and 'democracy' are on the horizon, if not well within it. And so the universals of the university are likely to go on proliferating and competing. 'The conflict of the faculties' is set to go on being elevated to quite new planes.

Conclusions

We may seem to have come a long way from our beginning observations and it is time to draw together the threads of our discussion and to summarise the argument of this chapter.

So-called policy-making in higher education tends to take place within a horizon of taken-for-granted axioms as to what it is to count as a university in the twenty-first century. These axioms constitute a narrow space that might be summarised as the global university. This university is at once oriented towards overt performance in the world and towards income generation with an increasingly limited set of subsidies from the state, understanding its mission as enhancing the global knowledge and learning economies and treating the student as a customer for its services. Accordingly, policy-making in higher education takes the form of a highly limited adjustment of elements that are constitutive of this global university (such as student fees, rights to raise income, financial autonomy, audit arrangements, performative criteria of value, research allocation mechanisms, the position of students and some balancing of the private and public sectors of higher education). Policy-making in higher education deals therefore only with relatively minor matters, and is virtually never a matter of re-envisioning the nature of the university in the twenty-first century.

This policy myopia pretends to a unity that neither does nor should characterise the university in the twenty-first century. The university is riven with conflict between ideologies of the university, a conflict that is likely to grow. This conflict is not to be disparaged or repudiated, still less neglected. On the contrary, its presence is testimony to a flowering of ideas and so of possibilities of the university. Accordingly, policy-making should become much more an attempt to stimulate universities' thinking about themselves such that policy-making, at least at the level of individual institutions, becomes a space for the creation of plausible and creative fictions as to the possibilities that lie ahead, fictions that at the same time recognise the ideological conflict that lies within universities.

In turn, perhaps for the first time in many instances, might be released universities' imaginative powers in relation to themselves. At the moment, policy-making is freezing universities' imaginations; in the future, policy-making has the challenge of stimulating that institutional imagination. That must surely be a necessary condition of universities realizing their potential in the twenty-first century. And so what emerges, in turn, is nothing short of a plea that policy-making itself be re-imagined into a much more challenging and creative enterprise.

Bibliography

Bakhurst, D. (2011) *The Formation of Reason*. Chichester: Wiley-Blackwell

Bhaskar, R. (2008) *A Realist Theory of Science*. London: Verso (first published in 1975)

Boutang, Y. M. (2011) *Cognitive Capitalism*. Cambridge, MA: Polity

Deleuze, G. and Guattari, F. (2007) *A Thousand Plateaus: Capitalism and Schizophrenia*. London: Continuum (first published in 1987)

Kant, I. (1992) *The Conflict of the Faculties*. Lincoln: University of Nebraska (first published in 1798)

List, C. and Pettit, P. (2011) *Group Agency: The Possibility, Design, and Status of Corporate Agents*. Oxford: Oxford University Press

Lyotard, J-F. (1984) *The Postmodern Condition: A Report on Knowledge*. Manchester: University of Manchester (first published in 1979)

Readings, B. (1997) *The University in Ruins*. Cambridge, MA: Harvard University Press

Rothblatt, S. (1997) *The Modern University and its Discontents: The Fate of Newman's Legacies in Britain and America*. Cambridge: Cambridge University Press

Sabri, D. (in press) Revisiting Assumptive Worlds: A Theoretical Framework

Scott, P. (2000) A Tale of Three Revolutions? Science, Society and the University. In P. Scott (ed.) *Higher Education Reformed*. London: Falmer: 190–206

Shattock, M. (2012) *Making Policy in British Higher Education 1945–2011*. Maidenhead: McGraw-Hill and Open University Press

Thrift, N. (2008) *Non-Representational Theory: Space, Politics, Affect*. London: Routledge

Walsh, L. and Kahn, P. (2010) *Collaborative Working in Higher Education: The Social Academy*. New York: Routledge

Editors' conclusion

Higher education and the market: Thoughts, themes, threads

Joëlle Fanghanel and Peter John

Massification and neo-liberalism

The recent General Election result in the UK is perhaps indicative of H. G. Wells' science fiction work of 1933 *The Shape of Things to Come*. The novel's prescience and provenance highlights the fact that a mere two decades after its publication only 5 per cent of 18 and 19 year olds in Great Britain attended university, despite the fact that a quarter of the age group achieved the requisite grades for entry (Todd, 2014). In 2015, however, almost 50 per cent of the UK population attends university – a huge increase, and one that gained its main impetus from the ending of the binary divide in 1992. This point of departure heralded the end of an elite system which was accompanied over the decades by the increasing liberalisation of funding, the re-forming of organisational structures, the birth of teaching audits, and research assessment exercises – all driven by the new flexible capitalism.

A consistent theme running across the chapters of this collection is that over a number of decades, universities have been re-shaped to create increasingly individualistic academics and consuming students. This has occurred through a combination of economic reform (often driven by cyclical booms and slumps) and neo-liberal policies and processes – all underpinned by a new enabling state where universities are more tightly audited, governed, managed and directed (Davies and Bansel, 2007). In return, universities are given greater freedom to recruit, to raise capital, to govern themselves and to compete in the positional market. In so doing, they have surrendered significant collective power and taken on a greater burden of risk, which has been transferred from the state to individual institutions and their senior managers (Davies and Bansel, 2007).

In this *Brave New World* students are re-cast as consumers, and are expected to act like rational purchasers in a constructed market. The market then gradually withdraws value from the public good while transforming higher education into a product to be bought and sold as a commodity (Brown, 2003; Davies and Bansel, 2007). This has led to a shift in behaviour, with academics and institutions being measured on the delivery of their teaching and research, their employability statistics, their knowledge transfer and their entrepreneurial intent. In consequence, each institution is now responsible for its own well-being and success. Fairclough (2003) argues that the success of this project has been based on a shift in discursive power away from the social good to a new linguistic practice, which re-calibrates the relationship between the individual, the institution, society and the state. For academics it re-sets the terms by which they are employed and understood; and the terms under which they operate, and articulate their careers. These terms are then cloaked in a form of inevitability and a 'way it is' discourse, which blunts opposition and challenge (Davies and Bansel, 2007).

Richard Sennett (1998), in his book *The Corrosion of Character*, examines the effect of these changes and asks:

> How do we decide what is of lasting value in one's lives in a society which is impatient, which focuses on the immediate moment. How can long-term goals be pursued in an economy devoted to the short-term? How can mutual loyalties and commitments be sustained in institutions which are constantly breaking apart or continually being re-designed?
>
> (Sennett, 1998:10)

Given that there will be no turning back from marketisation of the sector (Palfreyman and Tapper, 2014), how can Sennett's, and others' concerns, be addressed? And what does the future hold for higher education?

In this volume, contributors with an institutional frame of reference (at the *micro* level of academics and departments; or at the *meso* level of institutional leadership) tend to highlight more internal convergence, while authors focusing on the *macro* level of policy and global trends point to policy ambiguity, uncertainty and irony even, when explaining the effects of the market. One common thread which emerges is that the rise of the market, however defined (quasi-; multiple; flexible), is at one with the varieties of capitalism followed by nation-states and especially noticeable in the UK and the US with their distinctive strain of the liberal market (Hall and Soskice, 2001). Such economies (USA, UK, Australia, Ireland, some North European countries and New Zealand) are characterised by:

- Shareholder profit rather than co-ordinated intervention and investment
- Deregulation (Adam Smith's 'invisible hand')
- Limited emphasis on the public good
- Hierarchical organizational structures
- Corporate management and governance
- Low collective involvement
- Extremely wide wage differentials
- Elevated levels of state regulation that are leveraged in return for public funding

What these features of liberalism highlight is that during certain periods of market evolution, institutional distinctiveness tends to converge. However, the intra-institutional challenges that the changes pose are often refracted differently thus producing new forms of divergence. What the chapters in this book reveal are the ways in which common pressures (unleashed by the logic of the market) are processed, mediated and internalised by institutions operating within different market segments (Hay, 2000). It also shows that the current approach to the market in higher education is beginning to resemble what economists call 'pareto-optimal' efficiency, where one party's situation cannot be improved without making another party's situation worse. This can be observed at all levels of the system, within and across institutions. We now reflect on proposals made by contributors to this volume in relation to these characteristics.

Reflecting on possibilities: structural and agentic solutions

The macro level of higher education policy and governance

Without the advantages of hindsight, it is easier to identify what is not working than how malfunctions might be redressed. At the heart of the authors' concerns in this volume are questions asked by Collini (2011): what are universities for in the twenty-first century, and how should the personal benefits and collective goods they afford be balanced? More specifically, the authors comment on the very nature of the relationship between the *private and public dimensions*, and the extent to which they might become convergent (private contributing to public), rather than remaining divergent outcomes – as they are often presented by policy-makers. The question of the tensions between private and public benefits is the subject of Peter Scott's chapter while Bruce in Chapter 5 supports the idea of promoting a positive view of higher education's contribution to society and the economy so that the benefits of higher education are understood by all. The focus on higher education as a public good, and the tension with private benefits, is at the centre of the questions debated in this volume.

An important aspect of this logic of action and one which continues to traverse the sector is obsessive *short-termism*. Focusing on the *longue durée*, and on the associated benefits that Sennett highlights, is seen by many as providing an answer to this dimension of marketisation. Several authors reflect on the need to think long-term, and White's discussion of higher education as a 'post-experience' and 'inter-generational' good in Chapter 8 is a case in point. A long-view approach is also outlined in Chapter 4 where Cuthbert suggests that all higher education should be able 'to have its head in the clouds and its feet on the ground' whilst meeting short-term public and student demands, thus building a sector that is sustainably strong in its diversity. The issue of a sustainable and diverse sector is echoed in Longden's re-conceptualisation of league tables in Chapter 7.

Several authors also argue for a *better articulation between stakeholders* in higher education, particularly that between policy-makers and research. They are in line with wider concerns about this disconnect in education as a whole, and follow

Furlong and Oancea's (2005:6) plea for a 'tighter link between research, practice and policy'. G. Williams, Naidoo, Carasso and Locke in this volume all stress the need for policy research to be considered during the policy-making process rather than being sidelined. D'Andrea likewise maps the way this can be done with reference to a group that was led by Roger Brown to impact policy on learning and teaching in the early years of this century.

The need for *regulation* is widely accepted, but a significant amount of deliberation is directed at the sheer volume and manner of that regulation. Scott in Chapter 1 suggests that it is time for the UK to release its grip on quality assurance as 'the level of surveillance' is already well ahead of the rest of Europe and of the USA. In Chapter 11, Alderman proposes that regulation should stop at the door the Home Office, and that the QAA should have relinquished the opportunity to act as a border agency officer, whilst supporting the notion that private providers should be subjected to same health checks as the rest of the sector. These proposals represent useful responses to the challenges of liberalism in relation to the functioning and governance of higher education.

Meso level: higher education institutions

A number of questions in this volume are also raised about issues at the *meso* level of the system. These contributions focus on the relationship between higher education and the state, the forms of institutional governance that arise, the growth of corporate management and the engagement of academics and students. Authors suggest that *institutional self-improvement* provides a strong response to the challenge of state regulation. Several authors in the volume highlight the need for institutions to foster a philosophy of self-improvement (Cuthbert in Chapter 4) and the engagement of students in the academic endeavour (Naidoo in Chapter 3 and Williams in Chapter 18) in order to counteract the performativity cultures induced by liberal ideologies, and the perceived over-commodification of teaching.

It seems difficult, however, to sever the need for self-improvement from the emphasis on *collegiate institutional governance* that includes 'shared governance' (Middlehurst in Chapter 17); 'shared goals and values' (Dill in Chapter 19); 'collective action' (King in Chapter 10); and an outward facing approach – the opening-up of the academic community to external debates so that members are not 'insulated from the external pressures' (Cuthbert in Chapter 4). Dill quoting Calhoun talks of establishing a public sphere inside universities. This proposition complements King's suggestion that quality assurance should be more decentralised and owned by academics. These propositions hold a potential for debate and contradiction, and might encourage the development of what Barnett in Chapter 20 calls 'the antagonistic university' – a space where contradiction is seen as a way to advance thinking and practice.

Beside Barnett and his call for resistance to policy myopia, several authors highlight the need for institutions to foster *creativity and innovation* as a means of resisting marketisation (Scott, Bruce, Middlehurst, Dill). Whilst the university depicted in Chapter 20 may be difficult to realise, senior managers have a role to play in developing academics to understand the demands of academic practice in today's environment; in seeking to establish a dialogue of informed critique across its governance structures; and in supporting development, innovation and creativity. These are fundamental elements of the internal purpose of the university and none are inimitable to the market.

A useful antidote to the marketisation of universities is March's (1999) *Pursuit of Organisational Intelligence* which shows that institutions are organised by shared meanings and practices built over time; these core notions are not immutable but are characterised by varying degrees of tenacity (Hoyle and Wallace, 2005). March (1999: 55) goes further and draws a useful distinction between the 'logic of consequence' and the 'logic of appropriateness'. The first entails an orientation toward external functions, effects and outcomes while the second is associated with internal obligations, standards and practice. These 'appropriate' actions are often expressions of 'exemplary, natural, or acceptable behaviour according to the (internalised) purposes, codes of rights and duties, practices and methods and techniques of the constituent group and of the self' (March, 1999: 57).

It is this 'logic of appropriateness' that can help establish and shape the principle of subsidiarity which we believe may provide a way forward. Despite being a contested concept, all definitions have one thing in common: that shared tasks should be decentralised to the lowest level of governance (Marshall, 2008). The implication is that organisations should refrain from arrogating power and controlling tasks that can be performed better by groupings closer to the individual. An emphasis on subsidiarity might then become the focus for those who argue for more 'local' solutions in universities (Naidoo, Chapter 3) and challenge the ubiquity of *deliverology* (Barber, 2015). Dill (Chapter 19) proposes using Ostrom's (2005) 'commons' model as an alternative and it is here that the principle of subsidiarity might add some value in enabling a more nested approach to academic governance as well as providing a challenge to the apparently inevitable rise of the corporate university.

The micro level of the system: faculties, departments and academics

At the micro level of the system, the market experience has been challenging for academics. In particular, the need to manage the student experience and student expectations in *a consumer-focused context* while concurrently delivering research and other outputs that will enable their institution to be competitive. The relationship with students is of course central, and this was emphasised in several contributions to this volume. The emphasis on student choice as the corner stone in the rhetoric of marketisation is denounced by many contributors (see Naidoo, J. Williams, Carasso and Locke, Ainley, Brennan, Dill). They argue that the focus on *student choice* can have deleterious consequences as it cultivates a form of false consciousness in the public and the student. The role of educators is clearly to redress this falsity and to shoulder, with courage and professionalism, their responsibilities as experts in learning and specialists in their field – reminding students of their critical role in helping themselves to learn. It is in this spirit that a number of contributors affirm the prevalence of *academic judgment* to resist fads or trends including those in academic quality (Cuthbert), risk-based quality assurance (King), or the co-creation of knowledge (Naidoo).

A number of contributions also focus on the role of *critical enquiry* (Norton in Chapter 14) and *research-based learning* (Brew in Chapter 13 and Jenkins and Healey in Chapter 15) to help re-invent the relation to students and combat the consumer agenda. Notwithstanding the limits of co-creation, the advantages of working in co-creative mode have been recognised as a powerful way to promote dialogic learning spaces and to challenge the dominance of the market (see Naidoo, Brennan and Brew in this volume). At this level of the system, it is also important to underline the *resilience of academic educational values*, as evidenced in a number of seminal studies (Henkel, 2000; Becher and Trowler, 2001; Trowler et al., 2012), and the degree of *agency* held by academics for meaningfully engaging with students and practice (Fanghanel, 2012). These aspects shape any response one might want to offer to the market question.

Conclusion

Whilst a strong discourse of academic disempowerment may circulate in some chapters of this volume, the complexity of the questions facing universities, academics and institutional leaders calls for some reflexivity when assessing the way universities respond to the challenges of marketisation. Leaving aside simplistic dichotomies (the golden age versus the age of ruins for universities; the virtuous academic versus the subverted manager; the student as learner versus the student as consumer), institutions and academic communities need to learn the art of measure, nuance and agility in a highly competitive context. In order to succeed locally they further need to develop – as this volume has identified – dialogic, expert and critical academic communities. It is a long-haul goal, and the road to success is tortuous. The ingredient of trust has been identified by several contributors as central to successful academic endeavour, at all levels of the system, and across all stakeholders. We argue that it is indeed central, and needs to be checked, tested, balanced and reaffirmed at regular intervals, and in the light of available evidence.

Despite criticism, some market mechanisms have brought some financial rectitude to institutions and their various academic colleges, faculties, schools and numerous professional support departments. It is also worth recalling that the prelapsarian university was often a finishing school for the wealthy elite, where the idea of a transformative education was confined to a small but growing number of the meritocracy (Young, 1958). Resisting the consumerist approach is right and proper but providing alternative ways for the mass of students, who do not always have the necessary cultural capital to challenge their institutions, to feel they are getting a quality education and value for money is vital regardless of our market antipathy.

Whilst it would be foolish to claim to have found even limited solutions to the tensions identified in the early pages of this volume, we consider that the concept of subsidiarity might provide a useful starting point. In particular, by operating a 'separation of powers' whereby the state performs fundamental functions that cannot be performed at a more local level while enabling local institutional agency to execute the remaining tasks and decisions. At the moment, under a regime of constant recording of performance and league-table competition, institutions have very little space and time to innovate and challenge. Instead they have to respond on an almost daily basis to policy requirements and funding initiatives, so much so that they become *distended* – struggling to expand or diversify their activities as the market takes a grip. We suggest that this distention disperses their energies and their ability to focus on their primary functions.

We call therefore for some further reflection on the possibilities that might be afforded to the sector by a careful exploitation of the concept of subsidiarity where a deeper consideration of how institutions are structured might counter the challenge that positive modifications are not possible (or even desirable). As Carozza (2003: 79) shows, the multiple tasks that now make up the *distended* university mean that change is not suited to traditional academic *ex ante* reasoning but that tasks need to be assigned vertically and set within the multi-level system we propose (Regini, 2011). Perhaps the best way to conclude and to illustrate our optimistic intent lies with Karl Polyani (1971:11) who asserts that:

> As long as social organization runs in its ruts, no individual economic motives need come into play; no shirking of personal effort need be feared; division of labor will automatically be ensured; economic obligations will be duly discharged; and, above all, the material means of an exuberant display of abundance at all public festivals will be provided. In such a community the idea of profit is barred; haggling and haggling is decried; giving freely is acclaimed as a virtue; the supposed propensity to barter, truck, and exchange does not appear. The economic system is, in effect, a mere function of social organisation.

Bibliography

Barber, M. (2015) *How to Run a Government, So That Citizens Benefit and Taxpayers Don't Go Crazy.* London: Penguin

Becher, T. and Trowler, P.R. (2001) *Academic Tribes and Territories: Intellectual Enquiry and the Culture of Disciplines.* Buckingham: Society for Research into Higher Education and Open University Press

Brown, N. (2003) Neo-liberalism and the end of liberal democracy. *Theory and Event* 7 (1): 1–43

Collini, S. (2011) *What Are Universities For?* London: Penguin Books

Corozza, P. G. (2003) Subsidiarity as a structural principle of international human rights law. *American Journal of International Law* 97 (1): 38–79

Davies, B and Bansel, P. (2007) Neo-liberalism and education. *International Journal of Qualitative Studies in Education* 20 (3): 247–259

Fairclough, D. (2003) *Language in the New Capitalism.* Available at: http://www.cddc.vt.edu/host/inc

Fanghanel, J. (2012) *Being an Academic.* London: Routledge

Furlong, J. and Oancea, A. (2005) *Assessing Quality in Applied and Practice-based Educational Research. A Framework for Discussion.* Available at: www.esrc.ac.uk/ESRCInfoCentre/Images/assessing_quality_shortreport

Hall, P. A. and Soskice, D. (2001) *Varieties of Capitalism: The International Foundations of Competitive Advantage.* Oxford: Oxford University Press

Hay, C. (2000) Contemporary capitalism, globalization, regulation and the persistence of national variation. *Review of International Studies* 20 (4): 509–531

Henkel, M. (2000) *Academic Identities and Policy Change in Higher Education.* London: Jessica Kingsley

Hoyle, E. and Wallace, M. (2005) *Educational Leadership: Ambiguity, Professionals and Managerialism.* London: Sage

Knight, P. and Trowler, P. (2001) *Departmental Leadership in Higher Education: New Directions for Communities of Practice.* Buckingham: Society for Research in Higher Education and Open University Press

March, J. (1999) *The Pursuit of Organizational Intelligence.* Oxford: Blackwell

Marshall, G. R. (2008) Nesting, subsidiarity, and community based environmental governance beyond the local level. *Journal of the Commons* 2 (1): 75–97

Ostrom, E. (2005) *Understanding Institutional Diversity.* Princeton, NJ: Princeton University Press

Palfreyman, D. and Tapper, T. (2014) *Reshaping the University: The Rise of the Regulated Market in Higher Education.* Oxford: Oxford University Press

Polyani, K. (1971) *The Great Transformation: The Political and Economic Origins of our Time.* Boston, MA: Beacon Press

Regini, M. (ed.) (2011) *European Universities and the Challenge of the Market.* Cheltenham: Edward Elgar Publishing

Sennett, R. (1998) *The Corrosion of Character. The Personal Consequences of Work in the New Capitalism.* New York: Norton

Todd, C. (2014) *The Rise and Fall of the Working Class 1910–2010.* London: John Murray

Trow, M. (1973) *Problems in the Transition from Elite to Mass Higher Education.* Berkeley, CA: Carnegie Commission on Higher Education

Trowler, P. (2014) Depicting and researching disciplines: strong and moderate essentialist approaches. *Studies in Higher Education* 39 (10): 1720–1731

Trowler, P., Saunders, M. and Bamber, V. (eds) (2012) *Tribes and Territories in the 21st-Century: Rethinking the Significance of Disciplines in Higher Education.* London and New York: Routledge

Well, H. G. (1933) *The Shape of Things to Come.* London: Penguin Books

Young, M. D. (1958) *The Rise of the Meritocracy.* London: Transaction

Index

Note: Italicized page numbers indicate a figure on the corresponding page. Page numbers in bold indicate a table on the corresponding page.

Taylor & Francis eBooks

Helping you to choose the right eBooks for your Library

Add Routledge titles to your library's digital collection today. Taylor and Francis ebooks contains over 50,000 titles in the Humanities, Social Sciences, Behavioural Sciences, Built Environment and Law.

Choose from a range of subject packages or create your own!

Benefits for you

» Free MARC records
» COUNTER-compliant usage statistics
» Flexible purchase and pricing options
» All titles DRM-free.

 REQUEST YOUR FREE INSTITUTIONAL TRIAL TODAY | **Free Trials Available** We offer free trials to qualifying academic, corporate and government customers.

Benefits for your user

» Off-site, anytime access via Athens or referring URL
» Print or copy pages or chapters
» Full content search
» Bookmark, highlight and annotate text
» Access to thousands of pages of quality research at the click of a button.

eCollections – Choose from over 30 subject eCollections, including:

Archaeology	Language Learning
Architecture	Law
Asian Studies	Literature
Business & Management	Media & Communication
Classical Studies	Middle East Studies
Construction	Music
Creative & Media Arts	Philosophy
Criminology & Criminal Justice	Planning
Economics	Politics
Education	Psychology & Mental Health
Energy	Religion
Engineering	Security
English Language & Linguistics	Social Work
Environment & Sustainability	Sociology
Geography	Sport
Health Studies	Theatre & Performance
History	Tourism, Hospitality & Events

For more information, pricing enquiries or to order a free trial, please contact your local sales team: www.tandfebooks.com/page/sales

Routledge Taylor & Francis Group | The home of Routledge books | **www.tandfebooks.com**

Dimensions of Marketisation in Higher Education

Dimensions of Marketisation in Higher Education is a critical analysis of the various dimensions of marketisation in a global context, exploring governance, policy, financial, ethical and pedagogical aspects. Bringing together a selection of influential authors who draw on the work of Roger Brown, the book is a timely examination of the impact that policies regulating cost, entry and practices in higher education can have on universities, students and academics.

This book explores the tensions and dilemmas marketisation brings into the educational environment for academic leaders, managers and students, arguing that they can be managed through rebalancing the relation between the market and the educational dimensions.

Key topics include:

- The economics of higher education
- Students in a marketised environment
- Regulating a marketised sector
- Marketisation and higher education pedagogies
- Universities' futures.

Unveiling nuanced and multifaceted perspectives and providing readers with collective and forward-thinking critical analyses, *Dimensions of Marketisation in Higher Education* will be an authoritative reference book on policy and practice, appealing to higher education leaders, managers and scholars worldwide.

Peter John is Vice-Chancellor and Chief Executive at the University of West London, UK.

Joëlle Fanghanel is Associate Pro Vice-Chancellor at the University of West London, UK.